THREE PASSPORTS TO ADVENTURE

HAL AND HALLA LINKER

This is the story of America's favorite traveling family—Hal, Halla, and David Linker of television's "Wonders of the World." Now carried in thirty-four U.S. cities, "Wonders of the World" tells on film of the strange and fascinating places the Linkers have visited; but in THREE PASSPORTS TO ADVENTURE they tell of their own adventures in filming this series.

Hal Linker met beautiful, blond Halla on a filming expedition to Iceland, and after their marriage this lovely descendant of Viking seafarers left Iceland for the first time in her life to accompany Hal on his assignments. Son David Thor was born during a return visit to Iceland, but was issued a passport of his own at the age of seven weeks, made his first trip—the 7000 miles from Iceland to Los Angeles—at ten weeks, and had been around the world by his first birthday!

TV audiences are unaware of the dangers and hazards that have beset the trio in gathering their film library, and now THREE PASSPORTS TO ADVENTURE tells this story. You will read about their dangerous visit to Batista's Cuba, when an unknown revolutionary named Fidel Castro launched his first attack—on a barracks across the street

(continued on back flap)

Three Passports to Adventure

By
Hal and
Halla Linker

DOUBLEDAY
& Company, Inc.

Garden City,
New York

1961

Acknowledgment

To Elliott Schryver, who felt sure that we had a story to tell, and to Art Lauring, whose help and advice were invaluable.

Contents

	Preface	13
1	Khyber Pass Adventure	17
2	"Eg skil ekki Islensku"	24
3	Whale Ho!	41
4	"For Better or For Worse"	50
5	The Way of the Welsh	58
6	North to Lapland	69
7	To the Far East and Beyond	79
8	Monsoon!	96
9	Pakistan—The North-West Frontier Province	112
10	From Israel to Cuba	128
11	Belgium to Japan	140
12	Africa and the King with Four Hundred Wives	150
13	Congo Witch Dancers and Famous Watusis	163
14	Simba! The Search for Lions	173
15	The Vanishing Duck-lipped Women	185
16	King Tut's Tomb	197
17	"Wonders of the World"	209
18	New Zealand and American Samoa	218
19	Ticketless to Tahiti	226
20	Corrida and Casbah! Portugal, Spain and Tangier	241

21 "The Greeks Had A Word for It"   257
22 Odyssey to Odessa   274
23 Inside the Kremlin   290
   Epilogue   311

List of Illustrations

Following page 48:

Whale 100 miles off Iceland's coast.
Cutting the whale's tail off to prevent breaking in storm.
Ingolfur Arnarson statue in Reykjavík, Iceland.
Halla in the national costume of Iceland.
Grapes growing in greenhouses heated by hot springs at
Hveragerdi, Iceland.
After filming in the Welsh coal mine.
Chairing of the Bard Ceremony at the National Eisteddfodd in
Wales.
Morris dancers at Bampton, England.
Laplander family near Ivalo, Finland.
David meets a Swiss guard at the Vatican in Rome.
Hawaii.
The Philippines.
Hong Kong.
Rickshaw ride in Hong Kong.

Following page 120:

Elephant training school at Chittagong, East Pakistan.
Cobras in Dacca, East Pakistan.
Ganges River scene near Dacca, East Pakistan.
Working in jute mill at Narayanganj in East Pakistan.
On the Ganges, East Pakistan.
Making illegal arms, West Pakistan.
Near the Khyber Pass in the village of Kohat.
Saber dancer at Fort Salop, Northwest Frontier Provinces,
West Pakistan.
Davey's first birthday in Israel.
Halla and David in Tel Aviv, Israel.

9

After Davey's first trip around the world.
President Batista of Cuba and David.
Street fiesta in Santiago, Cuba.
Davey's second birthday in Santiago, Cuba.
Dancers in Cuban night club.
With Sergeant Jesús María García, Santiago, Cuba.
Filming the Brussels "Ommegang" procession.
Vigelund statues in Oslo, Norway.
Davey at the controls of a DC 6 B over the Pacific en route
    to Japan.
Young Japanese "Maiko" Geisha in Kyoto, Japan.
Cormorant fishermen at Gifu, Japan, on the Nagara River.
Pearl divers of Japan.
Japanese Festival at Haranomachi.
The Hairy Ainu of Japan.
Shinto priest.

Following page 192:

Watusi warriors at Astrida, Ruanda-Urundi.
Old-style hairdo on Watusi man.
Wagenia fishermen on the Congo River.
At monument marking source of Nile, Ruanda-Urundi.
Watusi woman, Ruanda-Urundi.
Vanishing duck-lipped women.
Halla and David with the Wagenia fishermen on the
    Congo River.
Congo witch dancers in village of Mai Munene.
Chief of the Mai Munene.
Night dance of the Mangbetu, Paulis, Congo.
Halla towers over Pygmy couple, Ituri Forest, Congo.
Watusi warriors of Urundi.
The Bakuba King meets with advisers.
Congo Mangbetu girls wearing *negbe*.
Leopoldville night club in the Congo.
Davey's birthday on the Congo River.
Firemen of Leopoldville.
Halla and David riding camel in Egypt.

Inside the tomb of Ramses VI at Valley of the Kings near Luxor, Egypt.
Guide Rangi and David in Rotorua, New Zealand.
David and Halla with the Maori of New Zealand.
Rare Kiwi birds, Auckland, New Zealand.
Kava ceremony, near Pago Pago, American Samoa.
Police at Apia, Western Samoa.
Filming the dances of Tahiti. Papeete.
Sunset at Tahiti.
A Fiji policeman.

Following page 264:

Lisbon's Tower of Belém, Portugal.
Portuguese country dancers.
Gypsies of Granada, Spain.
The Alcázar, famous castle of Segovia, Spain.
Segovia.
Boy dancer in Tangier casbah restaurant.
Davey and Greek Army Evzone friends, Athens, Greece.
Golden Horn, Istanbul, Turkey.
Russian guards in Red Square marching to tombs of Lenin and Stalin.
Famous big bell inside the Kremlin in Moscow.
St. Basil's Cathedral in Red Square, Moscow, Russia.
First anniversary on television thrilled us.

All photos by Hal Linker.

Preface

IN OUR SEARCH for "Wonders of the World" to see and film and share with our television viewers, we have never lost our deep and constant awe at the greatest wonder of them all: the Divine Power that brings together two people from different backgrounds and, perhaps, from areas remote from one another, and blends them together through a chemistry called marriage into a husband and wife team who not only love each other, but also sincerely admire and respect one another. Whenever we see newlyweds, our greatest hope for them is that they may be as happy as we are.

Hal & Halla Linker

Three Passports to Adventure

Chapter One

Khyber Pass Adventure

I BRACED MYSELF against the back seat of the ancient sedan, while Halla, my wife, huddled next to me. The car lurched and groaned over the deep, hardened ruts of a lonely road or rather, wagon trail, in the North-West Frontier Province of West Pakistan. It was almost midnight. The biting cold of a dust-laden wind came through cracks in the dirty windows and openings by the sagging door posts.

I envied my wife. A native of Iceland, I assumed that she would pass off the night chill as something of no consequence. After all it *does* get cold in her native country. But Halla was as uncomfortable as I was.

"I've lived too long in southern California with you," she told me through chattering teeth, "I'm cold, Hal!"

At our feet our son David Thor, eleven months old, slept peacefully, happily in a makeshift car bed. I leaned forward and touched him. He was a warm little furnace. The ancient car slewed around a turn. Once it had been a luxurious limousine with working shock absorbers. Now it jolted and rattled like a demoniac oxcart. The fenders slammed down on the frayed tires of the rear wheels. A cloud of dust poured into our compartment and almost hid the driver.

I gripped the old upholstery and closed my eyes. There were vertical drops skirting the trail. As the dust subsided I cautiously looked ahead. The driver, muttering in his own tongue, continued the rather one-sided wrestling match with the huge, bucking steering wheel.

The Pakistani was a slender, narrow-shouldered man—almost a starveling. Yet I could not help but marvel at his unsuspected strength. He had to have the stamina of a wrestler to cope with the unyielding steering geometry of the car.

I struck a match and checked my watch. Halla stirred.

"Are we almost there?" she murmured, half-asleep.

"Not yet."

We were on our way from Peshawar to Rawalpindi—a matter of 150 miles of wild travel through the Khyber Pass country noted for banditry and pure, native cussedness—to catch a plane. I tried to peer ahead. The fitful yellow headlights merely etched a monotonous tableau of ruts, rock, and looming granite cliffs.

Snatches of Kipling's tales of soldiering in the Khyber Pass came to my mind, and I felt my coat pocket for the tiny .25-caliber Czech-made pistol inside. The drawling comment of the watery-eyed, mustachioed Englishman we had met in Peshawar came back to mind.

"If you hit one of those bandit types with that toy and he found out about it, he'd be rather annoyed, he would!"

For a moment I wanted a Western-style Colt .45. "Better yet I wish we had a company of Marines!"

Halla stirred. "Did you say something, Hal?"

I cleared my throat. "I'll never complain about the Los Angeles freeways again."

The driver abruptly jammed on the foot brakes and grabbed the emergency-brake lever. The car slewed and came to a halt. Little David woke up and began to wail.

Revealed in the headlights of our car was a solitary figure.

His black eyes glittered beneath bushy brows. A turban came low over his swarthy forehead. He wore a long tunic and baggy trousers—the typical costume of the semi-wild, nomadic tribesmen of the Frontier Province. Crisscrossing his chest were two bandoliers filled with gleaming cartridges. All this could be seen with a glance, and then I realized that he carried an Enfield rifle. Of most importance was the fact that its muzzle pointed directly through the windshield toward us.

The caliber of an Enfield is .303. At that particular moment it looked like the opening of a railroad tunnel. I gripped my toy pistol.

Our driver quaveringly called out. The rifleman growled an answer and pointed toward a pair of ruts which wandered off into total darkness.

I leaned forward. "What's going on?"

The driver twisted the wheel, put the car into low gear.

"Answer me!" I demanded.

Halla tapped my shoulder. "How can he, dear! He doesn't understand English."

I sank back next to her, the car slowly wheezed down the path, I saw dim figures trotting alongside. They all carried Enfields.

When the car slowed, the driver pointed ahead. The beams of our headlights illuminated a ponderous iron gate. The car came to a halt. The driver got out and walked to a narrow slit in the gate.

Halla and I sat trying to look nonchalant while the armed, beturbaned shadows peered with curiosity at us. The driver was being addressed by someone inside the gate. He cringed and when he replied his tone was apologetic, almost wheedling—or so it seemed.

At times like these, imagination can do terrible things. Mine ran amok. We were lost. The driver would obviously sacrifice us to save his own skin. I would resist to save my family. I would have given anything to have had a black-and-white Los Angeles police department cruiser pull up alongside and hear a gruff voice say, "What's going on here?"

Halla gripped my hand. "Are we in danger?" Her voice was clear and calm. She always had confidence in me.

"I don't know yet," I replied.

The driver fished out some papers and passed them through the slit. For a long moment everything was quiet. We sat stiffly in the back of the car. The armed shadows scrutinized us, and the driver calmly—too calmly, I thought—lit a cigarette.

Abruptly the gate began to swing open accompanied by the creak and groan of rusty metal. A nattily uniformed figure emerged, stepped up to the car. The armed shadows fell back as the young Pakistani officer—his shoulder pips proclaimed him a captain—saluted.

"Sorry to delay you like this!" His voice had a clipped, British accent.

"Is anything wrong, Captain?"

"Rather. Automobiles are normally not permitted on this road after dark because of bandits. Nasty chaps. We had to make certain who you were." He paused and gazed at us. "I say, we didn't give you a nasty start, did we?"

"Not at all!"

"Righto." He fingered his small mustache. "Your documents permit you to pass!"

Now that Law and Order had re-entered our lives I felt as refreshed and alert as though I had been riding all night on a cloud. "What is this place, Captain?"

"A fortified bridge." He smiled. "When the sun goes down this bridge is locked until dawn. No one can pass without special permission, such as you have."

He paused and eyed my wife and son. "You can, of course, continue to Rawalpindi. However, despite the fact that we have no accommodations here for you, I'd rather you'd stay here until daylight. It would be much safer."

I remembered that there was only one plane a week out of Rawalpindi. "We've got to be on the plane when it leaves Rawalpindi in the morning!" I said. "They're expecting us in Lahore."

Halla smiled at the captain to reassure him, and the captain was visibly impressed by her smile. I could well appreciate that, though we no longer were newlyweds.

He clicked his heels and saluted, then turning to our driver, volleyed curt orders in Afridi. With a clashing of gears we were again on our way.

As we resumed our lurching, chill journey through this lonely, hostile land I contemplated the fate that brought our little family along this primitive road near the Khyber Pass in northern Pakistan.

This, I told myself, comes under the heading of "It's a living!"

Some men sell insurance or cars. Others fly airline jets. I happen to earn a living—and an interesting as well as a rewarding one—by traveling to the far ends of the earth and recording what I see on motion-picture film in color. I film for travel-adventure programs for television as well as for geographical societies in the United States.

Halla, my beautiful young Icelandic wife, has the wanderlust of the Vikings in her veins. Our adventurous existence appealed to her even though she was a wonderful homemaker and greatly enjoyed our home in Los Angeles. On this trip, we had filmed the gyrations of the fierce Khattuck tribal dances in the vicinity of Peshawar. We had shown the tribesmen in the village of Kohat surreptitiously making illegal rifles and submachine guns to use in their interminable feuds. We had wandered through the native bazaars with their spicy aromas of cookery and perfumes. We had explored the incredibly colorful Street of the Storytellers and watched as venerable sages clad in colorful costumes a hundred generations old held their audience entranced with fables and legends, as Omar Khayyám did centuries before.

We had photographed native actors performing their stylized drama in bustling market places and youths twirling madly in imitation of the dancing of maidens. By long established custom in the North-West Frontier Province girls are not permitted to dance in public, and this was the substitute provided.

We had even resorted to subterfuge to obtain motion-picture films in the Khyber Pass. Although permission had verbally been extended us in Karachi to shoot footage in the pass, the actual written permits had not caught up with us in Peshawar, so we had to "bend the law" a bit.

To get the necessary scenes we placed an extra camera under the mattress of Davey's car bed. While we temporarily surrendered one camera to the border guards, we managed to get our work done with the smuggled camera, and these scenes were later cleared with the Embassy of Pakistan in Washington, D.C.

After filming every vestige of romance and excitement in the North-West Frontier Province we were on our way to the Peshawar Airport to board the weekly plane for Lahore.

The day had been oppressive, and because we were exhausted the usual blast-furnace heat seemed worse than ever. As we drove to the airport we noticed an ominously black, earth-hugging cloud come sweeping toward us.

An airline official came running up. "Sandstorm," he panted. "Everyone head for shelter in the lounge. Safer there!"

In less than ten minutes the low-hanging cloud swept over the field and abruptly turned day into blackness.

Ten other miserable souls huddled with us behind the boarded-up windows while the howling wind shook the building and forced sand through cracks in the walls.

Halla and I watched Pakistani women wearing their Burkah veils that completely covered them. They in turn stole glances at us through the eye-level net insert in their flowing robes. The moment these women reach maturity they begin to wear these white, all-concealing costumes. From then on until they die, they must never be seen unveiled by anyone but immediate members of their family or by feminine companions. As we spat sand and grime, we almost envied them their "sand-armor" outfits.

In our group was a rather mannish Russian woman about thirty who sat to one side with a stolid disregard of the raging elements. Earlier I had noticed at the ticket counter that although she was listed as an agriculturist she carried a diplomatic passport.

I tried to be a "peoples-to-peoples" envoy by striking a casual conversation with this "Ninochka," but she responded with a level, dispassionate gray-eyed stare which slowly swept over me, Halla, and the baby and then dropped to a massive magazine. After that cold appraisal by which we were investigated, classified, and relegated to a mental filing cabinet, I gave up and morosely waited for the sandstorm to blow Peshawar off the face of the earth. It was then that a British-accented, disembodied voice came through the public address system.

"Ladies and gentlemen," it said with annoying sang-froid, "we regret to inform you that owing to the sandstorm the plane has been unable to arrive from Rawalpindi. We will arrange to send you to Rawalpindi by automobile. The plane will depart from there for Lahore early tomorrow morning!"

My heart sank. We were more than 150 miles from Rawalpindi, over the tortuous roads of the Frontier Province.

When we had returned to Peshawar from Fort Salop where we had filmed the Khattuck dances, the commandant had insisted on providing us with an armed guard, as we would not be returning to Peshawar until almost dusk. If things are that bad around here, I thought, then what will happen during a night trip through the heart of the bandit country?

I eyed the Pakistani women and Ninochka. The Russian woman must have been a front-line soldier during World War II. Probably at Stalingrad. She merely lifted her eyebrows and then went back to reading her tome, as though an all-night journey by car through the Khyber Pass were an everyday affair. Or didn't they read Kipling in Russia?

For a moment I was tempted to stay another week and catch the next plane, rather than subject Halla and the boy to the all-night ride. And then I remembered our hotel, Dean's.

It was built something like an American motel, with all rooms at ground level. The windows of our bedroom were mere slits near the ceiling, built so to foil thieves. After eight at night the entire establishment shut down tighter than a drum. Even the water supply was locked up. The ride to Rawalpindi might be the lesser of two evils.

When the airline manager bustled in with the plan of operation, we found that three ancient cars had been provided for the entire group. Five passengers were assigned to one car; five more, including Ninochka, to the second; while Halla, David, and I found that we would ride in solitary splendor in the third.

The driver of our car, we were told, spoke no English.

"However," said the manager, "he is an expert chauffeur, a good mechanic, and a trustworthy fellow! With any luck you should make it in fine shape!"

Hard on the heels of this "optimism" came his plan of operation. Our car would be the first to leave, so if trouble came, the following cars could help. That was comforting. Two hours out of Peshawar I looked back for the reassurance of the tailing headlights. All was blackness. I later found out that both cars had been forced to stop by engine trouble.

I faced front, keeping this information from Halla while our silent jehu continued to fight the wheel, and wondered at the strange way life works out.

How had we come to be wandering through this remote, wild part of the world with an infant son?

It began in Copenhagen one wintry November evening.

A tall, mustached young man had politely tapped me on the shoulder as I stood buying my ticket at the big City Terminal in Raadhuspladsen. He introduced himself.

"I beg your pardon," he said. "I couldn't help overhear you say you were just completing a filming trip around the world. Have you ever thought of going to Iceland?"

"Iceland?" I laughed. "I'm freezing right here in Copenhagen!"

The young man was persuasive. He was insistent. If I hadn't seen Iceland my round-the-world trip really wasn't complete. He introduced himself as Asbjorn Magnusson, Copenhagen representative of Loftleidir-Icelandic Airlines.

This six-foot-two, mustachioed Icelander was Cupid in disguise.

19906

Chapter Two

"Eg skil ekki Islensku!"

FLYING FROM Copenhagen to London I wondered if I had made a foolish decision. My original, globe-circling filming expedition was to have lasted a month, but the world had turned out to be such a Pandora's box of wonders that the trip had stretched to four and a half months. The color motion-picture footage already filmed was more than enough for lecture needs. And the deadline for the lecture series in the United States was almost upon me.

Still, Magnusson's effervescent briefing on Iceland had so beguiled me that I decided to disregard the looming deadline. During the few hours I had spent in his company the energetic Viking had painted an alluring picture.

Not only had he dispatched messages to his people in Reykjavík, Iceland's capital, arranging my flight from London, but he had wangled a seat for me on the SAS DC6 to London where I would transfer to the Iceland-bound transport.

As I sat by the window, my hands burdened by a mass of brochures provided at the last moment, I recalled snatches of his rapid-fire, enthusiastic description.

"Iceland is a land of frost and fire. We have volcanoes as well as glaciers and the midnight sun!"

"Volcanoes in Iceland?"

"Absolutely." He had nodded. "Our country is one of the most active volcanic areas in the world. It has about twenty active volcanoes. Even though its northern tip touches the Arctic Circle, Iceland is much warmer than you'd imagine."

"With all those fire-belching mountains I shouldn't wonder——"

"No, no—not because of the volcanoes." He had waved his hands. "The southern coast of Iceland is warmed by the Gulf

Stream. Even in the dead of winter the thermometer seldom drops to zero Fahrenheit!"

Recalling his enthusiasm about Iceland's weather made me smile. I felt that it should be taken with a grain of salt.

His people, Magnusson assured me, still spoke almost unadulterated Old Norse—the tongue of famed seafaring adventurers such as Leif Ericson, the Icelandic explorer who found "Vinland" in the New World in 1000 A.D., five centuries before Columbus set sail.

The island is small, only 200 miles wide by 300 miles long. At this time of the year the sun would only be shining about six hours a day. Nevertheless, with luck, I felt I could do the job. Magnusson's Company, Loftleidir-Icelandic Airlines, operated only a once-a-week round trip in the wintertime between Reykjavík and London. I would have seven days between planes to obtain sufficient footage.

The four-engine DC6 shuddered slightly. Wisps of vapor streamed over the wings. Then the patches disappeared and I could see the North Sea below.

I began to sift through some of the notes I had taken while Asbjorn raved about his homeland, which he called "the Land of the Sagas." He had described fantastic geysers, a waterfall "much higher than Niagara," and innumerable hot springs which not only keep Iceland's buildings warm throughout the year but also constantly provide natural hot running water for household uses and for all-year-round outdoor swimming pools.

"In fact our hot springs help maintain a greenhouse industry with fresh fruits and vegetables as well as flowers all through the winter. We even bake bread in the steam from those hot springs. It's called *hverabraud*—hot springs bread."

I recalled another of his remarks. "Our girls are among the prettiest—if not actually *the* prettiest—in the whole world!"

He had gone on to explain that since the Viking settlement of Iceland, starting in the ninth century A.D., the inhabitants have added a mixture of Irish, Scottish, and English to their blood.

"Those old-time Vikings," he said. "They used to raid the British Isles. They always managed to bring back to Iceland beautiful, long-haired 'treasure'!"

He pointed out that Iceland therefore not only has lovely blondes but also beautiful brunettes and redheads as well. "In my country you will rarely see an extremely stout or an extremely skinny girl."

Then he had paused and dryly added: "I don't know why I'm telling you about our pretty girls, of course you're more interested in scenery and folklore!"

"Of course," I had murmured politely. What interest could I, a thirty-two-year-old bachelor, have in Icelandic beauties—what interest, indeed!

The plane shuddered slightly. As I glanced out of the window the plane was plunging through a heavy fog. That was putting it mildly. I learned later that we had encountered the worst fog experienced by London in over a quarter-century.

Coming into Margate not the London airport, I discovered that the Icelandic plane, taking advantage of a freakish, momentary break in the fog, had departed three hours earlier.

It was a jarring letdown, since I had worked myself into a great enthusiasm for the impending visit. But I had learned during World War II, that the best-laid plans "gang aft agley."

I shrugged off my Iceland detour and took the first airliner to Los Angeles, California—starting point of my protracted trip.

The ensuing weeks were hectic. There were "miles" of film to be developed and edited. I had to prepare narration. There were lecture engagements to fulfill in cities of a dozen states. And I was also putting together my future travel-television series, "Wonders of The World!"

Iceland should have faded from my memory. But despite the feverish activity I could not erase Magnusson's glowing descriptions.

"Dear Mr. Asbjorn Magnusson," I found myself writing a few months later, "I am sorry that fog upset my trip to Iceland. However, you have so intrigued me that I think that next summer I could come to Iceland to make a full-length color film. If you and your government should happen to be interested——"

The answer came by return air mail. It was an enthusiastic invitation from Thorleifur Thordarson, director of the Iceland Government Tourist Organization. I was to sail in June from New York City as their guest aboard the Icelandic ship *Tröllafoss* and proceed to Reykjavík.

So it was that I soon found myself standing on a remote Brooklyn dock staring at the *Tröllafoss* (pronounced Trud-la-foss). The name meant "Waterfall of the Elves" in Icelandic. It was a tiny vessel, aptly named, I thought, and for a moment or two I felt a qualm about venturing across the North Atlantic in this elf-like ship.

Although it seemed sturdy, its 3,990 tons was lilliputian compared to the imposing bulk of ocean-spanning greyhounds such as the French Line's *Liberté* or the Cunard's Queens.

As I studied the little ship I found myself thinking of the invasions of Iwo Jima and Okinawa, the operations in the Marianas, the Caroline Islands, and the Philippines and the occupation of Korea, when I was an Intelligence officer in the Amphibious Forces of the Navy. The silhouette of the *Tröllafoss*, with its aft located superstructure and cargo hatches, closely resembled the tiny Navy "AK" supply ships which I had so often watched from the "APA" attack transports that had been my world then. The war was five years in the past, but it still seemed close.

Just as I put foot on deck I happened to glance forward. Flying from the bow was a flag which bore a huge, dark-blue swastika on a white background. I froze in my tracks.

A stocky, uniformed man (it was the ship's chief steward) touched the peak of his cap. "Anything wrong, sir?" His English was accented.

"Anything wrong!" I pointed to the swastika. "What the devil is that Nazi flag doing there!"

His blue eyes widened beneath bushy blond brows and then narrowed. He thrust his jaw forward and drew himself up to his full five feet, five inches. "That, sir, is *not* a Nazi flag!" His face flushed. "*Everyone* knows that the Nazi swastika is different."

I was taken aback. "But——"

"Our symbol has shorter arms. What you see on our flag is the old Viking symbol of the hammer of Thor, Norse god of thunder. We've used that symbol in Iceland for over a thousand years—before the Nazis ever crawled up out of the seven pits of hell. And we'll be using *our* symbol long after those murdering swastika scoundrels are completely forgotten!"

He paused to catch his breath. Then before I could utter a word of apology he plunged ahead. "What's more, sir, during the war we lost many of our men and fishing ships to Nazi submarines."

"Sorry," I murmured. "I didn't realize——"

His face softened. He finally smiled. "A natural mistake for an American to make. Welcome aboard, Mr. Linker!"

During the nine-day voyage I found the little world of the *Tröllafoss* happy and orderly. The stout little vessel not only carried a respectable amount of cargo but provided comfortable accommodations for about fifteen passengers.

My fellow travelers were mostly Icelanders returning to their homeland. Their names, redolent of their Viking backgrounds, intrigued me. Among them were Hallgrímur Lúdvígsson, Svava Brynjolfsdóttir, Oddur Thorarinsen. Also aboard as passengers were Thor Thors, Jr. (his father was then and still is Iceland's Ambassador to the U.S.) and Miss Evelyn F. Alden, a pleasant, elderly vacationing Philadelphia schoolteacher.

It was Oddur Thorarinsen, a young fellow of twenty-three, who took great delight in teaching me two "important" sentences in Icelandic.

"No matter where you go or what you do in my country just say what I am going to teach you." He was quite solemn.

He made me repeat over and over: *"Eg er Ameriskur kvikmyndatökumadur. 'Eg skil ekki Islensku!"*

When I asked what it meant, Oddur would frown. "First learn to properly say it. Later I'll tell you what it means!"

Phonetically it came out as: "Yegg air Ameriskoor kvik-mindatuckoo-mah-thoor. Yegg skeel ekki eeslenskuh." Everytime I repeated it and then pressed for a translation Oddur shook his head.

"Not yet," he would say. "You still do not have it right." Finally after practicing my phonetic Icelandic I asked the chief steward, Helgi Gislason, who by now, was a good friend: "Will I get my head knocked off for saying that in Iceland?"

He chuckled. "All you're saying is: 'I'm an American cameraman. I don't understand Icelandic!' "

Oddur sparked an interest in the Icelandic language which has steadily grown. The capital of Iceland, Reykjavík, can easily be pronounced if you break it down as "Rake-yah-vik." Also, more than a thousand years ago, in the days of Leif Ericson, the language was spoken throughout almost all of Scandinavia. On the European continent itself the original Old Norse gradually developed into three distinct languages: Swedish, Danish, and Norwegian. Only in Iceland, because of its isolation, did the Icelanders retain the almost pure tongue of their Viking forbears.

Oddur told me how his people have resisted the introduction of foreign words for new concepts. "Unlike the other Scandinavian countries we have not adopted words like 'television,' 'helicopter,' or 'telephone.' "

"In Icelandic a helicopter is *thyrilvaengja* which literally means 'beater-winged.' Television is *sjónvarp* which means 'picture-throwing,' telephone is *sími* which means a 'line.' "

"Take your profession, Hal." He smiled. " 'Cameraman' in our language is *kvikmyndatökumadur*. This word is made up of *kvik*, meaning 'quick,' *mynd* which is 'picture' (a quick-picture obviously is a movie) *toku* which is 'take,' and *madur*, a 'man.' So you see how our Old Norse deals with your profession. The word is actually a descriptive phrase. You are 'a man who takes quick pictures'!"

The voyage took us past Nova Scotia and Newfoundland and into the iceberg lanes just south of Greenland. The sight of those ominous floating mountains of ice was chilling. Gazing at those jagged white peaks and knowing that 90 per cent of their bulk was below the surface of the icy water I remember mentioning to the purser that I was thankful the *Tröllafoss* had radar.

"True," he had quietly replied. "Except for one thing. It's temporarily out of order!"

I involuntarily shivered. During daylight hours the icebergs could be spotted by our lookouts. However at night, without the protection of an all-seeing electronic radar eye, it would be another matter. I recalled the sinking of the *Titanic* after it had collided with a gigantic iceberg in 1912 in these same waters.

During the next to the last day at sea I renewed an old wartime acquaintanceship—fog. The *Tröllafoss* crept through an ominous shadow world while the fog horn maintained a constant, depressing, plaintive moan. Oddur remarked that it reminded him of an ancient Norse Norn grieving for a fallen Viking.

But the last morning of our voyage saw bright sunlight splash the sparkling blue water with dancing flecks of gold. It was as though the world had renewed itself. Everyone perked up. Even the sound of the propeller shaft seemed to assume a quickened, optimistic note. And when I saw the coastline of Iceland loom dead ahead, the menace of icebergs and the gray ghost-world of fog faded from my mind.

When Captain Bjarni Jónsson invited me up to the bridge I set up my camera and took a long-pan shot of the approaching coast. The island was brilliant with the green of early summer. Even

Mount Esja, which loomed in the background, hardly bore a trace of snow.

I turned to the skipper, a short, roly-poly individual. "Why do you call your country Iceland? It looks as green as my California!"

"That was because one of our ancestors—how do you Americans put it—'goofed' in publicity!" He lit his pipe.

"About the year 868 A.D. a Viking named Floki set sail for an island in the North Atlantic which had been seen from a distance by other Scandinavian explorers. In those days nothing much was known about this place. None of the Vikings had ever landed here." He waved his pipe stem toward the approaching island.

"Floki sailed his dragon boat all around the island and landed at the worst possible place—a peninsula on the northwest corner which juts out towards Greenland. To this day it is known as Isafjördur—Ice Fjord! Floki came ashore just as winter set in. He saw icebergs floating in from Greenland and one snow storm after another. He spent a miserable winter. And he decided to call the island 'Ice-land' from the icebergs he had seen, even though spring and summer showed him that the land was good and the climate mild." The skipper chuckled.

"When he returned to Norway no one wanted to go to a land with such a forbidding name even though Floki assured them that the land was so good that 'butter drips from every straw'."

No further attempts were made to settle here until after King Harald "the Fair-haired" set himself up as the ruler of Norway in 872. The Vikings were an independent lot. Many of them refused to swear allegiance to anyone, let alone Harald who was not exactly popular.

"A group of 'rebels' attached themselves to a Viking named Ingolfur Arnarson who was about to lead an expedition to the Iceland." Captain Jónsson eyed me. "Those Vikings were pretty much like the English, French, and Germans who later on left Europe to seek independence and freedom in your America.

"Ingolfur's group did not have good prospects. All they had to go on was Floki's unhappy winter experience and the ominous name Ice-land. They expected a hard life in a cold, hostile land. But they felt that it at least would be their own country; there'd be no king telling them what to do!"

He gestured beyond the starboard bow. "Luckily enough they

landed on the south coast. You can imagine how happy they were to learn that the island was green and not a land of ice."

He nodded toward Mount Esja. "As the leader, Ingolfur had to decide where to build the settlement. In those days our ancestors were pagan, Mr. Linker. They had gods for everything especially carved, wooden household gods that were supposed to ward off evil. Ingolfur let his household gods select the place where they would settle down!"

I looked at him questioningly.

He nodded. "Aye—he had his wooden gods thrown overboard. Wherever they washed ashore, he insisted, would be the proper place to settle permanently."

It was a compelling scene he had conjured up in my mind: the low Norse dragon boats with their rows of colorfully decorated shields fixed to the gunwales, the Vikings in full armor solemnly standing by as the wooden effigies were ceremoniously thrown overboard.

The captain told how it had taken almost a full year of searching from their temporary camp before Ingolfur's followers found the idols where they had been washed up on the sands of a bay on the southwest coast of the island.

"It must have been quite a moment," he continued. "According to our sagas Ingolfur lifted the gods and looked around to decide on a name for this permanent settlement. He saw steam vapor rising nearby from many hot springs. He decided to call this new place 'the Bay of Smokes'."

"Exactly where is that place, Captain?"

He laughed. "In the language of the Vikings, which is the language of Iceland of today, 'the Bay of Smokes' is Reykja-vík." He pointed to the harbor dead ahead. "And that's exactly where we are right now!"

As I stood on the deck of the *Tröllafoss* filming the activity of disembarkation a tall, blond, impeccably attired young man approached me.

"Mr. Linker?"

I nodded.

"My name is Thordur Einarsson. I'm with the Iceland Government Tourist Office." His accent was extremely British.

"Wonderful," I exclaimed, extending my hand and smiling with what I felt was proper American enthusiasm. "I'm so glad to meet you, Mr. Einarsson. I'm delighted to be here——"

His level blue-gray eyes were unsmiling. He gravely returned my handshake and kept regarding me without changing his expression. It was my first encounter with typical Icelandic reserve. My own smile grew strained and finally disappeared.

He was polite, but businesslike. He efficiently whisked me past the customs and immigration officers, gathered up my baggage and camera gear, hailed a cab, and accompanied me during the short ride from the dock to the Hotel Borg, my Reykjavík headquarters, a five-story building erected in 1930 on the central square of the city.

En route he methodically enumerated a list of places to visit and activities that I might wish to film. "We will see the geysers, waterfalls and hot springs," he stated with his clipped British accent which, to me at least, seemed unusual for a native Icelander. "Later I shall take you to the northern part——"

"Where Floki landed?" I cut in with a tentative smile, anxious to display some knowledge of his nation's history.

He coolly eyed me. "Right you are," he said and then continued where he left off. At the hotel he left me after seeing to it that my hotel accommodations were in order, saying, "I'll return at six to take you to dinner."

Dinner turned out to be an excellent meal served in the cheerful confines of the main dining room. In fact as the evening wore on my reserved companion displayed traces of thawing, especially when discussing his country.

"We are proud of our educational system," Einarsson emphatically said. "There is absolutely no illiteracy in Iceland. What is more we publish more books and newspapers here per capita, for our 155,000 population, than they do anywhere else in the world. D'you know that we have five daily newspapers here, just in Reykjavík alone?"

"How many people live in Reykjavík?"

"Only 55,000 now, but it's growing. One third of our country's population now lives in the capital."

"And here's something else," he continued. "Every Icelandic school child must actually know how to swim before he or she can be graduated from public school!"

I thought of how many lives might be saved in my own country if American elementary schools adopted the same requirement. It forcibly reminded me how much we could learn from smaller nations like Iceland.

"But enough of this," Einarsson interrupted my thoughts. "Tomorrow we'll make an early start to visit 'Geysir the Gusher.'"

"The Gusher?"

"In Old Norse *geysir* means 'gusher.' In fact that's where your English word 'geyser' originally came from—the name of the very erupting hot spring which is located about seventy miles east of here." He paused.

"I guarantee you'll find it spectacular!"

I covertly studied this young government official, originally so formal and distant, and now quite friendly. For a moment I was tempted to ask why he had been reserved at our first meeting. And then I changed my mind. There would be plenty of time not only to film all of Iceland but also find out what made its people tick.

Thordur met me the next morning with a car and driver and we passed through the streets of Reykjavík. There were no tall buildings in town, the tallest at that time being the Hotel Borg. Since that time they have had a building boom and a series of five fifteen-story "skyscrapers" has been built, plus many other new and modern buildings. Most of the houses were built of poured concrete and many seemed unfinished on the outside.

Many people were still living in Quonset huts at that time, since the war was only five years past and there was a housing shortage. At the foot of Bankastraeti we passed a two-story frame building, beautifully painted white and standing in a little park. Thordur told me that this used to be a prison about two hundred years ago, but in those days they had so few prisoners they turned it into a Government House, which it remains even today. Several government offices, like the Office of Education are housed there.

We also passed the statue of Leif Ericson as we left town. This statue was given by the Congress of the United States to Iceland on the one thousandth anniversary of the founding of the Icelandic Parliament in 1930. On the back of the monument are these words: "Leifr Eiriksson, Son of Iceland, Discoverer of Vinland. The United States of America to the People of Iceland on the 1000th anniversary of the founding of the Althing A.D. 1930."

On the outskirts of town the new housing developments were

already taking shape, with hundreds of two-story houses of substantial construction going up. I stopped to film these. On a small hill just on the outskirts of town are seven large tanks, like oil tanks. Into these tanks is piped the hot water from the hot springs about ten miles out of town and from these tanks comes the hot water to heat almost the entire city of Reykjavík.

The next hours found us following a road which wound through a strange, austere, treeless land. I stared at the traces of lava flows and watched steam rise from innumerable hot springs.

Einarsson noted my absorbed gaze. "Our country is still geologically young," he explained. "The volcanoes are quite active. In fact there have been many serious eruptions during the past thousand years. That's why we have no trees today although there were great forests when the Vikings first came here. However—" with a shrug—"we Icelanders have learned to harness nature——"

I thought of the elaborate network of insulated conduits I had seen which pipe hot springs water from miles away to heat Reykjavík. This was truly harnessing nature.

As we jounced along the rough road into the interior he pointed out that there were no streetcars or railroads in Iceland. "We depend on buses, automobiles, and two domestic airlines," he said.

I reminded myself of the Icelanders' seafaring heritage. Their little island was so small with all the settlements dotting the coasts, what need had they for extensive land transportation systems?

He pointed to the passing landscape. "The ground here is primarily crumbly, volcanic slag. It could never sustain the weight of railroad roadbeds, locomotives, or rolling stock."

When we reached the "Big Gusher" I was immediately reminded of a Gustave Doré illustration of Dante's *Inferno*. A group of tourists, primarily from Sweden and Norway, with many of the women wearing their national costumes, stood to one side watching the steaming, bubbling scene with fascination. No other Scandinavian country has hot springs and geysers like Iceland. Einarsson and the driver of our car watched from a respectful distance while I got my camera ready.

I pointed to the water-filled crater. "This looks more like a pool of violently steaming water," I said. "Where's the gusher itself?"

He checked his watch. "It should erupt at any moment. The government man prepared things five hours ago!"

Now it was my turn to look blank. "What d'you mean, a government man 'preparing' things? Do they make this geyser spout with an underground pump—or a heating device?"

Just then I heard a warning rumble. I turned in time to film just as the geyser violently roared, sending a tower of scalding water more than 125 feet into the air, time and time again.

When I had completed my filming of the hour-long eruption, Einarsson explained about the "government man." Some fifty years before, the Icelanders noticed that the gusher seemed to be diminishing. In fact, for a number of years, it didn't erupt at all.

"Our scientists discovered that the crater around the geyser's opening was growing larger. The increasing amount of water that then filled it gave more surface to the cooling air, thereby making it too cold to erupt," Einarsson said.

"Our engineers then entered the picture. First they cut a channel into the side of the crater. Now for special occasions a government supervisor lets out water to reduce the level of the water in the crater by six feet. Then he tosses in about a hundred pounds of raw soap. This changes the viscosity of the water and temporarily fills some of the subsurface holes. As a consequence the water temperature rises"—he paused, made an explosive gesture with both hands—"and then the grandfather of all erupting hot springs —Geysir the Gusher—obliges with a first-class eruption about five to seven hours afterward!"

As I thought this over it seemed to me to be a perfectly legitimate thing for the Icelanders to do, since people come to Iceland from thousands of miles away to see the "granddaddy of them all" and it would be a shame if the geyser couldn't be made to erupt for special occasions and tourists missed it completely because the weather happened to be too cool.

In the following weeks I covered much of the island. I flew to the northwest to visit the site of Floki's landfall. I visited Akureyri and Husavik. I explored the desolate Námaskard—a foreboding wilderness of boiling mud, strange lava formations, and sulphur pits, climbed the side of the volcano Mount Hekla, filmed the impressive Dettifoss waterfall, and flew to Siglufjördur, where I shot footage of Iceland's thriving herring industry.

Meanwhile I also learned of the Icelanders' proud tradition of freedom and equality which was established by their Viking ancestors so long ago.

Einarsson's pride was quite evident when he brought me to a

35

hallowed place, seventy miles from Reykjavík, and described how, in 930 A.D. the world's first parliamentary assembly, the Althing, was established here at Thingvellir, thereby making Iceland an independent republic more than two centuries before England's Magna Charta was signed.

"In 1930, on the occasion of the one thousandth anniversary of the founding of the Althing the British Parliament sent a message of congratulations to our Althing," Einarsson beamed. "It was addressed: 'From the *Mother* of Parliaments to the *Grandmother* of Parliaments'!"

He had gone on to tell how, after three hundred years of independence, the Icelandic Republic had been joined to Norway. "Then a hundred years later, in the late fourteenth century, the Danes took over from the Norwegians, but Iceland never gave up its dream of once more having freedom and independence. Finally," and his eyes had flashed, "we were able to cut loose from Denmark in 1944! We're now an independent republic with a president and a parliament, modeled somewhat on your American republic."

During these absorbing weeks when I got to really know Einarsson, I discovered that his seemingly "cold" attitude at our first encounter was actually nothing of the sort. Icelanders are straightforward, matter-of-fact people who do not believe in being demonstrative on first meeting.

I grew to realize that their normal way of greeting is a polite handshake and a serene, non-smiling exchange of straightforward glances. In many ways this directness can be attributed to the influence of the surrounding ocean, the fact that for generations Icelanders have gone down to sea in fishing vessels to wrest a precarious living from Davy Jones's cold lockers.

"Fishing is our main source of livelihood. Without the ocean we might starve," he once remarked. "We respect the sea but it is an inexorable enemy." I recall how he turned to me. "Your playwright, Eugene O'Neill, in one of his great works he called it 'that old devil sea.'"

"*Anna Christie*," I said.

Einarsson nodded. "Anna's father, the barge captain, he was a Scandinavian sailor. He knew the sea, its beauty, its ruthlessness, its ferocity—like we Icelanders!"

"We thought you'd like to know more about the seas around

Iceland, too. That is why we are arranging for you to go on an Icelandic whaling expedition in a few days!"

I caught my breath. "A whaling expedition! Me and Captain Ahab," I exclaimed.

His seriousness was dissolved by a sudden grin. "Come now. It isn't so terrible. I assure you that most of the time our whalers come back!"

The following evening I found myself dining alone in the Hotel Borg. Einarsson was spending some time with his family. As I sat at the table I began to plan a shooting schedule for the following day.

I wanted to film the amazing greenhouse industry where roses, carnations, bananas, tomatoes, and corn are grown by means of the heat piped directly from the natural hot springs. As I was having my coffee I glanced up from my notes just as two young couples entered the dining room.

One of the girls was a tall slender blonde. Her exquisite profile was silhouetted by the lights in the background. As I stared at her she happened to look my way. I was conscious of deep sea-blue eyes. She was a Viking princess come to life. Then she smilingly accepted her escort's arm and went to a nearby table.

I sat quite still, somewhat stunned by how I felt. I could not take my eyes from her. I was fascinated by the way she moved, the animation of her features when she spoke to her companions. And I found myself envious of the young man who was lucky enough to be with her.

Magnusson's words came back to me: "The prettiest girls in the world!"

My coffee had grown cold. I beckoned to the waiter and asked for a fresh cupful.

A thought struck me. She would make a beautiful model, typical of Iceland's charm, for the greenhouse sequence, and perhaps to wear the beautiful Icelandic national costume for my film.

Before I realized what I was doing I rose from my table and approached her. I found myself standing at her side. Her three companions curiously appraised me while she looked up into my eyes with an unflustered, direct gaze. "Excuse me," I managed to get out, "but, I mean, do you speak English?"

37

She nodded. "Yes, I do!" Her voice was low and clear and her accent absolutely charming.

I took a deep breath. Disregarding how I might have appeared to the others I plunged into what could have been deep water. "I wonder if I could speak with you for a moment—on a business matter!"

She turned to her companions, said something in Icelandic and then stood up. For a moment her eyes delved deeply into mine and then, as though reassured by what she saw, she turned and walked ahead of me to a secluded corner of the dining room.

Once there I introduced myself, explaining who I was and what I was doing in Iceland.

"I know, Mr. Linker," she interrupted. "The newspapers—they have discussed your visit here."

I heaved an inward sigh of relief. I had forgotten about the press interviews Einarsson had arranged. There had been stories and photos in all the papers and now I gave fervent mental thanks for them. I told about my contemplated filming of the greenhouse industry. "Would your fiancé—er—or husband object if I were to ask you to pose with a typical Icelandic costume in my motion pictures?" I asked.

She smiled. "He is neither fiancé nor husband, Mr. Linker. And I would be happy to pose for you—that is, if someone from the government will, how do you say it—" A pretty frown knit her brow as she groped for the proper words.

"Vouch for me?" I cut in.

"Yes." Her blue eyes danced. "That is it. Vouch for you!"

She told me her name was Halla Gudmundsdóttir. When I asked how she spelled her first name she replied: "H-a-l-l-a" although she pronounced it "Hod-la."

Noting my perplexed expression she said: "It is a proper Icelandic name. Why are you so surprised?"

"It's the 'd' sound. There's none in the spelling, where does it come from?"

She threw back her head and laughed. "We get it from the same place you get the sound of 'r' in your English word 'colonel'! You see 'll' in Icelandic happens to be pronounced as if it were 'dl'."

"Touché." I ruefully acknowledged her point. "By the way, you speak English beautifully. Where did you learn it?"

"In the Menntaskólinn here in Reykjavík. I'm told it's equivalent to a junior college in your country. I was graduated only a few weeks ago." I remember marveling at the amazing coincidence that if you took my name, a perfectly normal Hal, and added to it the initials of the city in which I lived, L.A., you would get her name, Halla.

I learned that she lived with her parents in Hafnarfjördur, about seven miles from Reykjavík. I told her I'd get hold of Thordur Einarsson, the Government Tourist Office man the very first thing in the morning and arrange things so that it would be proper for her to accompany us to the greenhouses.

Back in my room I simply could not get my mind away from Halla. I tried to analyse my feelings. A sudden thought made me ponder on the ways of fate. Had there not been that terrible fog the previous year, which had prevented me from catching the Iceland plane in London that November day, I would have undoubtedly proceeded to Reykjavík, taken my films during the seven-day period that year, and then returned to the States.

During all that time Halla would have still been attending classes at Menntaskólinn. And since I would not have had any reason to return to Iceland in the summer I would never have met her. The thought was unnerving. "Good old London fog," I sighed with relief.

The greenhouses I wanted to film were located some thirty-five miles from Reykjavík in a little town called Hveragerdi. En route we picked up Halla. At the hotel she had been striking enough clad in a simple tailored suit. Now, wearing an ornate, richly embroidered Icelandic costume with sunlight burnishing her long blond hair she looked more than ever like a Viking princess who had stepped straight out of the pages of a romantic Norse saga!

Hveragerdi proved to be a fantastic community where about twenty years previously the houses had been purposely built over hot springs so that each dwelling could have a natural hot-water supply in its own backyard.

The greenhouse industry was fascinating. I posed Halla amidst grapes and stalks of corn. I took close-ups and long shots showing her inspecting orderly rows of growing plants. I filmed her surrounded by flowers. The time seemed to fly as she cheerfully, willingy changed from one pose to another before my camera lens. Needless to say, after getting acquainted on this first trip I

39

lost no time asking her to go out with me again, and we saw much of each other in the ensuing days.

The whaling expedition seemed to take longer to get organized than Thordur had anticipated. That did not disturb me in the least since it gave me an opportunity to get to know Halla better.

We had dinner together several times and spent many evenings dancing while our food grew cold on the table.

Gradually I came to realize I was in love with her and that she was exactly the girl I had always been searching for throughout the world, and had never before found. Each evening when I took her home by taxi I would think only of the next day when we would meet again and not of the day when I would leave Iceland.

One night as I returned to the Hotel Borg, although it was fairly late, I was whistling "Some Enchanted Evening" when I entered the lobby and started for my room. The desk clerk called to me.

"Mr. Linker, Mr. Einarsson has been calling. It's quite urgent. He said to call him no matter how late you came in."

I picked up the phone. Einarsson's voice was jubilant.

"It's all set, Hal," he exclaimed.

"What's all set?" I asked.

"The whaling trip. You'll leave at the crack of dawn!"

Chapter Three

Whale Ho!

AN ICY, SPRAY-LADEN WIND lashed us on the open bridge of the small ship whose bow carried the unassuming name *Whale No. 3.*

Originally the weather had been mild and the sea calm when, as a three-ship flotilla, we had sailed from Hvalfjördur. Now, more than one hundred miles off Iceland's coast, an approaching storm darkened the sky and was beginning to churn the sea.

I stood beside the tall, blond, bareheaded young helmsman and watched his knuckles whiten as he gripped the spoke handles of the rebellious wooden steering wheel. His dripping hair hung down over his forehead.

His eyes, squinting against the rising gale, alternated between quick stabs at the swaying compass bowl and an occasional glance toward the desolate horizon. I knew he was concerned about our sister ships: *Whale No. 1* and *Whale No. 2.* They were nowhere to be seen. Our radio was out of order. We couldn't contact them nor could we hear the weather forecasts.

Our skipper, Captain Schulstock, left his station in a corner of the bridge and approached us. His teeth were clenched around the stem of a stubby unlighted pipe and his deep-set blue eyes, shadowed by the peak of a leather cap and framed by a network of weatherbeaten wrinkles, worriedly peered up at the low-hanging overcast.

He momentarily removed the pipe from his lips and yelled into my ear: "If this storm gets any worse we'll turn back!"

Just then a wavering cry drifted down from the lookout in the crow's nest on the swaying mast. *"Hva-a-AALL Blouse-ter!"* [Thar she blows!]

The skipper sprang to the railing of the bridge and peered ahead. He turned, shouted to the helmsman. The latter nodded and began to change the course of the 125 foot whaler. I made my way across the bridge to the skipper's side.

"There she is," he pointed.

I tried to shield my eyes from the stinging, salty spray. At first all I could see were waves. And then I spotted the telltale spout.

"She's a big-fin whale," Schulstock exclaimed.

As we started to close the gap between ourselves and our unsuspecting quarry the crew began to load the big harpoon mounted on a platform on the bow. The operation reminded me of naval gun crews preparing for action.

An explosive charge was placed in the breech of the gun, a long-shafted heavy harpoon was inserted in the barrel of the gun and then, much to my amazement, a second explosive charge was screwed onto the nose of the harpoon. It was explained to me that one explosive charge propelled the harpoon into the whale and then, as the harpoon entered the whale's body, a lanyard was automatically pulled which made the second explosive charge on the nose go off inside the whale. This opened the prongs of the harpoon inside the whale, prongs which were folded back alongside the nose of the harpoon until now.

We stalked the whale for those hours in the rising storm, since a whale comes to the surface and spouts or "blows" three times and then "sounds" or dives for the bottom searching for food. While down it can change direction and speed, so the captain has to try to guess where it will come up. After four hours the captain stopped the ship where he thought the whale might come up and made his precarious way down a narrow catwalk that connected the bridge with the harpoon gun.

Our ship climbed a towering wave, momentarily hesitated on the crest, and then dipped toward the trough. The whale appeared dead ahead. Captain Schulstock aimed for the hump in the middle of the whale's back and pulled the trigger. The harpoon gun roared with the ear-splitting blast of a five-inch gun.

The harpoon itself, trailing fathoms of rope, tore into the whale's hump. There was a muffled explosion from the second explosive charge.

The whale dove for the bottom trailing what seemed to be miles of rope. I noticed that the rope from the harpoon went through a device on the bow of the boat and then went directly up to a pulley high on the mast before going down to the winch. This made the mast of the ship a sort of tremendous fishing rod to take up the strain of pulling in the whale. But we weren't ready to pull this whale in yet.

The stricken creature's tail beat the water into froth. Captain Schulstock frowned, ordered the harpoon gun to be reloaded.

I watched and filmed as he bided his time and then fired a second charge. Again the whale dove. The line paid out at a furious clip and then began to slack. Captain Schulstock barked an order and a crewman started to reel in the line with a power-operated winch.

When the whale resurfaced we were almost on top of it. A wave momentarily exposed it to my startled gaze—it looked almost as large as a submarine!

Much to my amazement the captain ordered the whaling gun reloaded again and he prepared to fire a third harpoon into the whale. Noting my look of surprise he turned to me and said, "Mr. Linker, in the United States when you want a steak for dinner or leather for a pair of shoes you have to kill a cow. Well, to get a very important industrial commodity, whale oil, we have to kill a whale. This is business, not a sport, and I don't want the whale to suffer and die over a long period of time. This third harpoon is a humane harpoon," and he turned and fired the final harpoon. The whale was then dead, but a whale is a mammal, not a fish and if allowed to remain in the water too long it would tend to sink, so to keep it afloat they did a very simple thing, yet something that surprised me. They inserted an air hose about the size of a garden hose, into the whale's body and inflated the hulk with air to keep it afloat. Then it was lashed alongside the ship and I could see that it was a 70-foot whale, weighing about 70 tons, while our little ship was only 125 feet long. A chain was used for the lashing. The tail flukes of the whale stood up into the air about ten feet or more and the captain ordered the ends of the tail cut off lest strong winds or the sea cause the entire tail to break off. A hole was also cut into the tail for an identifying buoy in the event that we have to cast this whale off and go after another one.

We searched all that night for other whales, but it wasn't until the next morning as the storm seemed to be getting even worse that we sighted another spout. An identifying buoy was quickly attached to the tail of the whale we had caught and then to my surprise a 15-foot pole with a small black flag on top was inserted in it's back, so it could be seen from a distance, and the dead whale was cast adrift to float by itself while the crew tried to catch the second whale.

We didn't get the other whale, however. The fury of the storm struck when the captain had had only one chance to fire at the whale, and as I recorded it all on film, he missed when the whale dove underneath the ship and got away. We barely could get back to our first whale again, tie it to the ship, and head for shore when the full fury of the storm hit us.

Now the captain turned to the helmsman and ordered him to change course. The latter nodded and began to turn the wheel. I grabbed the bridge rail and stared at the attacking waves.

The howling wind, now of gale intensity, plucked rain from the scudding clouds and flung bullets of icy water into our faces. I was a somewhat uneasy spectator at the unfolding drama.

The skipper put his mouth to my ear. "We'll run for shelter near Snaefellsjökull."

I nodded. Any landfall would be to my liking; even Floki's "Land of Ice" peninsula would have been "paradise enow" at the moment. I looked over the turbulent sea. "What do you think happened to the other whalers?"

Schulstock shrugged. "If we're lucky we'll meet 'em when we land!"

I tried to snuggle even more deeply in the sou'wester and oil-skins I had borrowed from the captain. I certainly had not bargained for an experience such as this when I had decided to film the "summertime" whaling expedition. For a while, though, I forgot the storm as I thought of Halla.

As I happened to glance at the helmsman he caught my eye and grinned. I rather imagined I knew what was going through his mind. During the winter months he was a university student. It was only during the summer that he came to the coast of Iceland to ship out as a crew member on the sturdy little whalers. This was his vacation!

It was then that I became aware of a continuous series of thudding blows that made our ship shudder from stem to stern. This had been going on for some time, but I had assumed that it was caused by the battering waves.

Captain Schulstock's look of worry told me that it was something else. He muttered what could have been a prayer or an imprecation and made his way to the port side of the bridge. When I

44

caught up with him he pointed below. Looking down at the dead whale lashed to our ship, I saw the reason for his worry.

The huge mammal was riding almost on the surface of the water. As I watched the gargantuan body slammed into the hull. "That thing's liable to crack this ship wide open!" I exclaimed.

He nodded. "The banging against the ship has fermented the food in the whale's stomach. Look, it has formed gas which has bloated the tongue up like a balloon!"

I leaned over the railing. What I saw was startling. The gases had passed from the whale's stomach through a slit in the back of the tongue. The tongue itself was blown up to a grotesque, leathery sphere more than fifteen feet in diameter.

"That's what is making her ride so high," Schulstock said. "We have to puncture the tongue, let out the air so she'll again float low in the water!"

Even as we watched whale and vessel again met with sickening impact. The skipper turned, cupped his hands around his mouth, and bellowed orders above the fury of the wind. I saw a crewman spring into action.

"What's he going to do?"

"Tie himself to the railing and try to cut the tongue open to let out some of the gas!"

Sensing a thrilling sequence for my film I turned and made my way down from the swaying, lurching bridge to the lower deck. En route I picked up a length of rope which I intended to use to tie myself to a railing in case the weather got worse.

I braced myself in the shelter of a bulkhead on the low, main deck which was almost constantly awash. The inflated tongue of the whale loomed above me. I aimed my camera and waited.

The seaman on the deck above grasped a huge, scimitar-shaped blade called a flensing knife by its four-foot handle. For a moment he hesitated and then drove it into the bloated tongue. I pressed my finger on the camera trigger button and took pictures while gas came whistling out with a nauseating odor and the tongue began to collapse. Time and again the sailor cut and slashed.

I kept filming as the whale's carcass slowly began to sink back into the water. At last it rode barely exposed to the seething surface. The battering ceased. There was now a protective cushion of sea water between its inert hulk and the hull of *Whale No. 3.*

During that wild, storm-tossed moment I had not the slightest notion that the footage I had taken would someday be leased from me by RKO Pictures and incorporated in their Technicolor film *The Sea Around Us*—a production which won an Academy Award as the best full-length color documentary film for 1954.

Although common sense suggested that I should stop pressing my luck and retire to the captain's cabin until the storm subsided I decided instead to wander about the careening ship, filming additional storm scenes.

Meanwhile I continued to carry that length of rope, always planning to use it to lash myself to the railing and then promptly forgetting to do so whenever a new shot presented itself.

Not long afterward I noticed that the ship's motion seemed to be subsiding. I thought that it was because the whale was riding low enough to act as a help rather than hindrance, but actually we were in the shelter of the mountain and glacier called Snaefellsjökull on the west coast of Iceland.

The coastline of Iceland looked good to me. And the next day when I set foot on the dock of the whaling station at Hvalfjördur it was to find Thordur Einarsson waiting for me.

"Good old terra firma," I exclaimed, stamping my foot on the ground. "And the firma the better!"

He looked searchingly at me. "How was the whaling trip, Hal?"

"It was routine, just routine." I tried to be nonchalant.

A couple of my erstwhile whaling shipmates passed at that moment. They glanced over at me, said something in Icelandic, burst into roars of laughter, and went on. Thordur, at first, seemed startled. Then he grinned. "Routine, eh? You must have been carrying a rope around with you on the ship."

"Rope?" Now it was my turn to be startled. "Why—what did they say?"

His eyes twinkled. "They were saying that the weather was so bad the American tried to hang himself!"

The whaling station was over an hour's drive from Reykjavík and it was growing fairly late in the evening. I asked Thordur if he would mind waiting while I attended to an extremely important, personal matter.

He eyed me for a moment and then said: "Not at all, Hal."

I sought out a phone book in the whaling station office and began to scan the directory. I had left Halla's telephone number

46

with my passport and other documents at my hotel room. I went down the line of names beginning with G. I could find no listing for Gudmundsdóttir.

Strange, I did it all over again. Still no luck. There was a tap on the door. Thordur came in and looked questioningly at me. "Can I be of assistance?" he asked.

"I'm trying to look up Halla's phone number," I said. "But I can't find the name Gudmundsdóttir listed at all."

He smiled. "That isn't the name you want, Hal——"

"But—it's her name, I'm sure of it."

"Let me explain. In Iceland we use the Viking system of patronymics in which a person's *last* name is derived from his or her father's *first* name. Here's how it works. Supposing a man's name is Gudmund and he has a son who he names Harald. The boy's full name is automatically Harald Gudmundsson because this tells the world he is Harald, the son of Gudmund. Then when Harald Gudmundsson has his own son eventually and perhaps decides to name his boy Jon, the boy's full name is Jon Haraldsson, since he is Jon the son of Harald, just as his father was Harald the son of Gudmund. In other words, the last name merely tells whose son they are.

"What happens with girl's names?" I asked.

"Well," he explained, "Supposing that same man, Gudmund, has a daughter and he decides to name that girl Halla—her full name would automatically be Halla Gudmundsdóttir, meaning Halla, the daughter of Gudmund. Incidentally, Hal," he went on, "that's how your Halla gets her last name of Gudmundsdóttir."

Disregarding my perplexed look, he plowed on. "You can understand now why women in Iceland never change their names when they marry."

"I can?" I murmured, but Thordur continued, "Their last name merely tells whose daughter they are, and obviously that wouldn't change just because they get married. Supposing your Halla should marry someone named Jon Magnússon, for example——"

"Not if I can help it she won't," I muttered.

"—she couldn't take the name Magnússon since that would make her the son of Magnús. That's why Icelandic women always keep their maiden name, with the only difference being that before they marry they are called *Ungfrú* or Miss Halla Gudmundsdóttir and after they marry she would be *Frú* or Mrs. Halla Gudmundsdóttir.

"Okay, Thordur," I broke in, "now I know why she's *Ungfrú* Halla Gudmundsdóttir, but how do I find her telephone number?"

He smiled. "Since the first name here is really the important one, while the last name merely tells whose son or daughter we are, all listings in the phone book are by first names. Just look in the book under H for all the Hallas and then look down that list for the Halla who is the daughter of Gudmund!"

Using that magic formula, I found the number in twenty seconds flat. It was 9747.

As I listened to the faraway phone ring I felt more apprehensive than I had been during the worst of the storm at sea. What if she did not——

The receiver at the other end of the line lifted and I heard her voice. My words came out in a rush. "Halla, it's me—Hal—I'm back and I know it's late but I simply must see you. It's something that is absolutely important—" I paused. There was silence at the other end.

"Hello," I said. "Are you still there?"

"I'm here, Hal," she answered. "Of course I'll see you."

"Could you meet me at the Hotel Borg. I'll be there in about an hour and a half——"

Her voice was calm and steady. "I'll be there, Hal."

I had one other call to make. The day before my departure for the whaling expedition I had dropped in at a Reykjavík jeweler who spoke English. In response to my questions he had informed me that the Iceland custom when people decided to become engaged was to exchange wedding rings.

"For an engagement ring the woman wears a wedding ring on her left hand with the man's name engraved inside the band," he had explained. "The man wears an identical ring with his fiancée's name. When they marry the rings are changed to the right hand in accordance with European custom. Thus the wedding ring is the engagement ring until they marry."

I asked the operator to get the jeweler and I waited impatiently until he answered. When I told him I'd be coming by to get two wedding rings he pointed out that it was quite late. "Wouldn't tomorrow do?"

"It's an emergency," I pleaded. "I'd count it as a personal favor

48

The whale's tongue inflated with gas from the stomach, giving the whale greater buoyancy; the whale banging against the side of the ship threatened to sink us (100 miles off Iceland's coast).

The whale was so big the end of the tail had to be cut off lest the entire tail break off during a storm (100 miles off Iceland's coast).

Group of Icelandic youngsters in front of Ingolfur Arnarson statue—Reykjavik.

Halla in the national costume of Iceland.

Grapes growing in greenhouses heated by hot springs at Hveragerdi, Iceland.

Up from the filming in the Welsh coal mine.

The schoolteacher from Merionethshire who was chosen best poet in all of Wales is seated in his dark robes at the Chairing of the Bard Ceremony at the National Eisteddfod.

Morris dancers at Bampton, England.

The Laplander family we visited near Ivalo, Finland.

David meets a Swiss guard at the Vatican in Rome.

Aloha, Hawaii.

In the Philippines, cart drawn by carabao.

Hong Kong – through the city.

A first rickshaw ride in Hong Kong.

if you'd be kind enough to open your place so I could pick them up tonight."

There was a pause. "When will you be here, Mr. Linker?"

"Within an hour."

During the drive over the rough highway which wound along the rugged coastline I kept looking at my watch and mentally urging the driver to "step on it." Thordur sensed my impatience but politely made no comment.

He did not even raise an eyebrow when I asked him to let me off at the jeweler's. I raced in. The proprietor smiled.

"Are they ready?" I was breathless.

He nodded and showed me two simple gold wedding bands. Inside, one read "Halla." The other, smaller one bore my name.

"If the young lady's ring does not properly fit return it and I will make it either larger or smaller," he said.

I nodded, paid him, apologized for the trouble I had caused, and then rushed to the Hotel Borg.

Halla was seated in the lobby. For a moment I stood there, holding her hand.

I ushered her into the dining room. They were on the verge of closing but I talked them into serving us coffee.

"Halla," I began and hesitated.

"Yes?"

"During that whaling trip I had a chance to do a lot of thinking. I—I'm in love with you, Halla——"

I fumbled in my pocket and produced the rings.

"Halla—will you marry me?"

For a moment she did not say anything. It was the longest moment I have ever lived through. And then she put her hand over mine.

"Yes, Hal," she whispered. . . .

Chapter Four

"For Better or For Worse"

NEW HAVEN, CONNECTICUT, is a charming little city. But not for a young couple trying to get married on a Saturday. I had chosen New Haven because it was the residence of my married cousin, Mrs. Janice Price, and not far from Halla's arrival point, New York. But when we got there and tried to get someone to perform the ceremony it seemed that everyone with the proper authority had left for a long weekend. Even my cousin, a "native," seemed frustrated.

When after frantic search she finally did establish an official contact it was only to discover that insofar as the sovereign State of Connecticut was concerned Halla, being twenty, was a minor. She would have to obtain her parents' written consent before there could be a ceremony.

The man who told us that was an attorney named Herman R. Alderman. I recall thinking, even at that moment of dismaying news, that his name would be appropriate if he ever ran for public office.

We all sat there, blank-faced. Halla swallowed and then said in a tiny voice: "But my parents are in Iceland!"

Mr. Alderman rubbed his chin and stared at the ceiling of his office. "That, my dear, poses a problem."

Again there was a pause. And then Halla continued. "Would I have been permitted to come all the way from Iceland, alone, to get married if my mother and stepfather had not approved in the first place?"

"But it's a state law," the attorney cut in.

"—Would the American authorities, the U.S. consul in Reykjavík, have allowed me to come here on the regular Iceland quota if"—she looked at me and involuntarily grasped my hand—"if everything had not been properly arranged?"

Mr. Alderman frowned. A clock loudly ticked away in a corner. I had a sinking sensation in the pit of my stomach. Ever since Halla had embarked on her journey to my side things had seemed to go wrong.

First there had been the matter of the airline foul-up at New York's Idlewild Airport. When I had first pushed my way through the hurly-burly of the international section to the airline which was bringing my fiancée to the United States I had felt as though I was walking on air.

My first shock came when the uniformed ticket agent behind the counter blandly told me that no one had any "idea where the plane was."

"You mean—the flight hasn't left Iceland yet?"

"Oh, it left there, all right. We simply haven't heard from it since." His expression had been calm, as though not hearing from airplanes was routine.

I took a deep breath. "Let's start all over again," I said. "The ship left Iceland according to schedule?"

He nodded.

"Did it land at Gander, Newfoundland, for refueling?" I asked.

He shrugged. "Not so far as we know!"

I had tried to overcome the growing chill inside. "It's a four engine plane, a Constellation, right?"

"Oh yes."

"Can it fly non-stop all the way from Iceland to New York without having to refuel en route?"

He shook his head. "Hardly, sir. They'd *have* to land at Gander!"

"But according to you it's unreported at Gander—it's overdue there."

Again that nod. The chill within me expanded. "My fiancée is aboard that flight." I almost whispered.

An uncomfortable look crossed his face. "I'm sorry!"

I had gone weak in the knees. I remembered gripping the edge of the counter and thinking of Halla's mother and stepfather and how they had so completely entrusted their daughter to my care.

Her mother had come from Isafjördur, the small northwestern community where Viking Floki had landed. Isafjördur women, according to Icelandic legend, were reputed to be clairvoyant.

51

Regardless of whether it was true or not she had given me the compliment of telling her daughter, when we first met, that she felt "I was the right man for Halla." At the time I had not known what she had said. It was later that Halla gave me the translation of her mother's comment.

At the airport I remembered that scene. And then I lost my temper, pounded on the counter, and demanded to know the truth. "If something has happened to that plane and it has crashed in the sea somewhere between Newfoundland and Iceland I want to know—and right now!"

I had finally shattered his peculiar calm. He had retreated to an inner office. The next instant an older man, obviously the head of the staff behind the counter, had emerged. By this time a cluster of other people, waiting for the same plane, had collected at my elbow.

The older man wore a grave expression. "I hate to tell you this, sir," he had begun in a sepulchral tone.

I felt my brave, shining new world beginning to break into little pieces.

"—But due to a mix-up in communications we've made a mistake——"

I hung on his words.

"—The plane you're expecting was delayed for eight hours at the Keflavík Airport in Iceland. It took off from there only about half an hour ago." And then he smiled. "The plane with your fiancée aboard should be landing here about twelve hours from now—9 P.M. tonight, New York time!"

Sitting in Mr. Alderman's office, listening to that clock ticking away I felt once again the chills and frustrations that had started at the airport. The attorney's expression had not changed after Halla's last plea.

And then he had suddenly smiled. "Mr. Linker, your fiancée would make an excellent Portia!"

He glanced at the clock and then began to consult ponderous legal tomes while filling out a number of official-looking documents. He finally rose, stuffing papers into his pockets, and exclaimed:

"We'll have to rush if we want to catch a certain judge I know before he leaves the courthouse!"

Rush we did. And in the austere setting of the judge's chambers by virtue of a special waiver, Halla Gudmundsdóttir, my beautiful Viking princess, became Mrs. Hal Linker at noon on October 7, 1950.

Immediately after the ceremony I asked his honor if we could place a call to Iceland, to Halla's parents. We all stood by while my bride excitedly poured forth a happy torrent of Icelandic into the instrument.

We left immediately for our honeymoon in Washington, D.C. and after that to Hollywood. And as far as we are concerned it is still a honeymoon a decade later!

There are matrimonial "authorities" who like to claim that financial strain is one of the worst pitfalls for a marriage.

If such is so Halla and I should have run into difficulty from the very start. After I had carried my bride "over the threshold" of our small Hollywood apartment I had to take serious stock of our financial situation. Frankly it was not too good.

As a world-gypsying bachelor I had kept house as—well, a typical bachelor, save that the apartment was overflowing from floors to ceilings with a clutter of war and peacetime souvenirs, camera equipment, film-editing apparatus, cans filled with developed motion-picture footage, and volume after volume of books of information, plus a tremendous collection of magazines covering almost every known nook and cranny of the world.

This mass of what I chose to regard as orderly disorder had never bothered me. But when we entered the apartment, fresh from our honeymoon, and Halla stood still, staring at the tremendous clutter I found myself, for the first time, surveying my "castle" through her eyes. And I felt myself grow red.

"I know it's a mess, dear," I began.

"But it isn't," she excitedly exclaimed. "It looks so—so busy, so many things, books—" And then she had looked at me. "You do work so hard, Hal-minn!

Her immediate understanding, the use of the quaint Icelandic term of endearment, Hal-minn, which meant "my Hal" made me feel like a giant ten feet tall. Her understanding, co-operation, and love have been the same ever since.

I motioned to the film stacked in cans which overflowed the apartment. I pointed out to her that intrinsically those thousands of feet of exposed and developed motion pictures were worth many thousands and thousands of dollars.

I explained that virtually every cent I owned was wrapped up in that mass of coiled and packaged celluloid.

"These are what financiers would call 'frozen assets' Elskanmín. [This I had learned means "my dearest" in Icelandic.] To realize any income I will have to accept film lecture engagements whenever and wherever I can."

She nodded. "It's all right," she said. "I will be economical and keep house while you're gone on your lecture trips."

"You will do nothing of the sort!" I said.

Halla stared at me.

"You'll go *with* me. The apartment can keep while we're on tour!"

I could afford to say this since most of my engagements were in cities within the Pacific Coast area. Our honeymoon was neverending, as Halla accompanied me on trips to San Francisco, San Diego, Sacramento, Seattle, Portland, Bakersfield, and Fresno.

A gay and wonderful companion, she thoroughly enjoyed getting to see and know her adopted country. However there were times when I would have to accept lecture engagements in New York, Chicago, and other eastern and midwestern points. We desperately needed the money but I was reluctant to accept such assignments. I simply hated to be away from Halla.

She was practical, however. "This is your work, Hal," she would say. "I want to help you. Don't worry about my being alone while you're away."

We would daydream together. And when I told her how I proposed to somehow continue traveling around the world, filming nations, people, their customs, ways of living— "And you'll be with me, Elskan-minn," her blue eyes would sparkle with delight.

It was a wonderful life even if we were broke two thirds of the time. We were so thoroughly wrapped up in one another that when we drove to lecture engagements in our battered old sedan with barely enough gasoline to make the trip we felt as though we were traveling in luxury aboard our own yacht over far-off, exotic waters.

Sometime during the fourth month of this idyllic existence it was evident that shortly little David would come into our world. Of course at the time we did not know it would be a David. What did matter was that we were going to have a child. Our happiness was complete.

At the time of Halla's pregnancy I was averaging between $100 and $150 a lecture. The booking agent, of course, would take her 25 per cent slice first. And since I had to pay all transportation and living costs to and from each lecture I generally wound up with a net of hardly enough to make the entire effort worth while.

I certainly had nothing in sight to make me feel financially optimistic. The days of becoming a television program producer were still in the distant and inscrutable future.

I got in touch with Mr. Herman Ramo of the Finnish National Travel Office in New York. Would his people be interested in having Mr. Hal Linker "cover" Finland with motion pictures and accompanying lectures? They would!

While Halla slept I sat up and furiously searched out my financial resources. The Finns would provide one way passage for both of us from the U.S. to their country or round trip for me alone. I chose one-way for both. And since the airline connections would pass us through Britain it meant that I could cover England and Wales as well as Finland—two complete films in one journey.

My objective was to finish our trip in Iceland, where Halla could be with her mother at the time of the birth. I also hoped that I would be able to conduct a series of lectures showing my Iceland films to Icelandic audiences. Talk about carrying coals to Newcastle!

When I asked Halla if she would like to embark on a filming expedition which would get her to Iceland in time for the baby's arrival her eyes lit up. And then she clasped her hands in her lap and looked tenderly at me.

"Hal-minn, I'll go anywhere you want me to as long as it's with you. If it takes me back to Iceland I'll be happy only if it's good for you as well!"

I took her hands in mine and told her what I had done and hoped to do. "I'll have to borrow some money. And it'll be a calculated risk. Maybe Icelanders won't want to hear me talk about Iceland or see my pictures. But I want to do this, Elskan-minn. I have a certain feeling, an optimistic feeling——"

Her eyes misted. "All right. Then we will go. And you will be successful!"

It took a lot of doing to scrape together even a minimum of

operating capital. But it was finally accomplished. With high optimism and very much in love, we took off in May of 1951 for New York and then flew on a wing and financial prayer to Glasgow, Scotland, where we were to board a London-bound airliner.

The airport at Scotland was a dour place.

After our long flight across the North Atlantic, for the most part bucking head winds and encountering turbulent air, we made our way half-dead with fatigue to the British European Airways ticket counter at Renfrew Airport for our connecting flight which would take us to the capital of the British Empire.

A sympathetic ticket agent shook his head. "Haven't you heard?" he asked.

"Heard what?"

"We've been grounded—by a strike!" He gazed at me and Halla who drooped with near-exhaustion. "I'm afraid there are no planes going to London, Mr. Linker."

My wife was then in her sixth month. She had not once complained about the ordeal of the long journey which had taken us from our Hollywood apartment all the way to Scotland. But as she sat on the nearby hard waiting-room bench every line of her body betrayed her bone-deep weariness.

I stood there trying to think of some course of action. "What about a railroad connection to London?"

"There is an overnight train, I believe, but it's fully booked because of the strike!"

Again I stared at Halla. I flinched at the thought of telling her the cheerless news. Just then another uniformed BEA man came along. He wore a wide grin as he accosted the chap behind the counter. "Just got a wire," he said. "The strike *might* be settled this afternoon."

I almost grabbed him. "D'you really think so?"

He shrugged. His Scottish burr was thick. "Well, y'know how these things go——"

Our ship was a twenty-one-passenger Douglas Dakota—the British designation for the twin-engine DC3 which had seen wartime service as a Royal Air Force Transport plane.

We no sooner left the ground and the pilots retracted the landing gear when the Dakota nosed up into an overcast that seemed as

56

thick and lumpy as Scotland's proverbial haggis. Before long the plane began to bounce and sway.

Little by little hoarfrost obscured the windows. And when the flight engineer emerged from the cockpit and began to examine the leading edge of the wing by means of a flashlight I grew somewhat concerned.

"Anything wrong?"

"Ice," was his succinct reply.

My knowledge of aviation is typical of that of any groundling. Pilots frequently refer to people such as myself as "paddlefeet." But one thing I did understand at the time. And that was that ice belonged on lakes and rivers in winter, surrounding sea-food cocktail glasses in restaurants, or in highballs. But not on airplane wings in flight!

After the taciturn engineer popped back into the cockpit I tried to peer through the frosted window but could see nothing.

And then as the accumulation of "flight-fatigue" began to overcome me (Halla was already sound asleep, her head cradled against my shoulder) there was a sudden, sharp, crackling sound as though something had smartly rapped the fuselage.

I sat bolt upright. The cockpit door opened again and the flight engineer reappeared. He once more flashed his light through the window. Another blow jarred the plane.

I had visions of the wing rivets gradually popping off. After all the plane did seem slightly tired. "What's all that noise?" I asked.

"Ice cracking off," he said shortly. "The wing de-icer boots are finally working. Nothing to worry about, really."

Again he disappeared. I looked at Halla's golden head. Thank goodness she was sleeping through all this. The ice knocked at the thin dural frame of the Dakota for the third time. Nothing to worry about, the man said.

I put my arms around my wife. Nothing to worry about, eh? "That's what you think," I muttered to myself. "I have everything to worry about—right here, in my arms."

Chapter Five

The Way of the Welsh

ALTHOUGH WORLD WAR II was six years in the past, London was still cloaked in austerity. And as our taxi took us in search of hotel accommodations which were then as scarce as a satisfactory diet, we saw the looming shapes of bomb-shattered buildings on all sides.

The British European Airways (BEA) people had dispatched us to several hotels, but even they were pessimistic about our ability to obtain accommodations. Our financial situation, making it essential that we limit ourselves to lower-priced hotels, made our search even more hopeless. Even if we were to find local accommodations I dreaded the thought of traveling throughout the length and breadth of England and Wales seeking out an accommodation in each city. J. C. Henry, the Public Relations Officer of BEA was brought into the picture when we reported failure to find a room.

Mr. Henry came up with a suggestion that I grasped as if at a last straw. "Why don't you drop in on the Trust Houses organization?" he urged. "They're splendid people."

I learned that Trust Houses Ltd. was a privately owned organization which looks for and purchases historic inns and hotels that have run down in the past centuries and are now being offered for sale. They completely renew these establishments with the objective of keeping alive England's famous traditions of roadside hospitality. This has gained for them the unofficial blessing and co-operation of His Majesty's Government (King George VI was the reigning monarch at that time).

With little hope of solving our dilemma I took a red-double-decker bus to 53 Short's Gardens W.C.2, just off Drury Lane, while Halla waited in the airline office to hear the results.

58

The slip of paper I held in my hand from Mr. Henry told me to see M. G. Phillips who was the director. At the office I was ushered into a small office, where I found a charming elderly lady of about sixty seated behind a desk. "May I see Mr. Phillips, please?" I said respectfully.

"Do you mean M. G. Phillips?" she asked.

"Yes, that's the one," I replied, "I have business with him."

"Perhaps you can tell me what it is," she came back.

I hesitated for just a moment. Usually I prefer to take my problems right to the one who can help me and not have my words pass through a third party, but this time I found myself sitting down and telling her the whole story—our need for accommodations in London and especially while we were traveling around the island. I was even candid enough to tell her that our finances were low because of the films I had bought for the Finland filming as well as for the England and Wales filming.

She looked at me searchingly for a moment and then questioned me in detail about Halla's being along with me. I recall the approving smile she gave me when I explained that I thought families should always try to remain together and that although Halla was in a family way I felt we should still be together on this trip. She nodded approvingly when I mentioned that I wanted Halla to be with her parents in Iceland when the baby was born.

I watched her as she scribbled a note, rang a little hand bell on her desk, and handed the note to the young lady who came in. There was a murmured instruction and the young lady left.

"What cities in England and Wales were you planning to visit?" she asked. I rattled off a list of about fifteen of the main towns on our itinerary, which she copied down.

"Well, Mr. Linker," my unbelieving ears heard, "I think I can arrange for you to stay at our Trust Houses in almost all of those cities."

"But don't you think it will be necessary to check with Mr. Phillips, to be sure about it?" I protested.

At that moment the young lady entered bearing a letter, which my benefactress glanced at and then handed to me. It read:

TRUST HOUSES LIMITED

17th May 1951

To all Trust Houses Managers,

This letter will introduce Mr. Hal Linker. He and Mrs. Linker should be entertained as the Company's guests.

Yours faithfully,
M. G. Phillips

And then as my mouth slowly dropped open, she continued, "And if I may have that letter back for just a moment I'll be happy to sign it. You see, *I'm* M. G. Phillips, the Director!"

Ordinarily a very polite person, I am sure that I must have thanked M. G. Phillips before I left her office, but I honestly am not positive, since I returned to Halla in a daze at our good fortune.

"Well, that's one hurdle we've gone over," was the comment of Mr. Henry as he briskly rubbed his hands together. "Now to get you a car."

Like gamblers who keep going when they seem to have a run of luck, we decided that we should try to line up some transportation that very day. So it was that I found myself speaking to a Mr. Victor Bridgen, who operated a fine fleet of rental automobiles under the intriguing company name of Victor Britain, obviously derived from his own name. Like our benefactress M. G. Phillips he also must have been impressed by my story because as if in a dream I heard him telling me that his organization would be most happy to give us the free use of a Morris sedan for the entire period of our stay in the British Isles. "After all," he smiled, "we, too, would like you to have all facilities needed to get a fine film of our country. The better a film you make, the more people will want to come over to visit us from America. Just keep the car as long as you need it!"

Before we left London's sprawling confines we visited Westminster Abbey, a tremendous shrine of old England. I filmed the colorful ceremony of the changing of the Guards at Buckingham Palace. Although these tall, immaculately uniformed and highly disciplined troops are human beings, their ponderous, measured

60

stride and the inexorable pace of their maneuvering brought home to me, more than anything else, the almost superhuman, permanent quality of the English nation.

We even entered the incredible traffic of Piccadilly with our little Morris while I took footage of Eros perched on his stand and then drove to the Tower of London, scene of much of England's most glorious—and darkly tragic—history.

While within its massive confines we gaped at the beauty and incredible wealth of the crown jewels and visited the Chapel of St. John, an example of Norman architecture dating back to the time of William the Conqueror.

Even more intriguing to us was to watch the Yeomen of the Guard, the fabulous "Beefeaters." These stalwart, solemn-faced men, all decorated veterans of either World War I or II, were impressive in their military costumes which authentically date back to the sixteenth-century eras of Henry VIII and Queen Elizabeth I.

As they passed us, bearing their long pikes and halberds, their buckled shoes beating a slow, dirge-like cadence on the ancient stone flagging, it was as though we had been transported by a time machine into the past of four hundred years ago.

Halla gazed up at the tower and visibly shivered. "Now I can imagine how Mary Queen of Scots, or Anne Boleyn, must have felt up there while they waited for the headsman's ax!"

Driving the Morris through England's garden-like countryside was not without its more adventurous moments. Like all Americans I was used to driving on the right-hand side of the road. In England the traffic moves on the left.

As we went our merry way Halla sat more or less curled up to my left, chatting while she knit a wardrobe for our heir-to-be. Most of the time I concentrated on what I was doing behind the controls, which were on the right-hand side. Several times, however, during conversation I found myself absent-mindedly drifting to the right-hand side of the winding country roads.

At one time when I inadvertently did this an indignant bell tootling dead ahead startled me. I veered to the left side of the road in time to avoid a collision with an oncoming, tweedy, elderly bicyclist. I had a momentary glimpse of the highly indignant gentleman brandishing a furled umbrella. I could feel my cheeks redden with embarrassment. Halla, wearing a serene expression, merely continued to ply her knitting needles.

Proceeding and filming in easy stages was like a storybook experience for us. The Trust Houses where we stayed were delightful, colorful, and comfortable.

Since they were, for the most part, restored, authentic hostelries of Britain's historic past, our visit turned out to be one of the most pleasant travel experiences we had.

Windsor Castle was all that the books claimed. The beautiful gardens and sweeping vista of the surrounding countryside has hardly changed since the days of Chaucer.

Our wanderings took us to Oxford and Stratford-on-Avon, birthplace of Will Shakespeare. Halla was particularly fascinated by the Tudor atmosphere of Stratford, a shrine dedicated to the memory of the world's greatest playwright.

She excitedly told me that Iceland's theaters present the works of "the immortal bard." As we wandered afoot through the house where Shakespeare was born and visited the historic little cottage which was the dwelling place of Anne Hathaway, my wife could hardly contain herself: "Just think—here I am, actually seeing all these things I used to read about and dream of in school!"

En route to York and Chester we penetrated an entirely different England. On all sides we found traces of the Roman conquest and centuries-long occupation, all of which occurred almost two thousand years ago!

Seated in an inn situated within the shadow of York Minster, an imposing church noted for its beautiful stained windows, we were reminded by our host, the proprietor, that while Julius Caesar had "probed" Britain in the year 53 B.C. the actual Roman invasion did not take place until 43 A.D., almost a century later.

"Tremendous soldiers those old Roman blighters," he said over a pipe. "Forty thousand of them divided into four divisions, or legions, landed in what we now call Kent.

"They were finely trained, well-equipped veterans of campaigns in Gaul and the Euphrates. They knew amphibious warfare. They'd sew together animal hides, blow 'em up with air, and then pile their gear on these barges. While others on the offshore galleys kept up a barrage of arrows, lances, and missiles hurled by shipborne slings and catapults the advance parties reached shore, put on their armor, and established beachheads which protected the landing of the rest of the legions." He had paused and chuckled. "Old Hitler could have profited by studying Roman history!"

"The Roman emperor Hadrian built a continuous wall, a sort of Maginot Line which stretched some seventy miles across the neck of England—from what is now the Bay of Solway on the Atlantic side, to St. Shields at the North Sea."

"Actually how long did the Romans rule Britain?"

"Almost four hundred years!"

That was twice as long as the United States has existed!

When we drove to the site of Hadrian's wall it was to find only meager traces of that formidable barrier. It was a solemn reminder of how ruthlessly and inexorably time can obliterate the proudest and mightiest of civilizations.

From brooding Roman England we were told to visit the town of Bampton where we could obtain footage of the curious and exciting "Morris dancers" who have performed on each and every Whit Monday, since the Middle Ages.

"Morris dancing" we learned is the spoken corruption of what was originally called "Moorish" dancing. According to legend Crusaders and gentlemen-adventurers, returning from the Middle East, brought back with them their notion of Moorish, or Saracenic, dancing.

Somehow these dances became interwoven with the time of harvest, the Pentecost and the Easter season. Although there is no religious or mystic connotation the quaint and colorful custom remains, with pagan undertones.

We found Bampton jammed by visitors from all over England. The Morris dancers consist of several groups of townsmen who wear large black hats, white shirts, and white trousers. Suspended from the hat brims are ribbons which reach down to the small of the dancers' backs.

Above the knees are affixed additional ribbons which dangle below the kneecaps. Other ribbons, adorned by bells, encircle their ankles.

The "leader" of each group wears a costume strongly reminiscent of those worn by the court jesters of olden days. The music, played by fiddlers is stirring, vivacious, and has a strange syncopation which, at the time of our visit, had both Halla and myself swaying and tapping our feet.

The performers hop, skip, and bend without so much as a pause while they twirl and wave streamers of cloth from their gyrating hands. Meanwhile their leader darts amongst them, striking backs and shoulders with inflated, pigskin bladders that, although painless, produce considerable noise while he exhorts them with shouts of "On with it, me lads. On with it!"

The over-all effect of the yelling, furiously played music, jingle-jangle of bells, whopping bladders is so entirely un-English as to be delightfully astonishing. Although Bampton is the only locale where this performance has been faithfully repeated each and every May since the Middle Ages we discovered that the activity was beginning to spread throughout England—enjoying a popularity akin to that of square dancing in the United States.

Before proceeding to Wales we detoured for a visit to the eerie Salisbury Plains and the huge, Druid Stonehenge whose purpose remains locked in time. Arranged in a circular pattern these tremendous monument-like stones are thought to predate the birth of Christ by some two thousand years, perhaps more.

Although the sun was bright at the time of our pause there the air seemed more than normally chilled. There is a strange atmosphere at Stonehenge. People who believe in occult matters claim that the place is either haunted or accursed.

The old Romans and even the "barbarians" before them were mystified and somewhat apprehensive of the origin and meaning of these ponderous ruins. For many years wayfarers, we were told, avoided traveling past Stonehenge after dark.

It was a comparatively short drive in our Morris Minor to Wales, "Land of a Hundred Castles," which juts out toward Ireland from the west coast.

As we drove along winding roads, passing through fairy-tale villages we gradually became aware of the fact that we had penetrated yet another fascinating area of the world when we saw the intriguing and almost improbable names on signposts, names like Machynlleth, Pwllheli, Llanwrst and Amlch!

The Welsh, for the most part compact brunettes, spoke their own language, a Celtic tongue whose origin is almost as mysterious as Stonehenge. Later we were to discover that the Bretons of France's province of Brittany speak a similar language.

64

We had timed our arrival at Aberystwyth, site of the University of Wales, to coincide with the unusual, colorful annual Eisteddfodd, a festival performed in the Welsh language exclusively, by Welsh musicians, dancers, and poets. It was our good fortune that the Eisteddfodd had been scheduled for Aberystwyth at the moment of our visit. Each year the festival, which is world-renowned, is held in a different Welsh city.

I was able to film the unusual ceremony called "Chairing the Bard" wherein the individual selected as the poet laureate of Wales, is vested with special robes and seated in a thronelike chair for the high honor.

At the time the newly chosen poet laureate was a bespectacled schoolteacher who hailed from Merionethshire. Clad in flowing robes he maintained a solemn composure. But despite that, his pride radiated like sunshine. And that was as it should be. He was the recipient of the highest honor a Welshman can receive.

A highlight of the festival was the Gorsedd ceremony wherein participants parade attired in ornately colored, Druid-like robes. The various colors, we were told, signify the activity or profession of the wearer. Thus while one color indicates that the person practices law, another means that the wearer is a scientist or perhaps an educator.

The highlight of the impressive affair was the magnificent singing of the Welsh choral groups. Halla and I were entranced by the richness of their voices and their tremendous repertoire. We could have cheerfully spent days listening to them but, alas, "time was a-wastin'" and Halla was about to enter her eighth month of pregnancy!

At Cardiff, the Welsh capital, I visited the Welsh Coal Board. After showing my credentials and explaining the objective of our trip I plunged into the purpose of my facing the board.

"I want to go down into a typical Welsh mine and film the men at work," I said.

The board members, nonplussed, looked at one another. Their spokesman wryly pointed out that photography had never before "been permitted down below."

"Precisely why I want to make a film," I said. "American audiences are interested in what goes on in a Welsh mine."

Mr. Islwyn Evans, the senior officer present, cleared his throat.

"There's a lot of 'damp'—gas—which accumulates down there," he slowly said. "To take motion pictures I daresay ye'll be needin' light, Mr. Linker."

I nodded.

"Well, now, that means the use of electricity in one fashion or t'other. What if there should be a spark which would ignite the damp and cause a gas explosion!" He paused and eyed me. "T'would be a pity, that!"

"Ay," agreed another member of the board. The rest of them nodded.

There was an air of finality about them. Just as I resigned myself to foregoing a mining sequence Mr. Jones again cleared his throat.

"Now on t'other hand——"

His colleagues looked at him.

"No reason why our electricians couldna' inspect Mr. Linker's equipment an' make certain it will properly work, eh?"

They nodded. "Our electricians are canny, they are!"

Mr. Jones's weatherbeaten face crinkled in a smile. "Very well, Mr. Linker. We'll break all precedents, we will let you film!"

I could hardly keep from running to the car where Halla patiently sat and knitted while waiting for the outcome of my appearance before the board.

"We're in," I jubilantly exclaimed and sent the little car flying toward the Glyn Tillery Mine, a somewhat gloomy collection of miners, under the eye of Mr. Jones, equipped me with a miner's homes. It looked like the setting for the novel and subsequent motion picture *How Green Was My Valley*.

While Halla sat in the car parked by the mine entrance, obliging miners, under the eye of Mr. Jones, eqipped me with a miner's overcoat and cap, complete with a lamp. Since the Welsh are rather small people and I am somewhat larger in all directions, the fit, as you can imagine, was rather snug. I cut a strange figure bedecked as I was for my descent. Halla had to stifle a chuckle.

With whatever dignity I could muster I picked up my gear consisting of camera, tripod and portable lights and, accompanied by mine electricians and technicians, boarded an empty coal cart with a shift of eight miners who were going on duty.

"Back in an hour," I sang out to Halla. And then the cart started its descent into the tunnel which slanted twenty-five degrees into the depths. Daylight was abruptly blotted out and almost immediately I was smothered by pungent, damp darkness. We rode for perhaps a mile in the small, crowded cart before reaching the "end of the line."

At this point I envied the smaller Welshmen when I discovered with some dismay that we would have to crawl for another quarter-mile to the scene of mining activity, at the "coal face."

My progress was an interminable, back-aching crouch through the four-foot-high, granite-surrounded passageway. Frequently I had to cry uncle by dropping to my elbows and knees for time out. My guides were more than patient. When I apologized for being so slow they shrugged: "Don't worry 'bout it, lad. Takes time t'get used to muckin' about down here!"

Loaded down with my equipment progress grew more painful. At times I found myself crawling through sudden and unexpected pools of brackish water mixed with a mud of sodden coal dust.

When, finally, we reached the scene of action I was panting for air, soaked to the skin, my spine felt as though it was severed at the small of my back, and my elbows and knees were four throbbing aches. I was positive I would never again be able to walk upright!

The electricians and technicians helped me set up my lights. But when I turned them on the hot bulbs condensed the humidity and fogged my camera lens with moisture.

Even so, by dint of constantly wiping the lens "between takes" I managed to obtain the drama of the hardy little Welshmen burrowing away at their grueling and highly dangerous task. The scenes years later thrilled millions of television viewers when I presented my filmed episode "The Way of the Welsh." But at the moment all I could think of was to finish the job I should not have begun in the first place and get back to Halla.

When I finally re-emerged from the mine I was not only on the verge of sheer exhaustion but terribly worried about my wife. I had only intended to be gone for an hour. Instead my expedition had consumed over five hours!

Poor Halla, I thought as I hurriedly limped toward the car, she probably has worried herself sick. When I reached her side she was perfectly composed instead of in tears.

"I was afraid you'd be terribly concerned, sitting here all alone while I was gone for so long——"

She shook her head. "I felt you knew what you were doing," she smiled. "So I told myself not to worry." And then her eyes lighted as she held up another small knitted garment. "Besides—as you can see, Hal-minn, I've been busy too."

Chapter Six

North to Lapland

HELSINKI, at the occasion of our visit, was enjoying its "summer." At such times the sun goes down for just four or five hours, and even these hours are very bright.

Being a cinematographer operating against a deadline this made for additional filming time—if I chose to disregard my protesting body and literally work around the clock.

A sparkling, bustling metropolis of some 450,000 energetic souls Helsinki compares, in size, with San Antonio, Texas. In fact the entire little nation which lies like a slanting wedge between Russia on the east and Sweden to the west is about as large as New Mexico and Vermont combined, and supports a population of approximately 4,000,000.

Despite the fact that it was late June the weather was brisk. The thermometer registered 55 degrees Fahrenheit and winter-weight clothing felt comfortable.

We were en route by taxi to the Olympic Stadium, which had been originally built for the 1940 games that never came off because of World War II.

As we sped along the wide, scrupulously clean throughfares of "New Helsinki," built after the turn of the century, the 1952 Olympiad was still a year in the future. En route to the stadium we encountered magnificent parks and immense squares adorned by sculpture, not the least of which was the famed and oft-photographed "Maid of Helsinki Rising from the Sea."

In the stadium we filmed a parade and song festival of the Swedish-speaking Finns. For me, at least, it came as a surprise to discover that some ten per cent of the population retains Swedish as a basic language. This custom remains as a mild reminder of almost five hundred years of union with the Swedes.

The big issue for Finland became the vast struggle between the Swedes and Russians. Finland, trying somehow to preserve her political, religious, and economic freedom, found herself playing the deadly role of "innocent bystander" as Swedish and Russian armies rolled back and forth over her soil, hacking each other to bits. During this protracted struggle, untold thousands of Finns perished amidst the flaming, war-torn rubble of their hamlets and cities. After each encounter between the contending giants the surviving Finns weariedly buried their dead and rebuilt their cities.

At the beginning of the nineteenth century it became evident that the Russian Bear would again sweep over Finland. Sweden's power was waning. Already Moscow was rumbling about "absorbing" the little nation which was determined to hang onto a democratic form of living. Finland was joined to Russia as an autonomous Grand Duchy, pledged to swear allegiance to the czar. In return for this gesture the Finns required that they be permitted to retain their own brand of national existence.

The Russian Bear agreed—in the treaty. But for the next hundred years she tried by means of the worst kind of oppression, enforced by saber-slashing Cossacks, to reduce the Finns to earth-groveling serfdom.

It was not until the Bolshevik Revolution of 1917 that the Finns saw a glimmer of freedom's light. While the Russians were preoccupied with their own internal affairs the Finns boldly declared their independence and set up a parliamentary form of government headed by a duly elected president.

Paavo Nurmi, the world-famous Finnish Olympic running champion who now owns a haberdashery store in Helsinki, summed it up for Halla and me during our visit to his establishment. The still lean, almost legendary runner who, during the Olympiads of 1922 and 1926 earned the title of "The Flying Finn" said: "We do not fear the Russians. We're just wary of them—as we've always been."

Before leaving for northern Finland and Lapland we set about filming Turku, second largest Finnish city and former capital.

Founded in the thirteenth century, Turku has a medieval castle and a picturesque, photogenic cathedral which dates back to 1295 A.D. Interestingly enough the large clock in the main tower of the cathedral has only the hour hand. Finns told us that in those days minutes were of no great moment. People were only concerned with the hour.

70

Back in Helsinki I had to face the matter of our financial situation—something I had been trying to postpone. In the first place when we arrived in Finland I learned, to my horror, that my "deal" with the Tourist office covered only part of our expenses. Most of our hotel accommodations and the greater portion of meals and other incidentals were to be borne by me.

Meanwhile there was the matter of Halla's condition. Was she able to cope with our trip to northern Finland and Lapland? On our Helsinki list of "must" sequences was a visit to the unique Childrens' Castle, a super-modern childrens' hospital and training school for nurses.

Built by the late Baron von Mannerheim and his wife, Baroness Sophie, the "castle" proved to be one of the finest of its type in the world. With a tremendous understanding of children, the Finnish medical people had built the hospital with an eye to large, airy rooms and spectacular "view windows" which brought the surrounding countryside right to the beds of the little patients.

The atmosphere was bright, cheerful. Doctors told us that the absence of the usual "hospital gloom and odor of medication" worked wonders in child therapy.

While I filmed this unusual establishment Halla was given a thorough medical checkup. A youthful, rosy-cheeked woman obstetrician assured me that it would be perfectly all right for her to "travel a bit longer."

However, overriding even this welcome bit of gratuitous assistance was the growing worry about money. And then I had a thought. With me was my film on Iceland which I intended to use for fund-raising lectures in Iceland. Perhaps the Finns would like to see and hear an American's impression of Iceland.

I suggested to the head of the hospital that I stage two lectures: the first to be a fund-raising appearance for the "castle" followed by a second performance "for the benefit of Hal and Halla Linker, and child-to-be."

The hospital people enthusiastically endorsed my proposition. Finnish newspapers dutifully publicized the charity showing of the hour-long color film: "Sunny Iceland, Land of the Vikings."

I gave the lecture in English, as advertised. The audience attending the first showing was more than we had dared hoped for. More important were the enthusiastic reviews which appeared in the newspapers.

When the time came for the "commercial" showing I almost had a packed house, thanks to the favorable publicity. Afterward I counted the "gate." Halla, who was sitting by, knitting, paused. "Well, Hal-minn?" she quietly asked.

I couldn't help but grin. "The monetary transfusion has been a success. The patients will 'live'."

Finland is often referred to as the country of 60,000 lakes.

Of the innumerable, picture-book waters we visited the lake at the summer resort of Aulanko National Park was the most spectacular.

Before setting off on one of the sleek white tourist launches which vacationing Finns call "water buses" we first explored the town of Hämeenlinna, birthplace of the late Jean Sibelius, Finland's great composer.

The tiny hamlet itself was overshadowed by a towering, formidable castle. Its sheer walls, battlemented towers, suggested both grim and heroic deeds of the past. I could visualize determined, dogged Finnish warriors, armor a-glitter, as they withstood the onslaughts of wave after wave of invading armies. I hastily thumbed through my copy of an official guidebook. According to the terse description, "nothing of importance ever took place at Hämeenlinna Castle!"

The candor of the Finns was refreshing, to say the least. When I told Halla that evidently history had by-passed the massive pile of medieval architecture, she nodded. "I rather thought the castle had a disappointed look about it!"

We made arrangements to hail a northbound "water bus." But after looking over the launch I decided it would be interesting to film it rather than just ride in it. I left Halla with all of our baggage aboard and rented a small motorboat.

We left the pier, my rented craft pacing the larger boat while I used it as foreground atmosphere in my filming. When I signaled my boatman to throttle back while I changed film, Halla's "bus" continued on its way. We began to overtake it when I happened to notice a military post on the nearby shore. A drill formation was in progress.

I asked my boatman to land at the army post. For a moment he seemed concerned about catching up with the water bus. Finally

I prevailed. And when I stepped ashore it was to find the soldiers there eyeing me with something like astonishment.

A young lieutenant confronted me, suspicion written over his features. After I had convinced him that I was merely an American cameraman on a Finnish government-approved filming expedition and not a spy he agreed to take me to his immediate superior, a captain.

The latter, a heavy-set older man, looked perplexed when I requested permission to film the troops in drill. In heavily accented English he said he had never run into a situation such as this. "I'll have to consult the major!"

By now I was curious to see how far up the military ladder I would have to climb in order to obtain my footage. The obvious buck-passing from low to high echelon made me feel right at home. It was just like my Navy days.

Like the two junior officers the major ruminated with considerable chin-pulling. Abruptly he turned to the lieutenant and captain. From out of his clipped military Finnish I could catch one word that sounded like "Colonel!" So that was it. Onward and upward—to the boss man himself.

The post commandant was a distinguished individual with broad shoulders and an almost painful military bearing. In fact had I been a casting director seeking a "typical colonel" I would have selected this man like a shot.

He listened to the evidence, absently stared at the distant horizon and then nodded an approval. While my boatman grew more fretful about whether or not we would be able to overtake the long vanished water bus I started to film scenes of the soldiers—draftees, in fact—as they performed "squads east and west."

After I finished I uttered hasty thanks and farewells to my military hosts and jumped into my boat. The boatman's normally long face seemed still longer as he shook his head and sent the craft at wide-open throttle down the lake.

"We never catch big boat," he said. "Too late!"

His gloom suddenly became contagious. I put myself in my wife's place. There she sat, alone in her eighth month of pregnancy with a mountain of baggage and equipment but neither money nor husband!

Our destination was a town called Vehoniemi situated at the beginning of the locks of a canal which connected Aulanko Lake

73

with another. By now I realized that I would never catch up with Halla by boat. And then I spotted a small community dominated by the buildings of what turned out to be an agricultural college. It looked like civilization. Civilization, in turn, meant automobiles.

I told the boatman to land, I paid him off, leaped out with all of my camera gear, and scrambled up the bank to the main (and only) street of the little village where I searched for a taxi or car which could speed me to Vehoniemi in time to meet Halla's water bus.

After a frustrating session involving sign language, pidgin English, and the few words of Finnish I had managed to assimilate I was able to rent a car. The fee was exorbitant, the vehicle itself hardly better than a contraption, and the grinning owner drove like a maniac! But we got to our destination exactly two minutes before Halla's boat made its appearance. I perched myself on a conspicuous spot and proceeded to take motion-picture footage of the approaching water bus. From where I stood I could see Halla's look of incredulity when she spotted me.

When I joined her she readily admitted that she had been confused when she saw my boat fall behind. After I failed to re-appear she had become downright worried. "I was ready to leave our baggage here and go back to find you. And then I looked up—" her eyes kindled—"and there you stood, filming away!"

From the air above Rovaniemi, capital of Finnish Lapland which straddles the Arctic Circle, we could see the destruction which had been wrought by the retreating Germans six years before. After the terrible winter of 1939–40 when the stalwart Finns had fought off a Russian invasion of their country, they had been forced to yield some of their territory. Once more Finland found itself involved in fighting the Russians when World War II broke out. This time they received assistance from Germany in their battle with the Soviet hordes. When the war ended in the defeat of the Axis, the German troops in northern Finland refused to lay down their arms, and the Finns themselves had to fight their erstwhile allies to convince them that the Nazi cause was dead. In that fighting the Germans had burned all of northern Finland to the ground.

On landing we mutely drove past extensive rebuilding activity. People worked with high optimism, but we could not help feeling

74

depressed by the scars of Nazi fury that still remained. More than anything else Rovaniemi, to us, illustrated the sores and boils which this somewhat Job-like nation has endured since its inception.

We had arrived at the height of the annual summer Festival of Lumberjacks. The streets were crowded with Finns, and, of course, the striking Laplanders themselves.

These people were more than picturesque in their colorful costumes. Many of them were blue-eyed, blond, and as Nordic as Scandinavians. Their dress featured intriguing boots with turned-up toes, like those worn by the Turks of old. We were told that they affect this style for a practical purpose. Since they spend much of their time on skis and snowshoes the upcurling tips of their footgear help keep the snow equipment firmly anchored to their feet.

The festival itself was a photographer's dream from start to finish. There was color and action galore. The lumberjacks began their unique celebration by boarding long, low, vividly painted rowboats. At a given signal they swiftly rowed with the tide down the turbulent Rovaniemi River to the end of the specified course marked by a railroad bridge.

Once at the bridge they abandoned oars for long poles and began to madly push their boats against the surging current back to the original line of departure. This description makes it sound easier than it actually is. The opposing current is strong and the water icy cold. The return trip necessitates the contestants navigating close to shore so that their poles can reach bottom. And since the poling is only permitted from one side of the boat the operation called for split-second co-ordination lest the craft nose too far into the current and turn over.

The main event consisted of a log race wherein the contestants, wearing only smooth-soled footgear (hobnailed boots are considered "sissy" stuff by these stalwarts), launched themselves on the river on individual logs and tried to balance themselves on their slippery platforms as they urged the rolling, bobbing tree trunks to greater speed in a watery race back to the railway bridge.

We were in a motor launch, filming this tricky operation, recording a number of the finishers as they wound up under the railway bridge. A launch, hovering there, darted like a mother hen to pick up the contestants.

I was in the act of rewinding my camera when I remarked to our skipper that the launch seemed to waste no time fishing the fallen warriors out of the water.

"That's because there is a dangerous rapids downriver from the bridge," he replied.

We were pacing Competitor Number 7 shortly thereafter when alarmed cries indicated that something had gone wrong. Halla grabbed my arm.

"Look Hal," she pointed. "The pick-up boat is rescuing Number 6 on the opposite side of the river but Number 7 is being swept away. They won't be able to get to him!"

She was right. I yelled to our boatman and we set off with wide-open engine after the luckless contestant. Our course intercepted him. I managed to obtain "grab shots" of Number 7 as he waged his losing fight against the rushing water.

The lumberjack's eyes were desperate until he saw us bear down upon him. At the last moment I laid my camera aside and helped grab him. The boatman reversed his engine. For a long moment current fought power and then, as we tugged and hauled exhausted Number 7 aboard, our engine won out and we slowly came about and headed back to the bridge.

When we left Rovaniemi in a mail bus for a quick dash to the northernmost extremity of Finnish Lapland, a settlement named Ivalo, we found ourselves being jounced over an unpaved, dirt trail that led through the "fells," a barren wasteland of rolling hills, stunted bushes and tough, lichen-like grass extending to the foreboding reach of the Arctic Ocean. The somber, wild desolation was so bleak as to be inspiring.

Ivalo was a cluster of buildings inhabited by rugged people. At the inn I made my acquaintance with the famous Finnish *sauna* steam bath. This favorite pastime of the doughty Finns may, in part, explain why they have thus far survived so much hardship.

One enters a small, shacklike affair which provides a series of steplike benches rising from the floor to the ceiling. In one corner of the structure is a fire which heats rocks that are about the size of basketballs. When I undertook to partake of this experience I, of course, had to strip to my skin. I entered the *sauna* and almost experienced a shock when the attendant, a woman, entered.

Without the slightest glance in my direction she emptied a

bucket of water on the heated stones. There was an ear-deafening roar, reminding me of the escape valve of an old-time steam locomotive. The place immediately filled with what was, literally, live steam.

It was then that I learned the purpose behind the series of step-like benches mounting to the ceiling. The steam rises. And the higher one goes the hotter it becomes. I climbed two thirds of the way and then came to a halt. The atmosphere higher was un-breathable—for me, at least!

A fellow bather (a Finn, of course) perched on the top bench. Through the vapor I could see him grinning. These hardy people love this routine, particularly in the dead of winter. After a liberal sojourn in the skin-boiling vapor they dash out of doors, flesh lobster-red, and roll in snow or else dive into pools of icy water. They practice this activity almost from the time they begin to toddle. Furthermore steam-bathing is not confined only to males. Finnish women also are fond of the *sauna*.

We thought that Ivalo was just about the end of the Finnish world, but the hotel manager told us that there was still another place—Lake Inari—which was even farther north.

"We've gone this far toward the top of the world, we might as well go the full route," I told Halla.

We rented an ancient car and lurched and bounced for some twenty-five miles over a vague road to an area aptly named the Devil's Boulder Field. Snow and ice still partly covered the frozen ground although it was June—early summer.

When we remarked upon this, our chauffeur related an anecdote about the homesick Laplander who, after leaving his home near Lake Inari, to live in the south, happened to encounter a traveling neighbor.

"Tell me," begged the expatriated Laplander, "did you have a nice summer?"

"Oh yes," his friend replied. "It was marvelous. We had it on a Wednesday!"

At the lake itself we were 150 miles north of the Arctic Circle. At night the sun here merely hovers just above the skyline like a huge, dull-red balloon for several hours during the so-called sum-mer. It does move, however—sideways—across the horizon.

The effect was eerie. I set my camera on its tripod and filmed the languid, horizontal movement of the sun, by "time-lapse" photography, one frame at a time.

At that moment I happened to spot some reindeer grazing in the distance. No film about Lapland could be complete without them. I finished "shooting the sun," moved the camera from the tripod, and headed across the wild terrain toward the animals.

The driver shouted something at me. I paid no attention. I was out to film reindeer. The animals glanced up at me and shied away. I began to stalk them. Before long I found myself a long way from the car where Halla patiently waited with the Finnish driver of the car.

The latter waved his arms, jumped up and down and, in general, made a lot of noise. I was annoyed. The idiot would frighten off the reindeer and ruin my chances for a decent sequence. I waved back, trying to convey the thought that he should stop making so much noise. Halla appeared at his side and also waved.

I shrugged. Whatever it was it could wait. Right now I was after reindeer. I forced myself to move slowly. The furry, horned animals finally decided that I was anything but dangerous. They again began to graze while I obtained my shots.

When I rejoined Halla and the driver the latter wore a worried look. "You shouldn't have done that, Mr. Linker," he exclaimed.

"Done what?"

"Gone after those reindeer. It's dangerous!"

"Dangerous?" I stared at the now distant, peacefully feeding reindeer. "Why if one of them had charged me I would have ducked behind a tree."

"It's not the reindeer," he said with an exasperated look. "It's the explosive land mines left by the retreating Germans. The fields are full of them. Hardly a month goes by without an animal or a person, stepping on them and getting blown to bits!"

From then on I filmed reindeer from the car.

Chapter Seven

To the Far East and Beyond

MR. ROBERT J. GIBBONS, U.S. vice consul in Reykjavík, was in good humor as he officially stamped a document. He looked up at Halla and me. He was the same man who had arranged for Halla to immigrate to the U.S. so we could be married.

"That does it, Mr. Linker," he said. "As of this date, September 7th, 1951, David Thor Linker, age seven weeks, is registered as a citizen of the United States." He smiled. "Congratulations, sir. And to you, Mrs. Linker."

Halla returned his smile and looked down at our son's tiny pink face.

I cleared my throat. "One more thing, Mr. Gibbons. I would like to have a passport issued to him."

The vice consul blinked. "But that isn't necessary. He can always travel on your passport."

"True. But Mrs. Linker and I would appreciate his having his own passport."

Aside from the fact that Halla and I wanted our son to have his own individual recognition "from the very beginning," so to speak, there was a practical reason as well. Halla, still an Icelandic citizen at the time, had her own passport. And because my career, which included my wife and son, would keep constantly on the move I wanted to make sure that should anything temporarily part us, no matter when or where, they would be able to move with complete freedom instead of having to wait, immobilized, because of a single family passport which might read: "Hal Linker and son."

Mr. Gibbons pursed his lips. He chuckled. "Why not! Your son will probably be the youngest Yankee world traveler in captivity!"

He shoved the forms toward me. "We'll need full information about his 'past activities.' I think we can forego any letters of

79

reference and the statement that he has never been convicted of a major crime! But you will have to get some passport photos of him."

Now it was our turn to grin. "It so happens that I have the necessary pictures with me."

I produced the snapshot I had taken twelve hours after his birth. While an Icelandic nurse had held him up to view behind the window which separated the nursery from the visitor's area of the Reykjavík Hospital I had taken a dozen flash pictures of our son. The photo we had chosen showed David Thor with one arm up seemingly in the act of waving "hello" at the world.

The physical description for the passport was haphazard. Davey had a fuzz of brown hair and since all babies are born with blue eyes it was hard to decide how he'd look in a year or so. I recall our solemn consultation while David yawned in utter boredom in his mother's arms.

Mr. Gibbons studied Halla and myself. "We'll begin by describing him as having blue eyes. As for the color of his hair—since his mother is blond and you are brunet his hair will probably be dark, so let's leave it as being 'light brown.'" He took out a tape measure and said, "Height, one foot, six inches."

Finally it was done. Halla and I proudly examined Passport No. 233 issued to one David Thor Linker, United States citizen, age seven weeks. We showed the precious document to little David. He could not have cared less! But we now had three passports and they were to turn out to be our "Three Passports to Adventure."

The original passport served little Davey Thor for four years. Since that wonderful day in Iceland a succession of two more passports and innumerable visas have marked the progress of our son's growth and travels.

Affixed to his passports are visas for Pakistan, the Philippines, Japan, and Hong Kong. Sifting the pages I find the entrance and exit visas from Rome's Ciampino Airport, an Israeli visa, notations attesting to the fact that little Davey visited the Belgian Congo, Egypt, Turkey, Russia, India, Tahiti, and all in all about sixty countries to date.

His second passport, No. 2863, issued September 6, 1955, at the embassy of the United States in Tokyo shows that David Thor, age four, by then was three feet, six inches in height, had blond hair and hazel eyes.

His third passport, No. 51588, dated September 7, 1959, was issued by John G. Degen, Jr., of the American consulate in Curacao, Netherlands Antilles. In this, his current passport, Uncle Sam has gravely recorded the fact that citizen David Thor Linker, is eight years old, four feet, five inches tall and still blond and hazel-eyed.

Since that day in Reykjavík nine years ago David Thor has traveled with us over 200,000 miles—almost the distance between this planet and the moon! He has celebrated his eight birthdays in as many foreign lands. He has playmates of his own age scattered throughout the world. He has ridden in every conceivable type of conveyance, with the exception of a submarine, balloon, an American Indian papoose cradle, yak-back, or space ship. And the way the world is progressing David should have used the last mentioned by the time he is eighteen.

Our saga of the "Three Passports to Adventure" began in earnest three weeks following our son's visit to the U.S. consulate in Reykjavík.

During the time immediately before Davey's birth and until our departure from Iceland I had fulfilled a very successful series of film-lecture engagements throughout the little island republic. Although the subject of my film shows (delivered in English, incidentally) was my color film about their own little nation my audiences responded with gratifying enthusiasm. I received fine notices from all the newspapers. They were pleased at how well I had captured the spirit of their country.

The income from the lectures was badly needed. I was "film-rich" but "money-poor" as before. Our motion picture travels through England, Wales, and Finland had drained my finances almost completely.

We both knew that eventually my large stockpile of color motion-picture footage would pay off. But meanwhile there was the pressing matter of now. As a bachelor I had never worried about the lean intervals in between paydays. But with Halla and Davey present it was another matter.

I frankly discussed the situation with Halla. "As soon as you feel up to it we should return to the United States where I can appear in lecture engagements. In that way we could get financially 'well' to enable us to keep traveling and filming."

Halla smiled. "I'm up to it right now, Hal."

Little Davey's first trip at ten weeks of age took him 7000 miles from his Iceland birthplace to his home in Los Angeles, California. But we did not spend too much time in the film capital. Fortunately there were requests for my appearance in more than a dozen different cities. I barely had time enough to edit my new material before we found ourselves shuttling back and forth across the U.S. in airliners and trains.

Little Davey thrived on his nomadic existence. Halla and I bought a tiny portable crib made of plastic with conveniently attached handles. This unique gadget had a mattress and a board on the bottom and looked much like a flattened-out shopping bag.

Sometimes I would take one handle, Halla the other, and Davey would be suspended in cooing, gurgling ecstasy between the two of us.

During our U.S. lecture tour Davey would snooze in his "flying crib" backstage while his mother sat by his side, reading or knitting while I was in front of the audience fulfilling my engagement.

During that winter I was also putting the finishing touches on the basic format for my future television travel program "Wonders of the World." It was obvious that television would need educational programs. And I knew during the winter of 1951–52 that travel was an absorbing topic that fascinated people everywhere, regardless of race, religion, or political ideologies. I gave several television shows in Detroit for George Pierrot's television series. Thus I got my feet wet in TV.

As the spring approached Halla and I began to plan our next summer's filming expedition. Although our income was steadily growing it was still far from handsome. We sat up into the wee small hours on train coaches to save money and to allow for future investment in new cameras and tape recorders.

I remember looking up at Halla one night in a hotel in Des Moines and shaking my head. "If we go back to Europe we do it in better style than last time, Halla."

I remember her looking thoughtfully at me. "Remember that French general—the one who served under Napoleon?"

"What does that have to do with our financial problem?"

Her eyes twinkled. "As I recall it, from history, it was during a battle. Napoleon asked him how things were going. He answered: 'My right flank is shattered, my left flank has been destroyed. I am outnumbered in the center. I shall immediately attack!'"

"All right," I said. "So be it. We will attack!"

Halla put her hand on mine. "Actually," she said softly, "we are rich, right now. We see interesting places, meet wonderful people. We eat, we have shelter. And what's more we're always together. No girl could want more than that."

Her glowing remarks removed any doubt from my mind. I felt that I had the wealth of Croesus and the strength of Samson. The world was ours.

And then, as though endowed with her mother's clairvoyant ability to foretell the future, she added: "Besides I have a feeling that we will get wonderful news!"

She was absolutely correct. On our return to Los Angeles I found a letter from Philippine Airlines awaiting me. I had previously put together a commercial film for them called "A Visit to Hong Kong and Tokyo," on which I had made a tiny profit.

Taken from footage I had shot during my first, "pre-Halla" round-the-world trip, the film had been successfully used by the company's sales department as a means of inducing people to travel on the airline. Now they wanted me to make two additional films for them; one of Calcutta and one of Israel.

Looking at the globe in my workroom it was obvious that by the time we finished the picture in Israel we would be more than half-way around the world.

"Let's go right on through Europe after we finish there," I said to Halla. "I'll be able to get additional material for our lecture engagements and the television show as well."

And then, because I wanted to make her happy, I added the crowning touch: "Besides it'll give us a chance to stop off at Iceland so your folks will see their grandson!"

A country which had long intrigued me was Pakistan. No major color film had been made there since that nation received its independence from Britain in 1947.

83

I wrote to the government of Pakistan, requesting co-operation when we would arrive there during my airline assignment. The Pakistani embassy in Washington, D.C., not only immediately pledged full co-operation but also inquired into the possibility of my doing a separate film which they could use to encourage both tourist travel and commercial interest in their new nation.

A contract was arranged calling for us to receive $2000 for the film. A retainer of $500 would be paid prior to our departure; the balance would be forthcoming upon delivery of the finished sound film to the Pakistani embassy.

Halla and I celebrated. The $500 retainer would more than help carry us during the trip. Our itinerary called for us to leave the West Coast early in June and proceed via Honolulu and Hong Kong to India. From there we would go to East Pakistan, film that segment of the Moslem nation, return to Calcutta for the airline sequence, and then fly to Karachi, the West Pakistan capital, to finish the government film.

"After that," I told Halla, "we'll film in Israel, then we'll go on to Reykjavík."

As the target date for our departure got close to hand I grew concerned. The $500 advance had not arrived. In fact the official silence from the Pakistani embassy was deafening!

A series of long-distance calls finally gained a verbal promise that the money would be waiting for me in Honolulu "in care of the Philippine Airline people" when we arrived there.

Shrugging off a tiny sliver of worry we packed camera, film, and other gear, and with the portable crib in operation once again, boarded the silvery DC6 which took us across the sunny Pacific to Honolulu.

The airline people had notified the press of our arrival. And when we stepped off the ship our "Aloha" was somewhat formidable, consisting of news photographer's flashing light bulbs and graceful grass-skirted Hula girls who draped beautiful orchid leis around our necks.

Little Davey happily waved his chubby arms and feet in acknowledgement of the friendly welcome. Halla was entranced. It was her first experience with the beauty and warmth of the island paradise of the Pacific, now our fiftieth state.

The reporters thronged around us when the photographers finished taking their pictures. One of them, more or less acting as

84

a spokesman, said: "Honolulu must be quite different from your native Iceland, Mrs. Linker!"

"Oh yes," Halla answered breathlessly.

"What was the first thing you noticed here when you got off the plane?"

She smiled. "The smell!"

The reporter's face went white. "The smell?"

"Oh yes," she nodded her golden head. "The smell."

The gentlemen of the press were obviously taken aback. I plunged to her rescue, visioning condemnatory black headlines.

"Halla," I began. "Don't you actually mean by 'smell' the beautiful aroma of the flowers?"

"That's what I mean, Hal," she spread her arms wide. "It's wonderful, the nice smell here!"

I turned to our audience. "A matter of semantics," I said.

The gentlemen of the press relaxed. Quite noticeably, in fact.

A visit to the Islands of Hawaii was then and, for that matter, always is, a trip to Paradise Gardens for us. During the week we spent there filming there was only one disturbing note. The Pakistani advance fee we were so heavily counting on had not arrived. Instead there was a cryptic message assuring me that it would be paid when we reached Karachi, West Pakistan. We had less than $100 with us, and no one we could borrow from. We decided to push on to the Orient anyway.

Our flight from Honolulu took us via Guam to Manila, headquarters of our sponsoring airline. When we landed the midsummer tropical sun felt like a blast furnace.

It was Halla's first experience with the true Orient, and the glaring, merciless heat plus the extreme humidity was unnerving for her.

At this time Manila was still recovering from the scars of World War II. Today, with the exception of Corregidor and Intramuros, there is hardly a trace of the fighting.

Actually the Philippines, a republic of fifty-one provinces comprising over seven thousand islands, is a delightful winter vacation spot.

But when Halla first landed there in June the climate was anything but agreeable. During our ride from the airport to downtown Manila we passed the sweeping expanse of Manila Bay, the beautiful Luneta public park, and arrived at our hotel, the newly constructed Bay View Hotel on Dewey Boulevard.

Our room was not air-conditioned. And while it was merely uncomfortable for little Davey and myself the stifling heat that first night proved almost unbearable for Halla. She never once voiced a complaint. But the wan look on her face the following morning prompted me to change to an air-conditioned room.

"Hang the expense," I snapped, disregarding our dwindling funds, "full speed ahead!"

During our stay in the Philippine capital we encountered considerable rainfall—a foretaste of what we would encounter during the Monsoons of East Pakistan and India.

I had a "scenario" of required footage to take. A key sequence consisted of a visit to the site of Intramuros, the ancient Spanish walled city now in ruins as the result of the fighting and the wanton destruction by the Japanese when American forces invaded Manila toward the end of the war in the Pacific.

As we plunged from the modern city into that old part of Manila, Halla stared at the people and noticeably seemed to shrink back. And when we got out of our taxi and walked along the teeming, jammed narrow alleyways my Icelandic wife perceptibly paled.

I stopped and anxiously looked at her. "Don't you feel well, darling?"

Her eyes were fixed upon the dark-complexioned men, women, and children who were staring at her while jabbering in Tagalog and Spanish.

"These people," she whispered. "They—they look so—so strange and mysterious. I'm afraid——"

My jaw dropped. I whirled and eyed the people who watched us. One of them suddenly grinned and waved: "Mabuhay!" the classic Philippine equivalent of Hawaii's "Aloha."

I eyed Halla. She was hanging onto my arm. "Darling," I soothed her. "I'm afraid you've been watching too many old movie thrillers back in Iceland. These people are like people in America, Iceland, England—anywhere else in the world. They raise families, work hard. We're as safe here as we would be at home."

"But the way they keep staring at us, Hal," she breathed.

"At you, my Viking princess. At you!"

She looked at me. Seeing the grin on my face she first blushed and then laughed. "You're right, Hal," she said. "I guess I did see too many crazy movie pictures!"

A little boy tore past us. His teeth flashed in a big smile. "Mabuhay!" he yelled over his shoulder.

"That means welcome," I whispered to her.

She tossed her blond head back, raised her arms, and sang out. "Mabuhay to you!"

From that moment on Halla was completely relaxed. And during our stay, while we visited and filmed the Malacanan Palace, official residence of the President of the Philippines; Santo Tomas, one of the world's oldest universities, founded in 1611 and which, during the war was a Japanese concentration camp; the beaches at Batangas and Bataan as well as the grim "Rock" of Corregidor, fortress at the entrance to Manila Bay, Halla never again was afraid in the Philippines.

Hong Kong, our next stop, was for Halla a place of enchantment. When my Icelandic beauty set eyes on the Crown Colony prior to landing it was a case of love at first sight.

After landing, the teeming, multitudinous sights, colors, and odors made Halla gasp with excitement. "It's just like what I've read in novels, Hal," she exclaimed.

Riding in a taxi from the airport to a "reasonably priced" hotel, the Chinese-owned International Hotel, she held little Davey up so he too could drink in the exotic atmosphere. When we arrived at our headquarters I found that our room, non-air-conditioned, was about as large as three small bathrooms put together! We couldn't afford a better hotel, I felt. But after one sleepless night in the muggy confines of that tiny room I decided to "live it up" and take advantage of modern design, air-conditioned living, even if it did mean losing a slice of our carefully hoarded funds. To do that we moved to the Miramar Hotel.

Our sojourn was fascinating, even to me after having spent considerable time there during my earlier visit. Seeing places like Sai Ying Pun and Wanchai district's "ladder streets" and narrow lanes with steep flights of stairs through Halla's wide, entranced eyes was like encountering it for the first time all over again.

We wandered through the Chinese bazaars and visited the establishments on Cotton and Nathan Roads where tourists and "old hands" alike shop for genuine bargains in woolen, cotton goods, real and artificial silk.

I filmed the fantastic Tiger Balm Garden and the Hong Kong reservoirs which were first constructed in 1851 by the British.

We rode the little "walla-walla" water taxis across Hong Kong Harbor and traveled on the Peak "tram"—over 1000 feet up—to the top of Victoria Peak overlooking Hong Kong, then over to Repulse Bay and the Lido. We went to Shek-O Bay to swim and followed this by going over to take footage in the colorful fishing village of Aberdeen. Halla couldn't take her eyes from the hundreds of fishing junks riding at anchor.

I explained to her that ninety per cent of Aberdeen's population spend all of their lives aboard the fishing junks; only ten per cent live on shore. "There is something in common between these people and your Viking ancestors," I said.

She looked up questioningly at me.

"The Aberdeen natives are, for the most part, descendants of the pirates who, hundreds of years ago, used to raid Hong Kong." With my tongue in my cheek I went on. "Now they've settled down, as you can see, just like the Vikings who used to raid throughout England and the Continent!"

Halla did not speak to me for all of ten seconds.

A truly appetizing experience was our visit to one of the floating restaurants—a sort of king-sized houseboat, Chinese style, anchored in the middle of the Aberdeen harbor. To get there the three of us (yes, little Davey was right by our side as always) rode out in a water taxi operated by a Chinese woman and her daughter. The practice of mothers and daughters manning these rather tiny sampan-like craft is universal here. The woman operates a large, long oar in sculling fashion astern while the girl, perched in the bow, more or less "assists" with a smaller oar.

Our dinner on the floating restaurant was excellent sea food prepared as only the Chinese know how. In fact our visit to Hong Kong was a gastronomic, as well as scenic, adventure. Halla and I enjoyed the exquisitely prepared and succulent rice, shark-fin soup, bird's-nest soup, suckling pig, sweet almond cream and northern Chinese delicacies like Szechuan and Peking duck!

Halla, blessed by a metabolism which efficiently makes use of every type of food, could enjoy each course as often as she wished without worrying about her trim waistline. As for me——!

Our plane broke through a low overcast and circled over the sprawling city of Calcutta—the teeming metropolis which, during the days of British rule, was the empire's second largest city. Rudyard Kipling at one time called it "The City of Dreadful Night."

When our plane touched down at Dum-Dum Airport we sensed, almost immediately, the feeling of antiquity of this ancient civilization.

The airport terminal building itself was bustling with flashing-eyed women clad in saris, tall, beturbaned, grave-faced, mustachioed uniformed guards, and a horde of eager "bearers" who descended upon us like the proverbial plague of locusts.

We managed to elude most of them and make our way to a cab. Our destination in Calcutta proper was the Great Eastern Hotel which lies in the heart of the city of 5,000,000 inhabitants.

When our cab turned off Chowringhee, the wide, tree-lined avenue lined on one side by shops and restaurants and on the other by the Maidan, a vast park, we could see a swarm of men assembled by the hotel entrance. I remarked to Halla that "something must be happening."

I was entirely correct. Something did happen. These people were porters, called "bearers" here. And what ensued was a repetition of the airport scene except that this time there was no escaping them. We were in their clutches.

At the time we were traveling with twenty pieces of baggage. The bulkiest items were little Davey's property. In addition to his portable crib we also had a heavy folding play pen of wood, a folding aluminum stroller, and a two-months' supply of American baby food and condensed milk. The matter of insuring his proper diet had, of course, preoccupied us prior to our departure from the U.S.

Before we had taken off for Honolulu at the start of our trip Halla and I had estimated how much fuel we would have to bring for little David. When we left the Philippines we had one hundred fifty pounds of excess baggage! This amount consisted of our son's food, crib, play pen, and stroller. Fortunately my contract with the airline took care of the excess baggage charges.

Halla clutched little Davey while I was assailed by the porters. Before I knew what was happening our belongings were grabbed by a forest of brown-skinned arms. And dazed by the entire situation, we found ourselves stalking into the hotel lobby followed by an entourage of fourteen porters, some solemnly clutching an item of baggage even as small as one briefcase!

Once in our room in the old wing of the building I found myself confronted by outstretched palms, eager for "baksheesh"—tips. Fortunately I had changed currency into Indian rupees and annas at the airport. I carefully plunked anna coins into each hand and was rewarded by the universal Indian acknowledgment: a solemn-faced nod toward one shoulder, the head slightly inclining forward to meet an upraised palm and the automatic comment: "Atcha, Saah'b!"

Although India is now fiercely independent the impact of Britain's long rule remains. When we went down to the ornate, air-conditioned dining room with its balconies and mirrored walls we found another army of servitors, this time turbaned waiters and bus boys, grouped in squads around each table. We counted seventy-eight waiters on the floor serving sixteen customers! At each table there was the Number One waiter—a mustached, high-turbaned individual who resembled a trooper from the fabled Bengal Lancers. In addition there was an individual, equally as resplendent, who took care of our desires insofar as wine was concerned. There were the attendants who had specific duties such as seeing to it that our water glasses were constantly full while the next one would rearrange our dishes and still another would deftly keep us supplied with knives, forks, and spoons.

It was all rather heady for us. By the time we had finished our first Indian repast, I was feeling somewhat opulent. "Just call me Sultan Hal," I grandly informed Halla. Then I remembered that we had only about $25 to our name!

Outside the hotel it was a different matter. Mother India with her hundreds of millions of children has been hard put to provide enough food for all. The streets of Calcutta brought home that depressing fact. Everywhere we went we encountered poverty and beggary.

Halla in particular was shocked by the emaciated mothers who, clad in rags, wandered through the streets, their undernourished children clinging to their tattered skirts while they held their hands out and uttered a singsong, plaintive appeal for "baksheesh!"

We quickly discovered that this poverty extends even into the hotel itself. Each room has its own bearer or servant. This individual hovers constantly just outside the door. His only task is to execute the slightest wish of the occupant, regardless of what hour of the day or night.

At night the bearer merely curls up and sleeps in the lobby just outside the hotel room door. Halla was quite overcome when she discovered this. And when we went for a rather late after-dinner stroll, she was even more astonished to find the sidewalks virtually covered with homeless people who curled up and slept on the hard pavement, or if more fortunate, in doorways.

However not all of Calcutta was this depressing. We visited and filmed Dalhousie Square where imposing government and commercial buildings stand in a square around the waters of a large reservoir.

We visited the Hooghly River and the Botanic Gardens where I filmed Halla and David beneath an ancient banyan tree whose spread is so huge that several hundred people can sit in its shade.

No one can visit India without becoming acutely aware of the caste system and the ancient, mystic religion of Hinduism. The Hindus worship a number of gods. And of the deities the one most foreboding to us was the goddess Kali, "wife" of Siva.

Kali typifies hate, destruction, and death. When we visited her temple Halla looked at her statue and shuddered. Black, she is depicted with four arms and red palms and eyes. Her tongue, face and breasts are bloodstained, her hair matted, and her teeth like the fangs of a carnivorous animal. She wears a necklace of skulls, corpses for earrings, and a girdle of serpents!

This, then, is the symbol of Kali, the black goddess. I learned that worshipers of the sect offer blood sacrifices to her during certain ceremonies.

When I told Halla that I was going into the temple to film the sacrificial area she got worried. I assured her that it would be perfectly safe, but I nevertheless made her wait in our car just outside the temple.

The sacrificial area was gloomy. Despite the afternoon heat I felt myself shuddering. The blood-red eyes of the fierce goddess seemed to bore through me while I set up my camera and started to take pictures of the sacrificial blocks where lambs, sheep, or goats are slaughtered during the weird ceremonies.

The sacrificial blocks rather resemble the stocks of the American colonial period. I learned that the necks of the sacrificial animals are placed in the stocks and then they are beheaded or else their throats are cut. The blood is allowed to flow freely and stain the ground. While I filmed this macabre chamber the earth was still saturated with the gory residue of past ceremonies.

When I had finished I noticed that I had a silent, glowering audience of people who could only have been Kali-worshipers. I shouldered my tripod and tried to be nonchalant as I walked toward them, bound for the exit. They continued to eye me and only at the last moment stepped to one side to let me by.

By the time I reached our car I was feeling quite chilled despite the burning sun. And as I started to get in Halla stared at my shoulder.

"Anything wrong?" I asked.

"Your shirt," she exclaimed. "Those dark stains. Where did they come from?"

I twisted my head and looked. Surely enough, black, irregular stains covered one complete shoulder of the short-sleeved sports shirt I was wearing.

"It's a mystery to me," I said.

And a mystery it has remained to this day. The shirt had been laundered many times over. And yet, up until the time it was worn out, the stains not only never did disappear but did not show any sign of fading.

Hindus cremate their dead. The Parsees, a race descended from the ancient Persians, place their dead in tall "towers of silence"— gaunt structures resembling old-fashioned brick factory chimneys. The Parsee dead are placed on iron grating at the top of the towers. There they await India's ubiquitous scavenger, the vulture. Eventually the stripped bones drop through the bars of the grates down into the black depths of the towers!

Lining the Hooghly River banks are a number of burning ghats ("ghat" means place in Hindustani). At these rather exposed establishments the process of cremation is a family affair.

Relatives of the deceased not only pay for the firewood but frequently build the funeral pyre and then keep it going until the remains are entirely consumed. I discovered, during our visit to one such ghat that a mark of prosperity consists of how much wood a family can afford to purchase for a cremation. I was told on good authority that impoverished families (which means virtually 88 per cent of India's population) can only pay for "token" burnings. Fortunately I was able to film a scene of a "prosperous" cremation. This simply meant that the body was reduced to ashes which, in turn, were cast into the Hooghly at the foot of the burning ghat.

I recall that while filming the funeral pyre Halla, with amazement, exclaimed, "Hal, look!"

I raised my head from the camera view-finder and glanced to where she pointed. There, at the foot of the burning ghat, in the murky water where the ashes were thrown, a group of cheerful, shouting youngsters were gaily swimming about!

Although our stay in India was drawing to a close I found we were lucky enough to be present during the celebration of the Juggernaut festival.

The most spectacular display takes place at the city of Puri, quite a distance from Calcutta. I was advised, in order to obtain footage of the ceremony, to go instead to Barneghat, a small town approximately thirty miles "upriver" from the city. I was also told that it would be "safer" to leave Halla and little David at the hotel since the religious celebration, involving the appearance of the fabled "Car of the Juggernaut," drew fervent and somewhat fanatic pilgrims from all parts of India.

Essentially the spectacle is a re-enactment of the journey of the Hindu god Vishnu or Jagannath, "Lord of the World," from his temple to his "country estate" for the purpose of resting. The original journey, according to legend, took seven days. The celebration, therefore, is a re-enactment of the god's journey, his self-reward for having created the world. And the pilgrims fight for the honor of grasping two huge ropes attached to a five-story-high car mounted on towering wheels.

When I got to the scene of the celebration the sun beat down with almost paralyzing intensity. The streets of the rather tiny village were absolutely black with teeming multitudes.

I set up my camera at a police post overlooking the jostling, shouting throng and then guarded by a circle of policemen prepared for the spectacle. The Car of the Juggernaut loomed in the background, dwarfing the swarming mass of surrounding humanity.

Gazing at this formidable vehicle I could not help but admire the brilliant gold and crimson adornment. Pyramidal in shape, the massive car has carved blue horses on the lower level while above

93

are figures representing Vishnu or Jagannath and his "brother" and "sister."

Priests appeared on the upper deck of the Car of the Juggernaut. I heard a stentorian voice rise above the hoarse murmur of the crowd. The next moment there was the blast of a trumpet, a clashing of cymbals, the priest waved a cloth, and then hundreds of pilgrims, literally screaming with ecstasy, grasped the huge manila ropes attached to the car and hauled it several yards toward us.

The scene was awesome. And the roaring mob caused me to look with gratitude at the grim-faced, efficient Indian police who kept a sharp eye on the turbulent pageant.

The people tugging on the ropes relaxed and the huge car came to a halt. During the momentary interval of comparative quiet I turned to a nattily uniformed, big-shouldered sergeant.

"Is it true that people used to throw themselves beneath the wheels of the Juggernaut, thinking that by dying that way they would attain a better existence in their reincarnation?"

He gave me a fleeting smile. Undoubtedly my rather hazy knowledge of the Hindu religion was amusing. But then he nodded.

"There used to be many people who were carried away by the excitement," he paused as the horn, clashing cymbals, and overwhelming roar of the pilgrims indicated that the car was in motion once more.

When the haulers again paused, their bodies glistening with perspiration and their chests heaving from exertion, the sergeant slowly continued. "Actually the idea of being crushed under the wheels of the Juggernaut is offensive to our religion. But there used to be fanatics." He looked at me.

"Even today there are some people who are impelled to throw themselves under the Juggernaut. Most of the time we can prevent this. Once in a great while—" He shrugged.

The clashing, discordant signal returned, signifying another segment of the strange journey of the car. I turned to my camera and filmed more of the incredible ceremony. And then I stiffened with something like dawning horror.

A woman, carrying an infant, darted from the sidelines and rushed straight for one of the huge wheels. A couple of turbanned police bolted after her. I caught my breath. Clutching her infant with one hand she raised her free arm and hurled something beneath the wheel.

94

I turned to the sergeant just as the patrolmen reached her and pulled her away. "Was—was she trying to—" I said huskily.

He shook his head. "She was throwing coins under the wheels. Symbolic," he said.

"But your men—they certainly got her away from there in a hurry."

The sergeant stroked his mustache. "They wanted to make certain that it would be only coins she would sacrifice."

Chapter Eight

Monsoon!

THE GATHERING NIGHT dripped with oppressive humidity as Halla and I stood arm in arm on the rambling veranda of the Government Circuit House in Dacca, the capital of East Pakistan. This Circuit House was a two-story U-shaped structure of about twenty rooms, in which the British "raj" formerly housed the Crown circuit judges on their yearly rounds in the days of the British rule of India.

We had flown in from Calcutta the day before only to find that there were no hotels in Dacca. Fortunately the Pakistan government officials had been able to arrange for us to stay in one of the high-ceilinged rooms of the Circuit House. Now the bearers were setting the tables for the evening meal.

Little David was tucked away in his crib, covered by a tent of mosquito netting, commonly called a "bar" in this part of the world. Now the late afternoon heat pressed down on us. We had drawn our bed and Davey's crib to the center of the room, directly under the wide-bladed overhead fan, so that the air stirred by its blades would penetrate the fine mesh of the mosquito netting and provide some measure of comfort. After that, Halla and I, our clothing sodden with perspiration, had wandered outside for a few gasps of "fresh" air.

A bank of black clouds on the horizon warned us that the monsoon rains were close at hand. Occasionally a flicker of lightning fitfully bathed the ancient, heat-baked Dacca landscape with harsh brilliance.

Halla was so fascinated by the approaching storm that she temporarily forgot her discomfort. She turned to me and remarked, "I've often wondered why in the Hollywood movies they are allowed to show lightning as a jagged streak across the sky.

What an imagination they have." In her native Iceland she had never encountered a true thunderstorm. She had witnessed "sheet" lightning on the horizon but never an actual zigzag bolt. For her the possibility of an electrical display was a new and dramatic experience.

A gust of superheated air stirred dust in front of the veranda. Several large drops of water splashed on our foreheads. I had just opened my mouth to suggest that we go indoors when the sky overhead was torn apart by a tremendous blinding bolt of zigzag lightning that jumped from one cloud to another, what seemed to be only an arm's length away. The next instant a thunderclap rocked the house with a nerve-shattering impact. For a long moment I froze, almost blinded and literally petrified by the closeness of the flash. My ears rang and I could smell the ozone. It was my worst encounter with an electrical storm on land or at sea.

Halla, blissfully ignorant of what damage lightning can do, smiled and her voice rang with delight. "Wasn't it thrilling, Hal! Is that what lightning is really like?" As the color drained back in my face it was on the tip of my tongue to point out that had the bolt hit the ground instead of leaping horizontally from one cloud to another it would have been somewhat more than just thrilling. Instead we beat a hasty retreat indoors as the main body of the storm broke around us accompanied by a slashing downpour.

There were two other guests in the Circuit House. One was a short, pleasant-faced, talkative English traveling salesman almost unbelievably named Archibald Fairfoul, and the other a lanky, good-humored ex-Kansas farmer, Jess Wahlgren, who was in Dacca under a UN Point Four grant to help improve Pakistani agriculture.

They both looked up when we rather breathlessly entered the dining room.

"That's quite a storm," I said, mopping my brow.

The Englishman shrugged. "Mild, compared to some I've seen here——"

The Kansan chuckled. "You don't call that a storm, why back in Kansas I've driven through rip-snorters that make this thing seem like a spring shower!"

Halla was intrigued. She turned to me. "Hal—when we return to the States you must take me to Kansas to see a really big storm!"

Another bolt, obviously directly overhead, made the ceiling fan slightly sway. I looked at her. "Take my word for it, dear. This storm is big enough for anyone—including a Kansas farmer!" The latter threw back his head and laughed. A bearer entered the room. "Dinner is sairved," he announced with a slight bow.

Although the food was deftly served, frankly we often debated whether the food had been cooked in tiger fat or paraffin oil. Over coffee and tea while the Englishman and Kansan began to shop-talk about their respective interests, Halla and I, at our end of the table, discussed our immediate plans. We had decided to take a motor-launch trip some ten miles down the Ganges River to the Adamjee jute mill—at that time the first such mill constructed in Pakistan since that Moslem nation had won its independence from Britain.

However, before taking that trip I felt that we should spend several days in Dacca itself, filming activities on the streets. As I explained our schedule to Halla we became aware that our companions were engaged in a rather heated debate.

We could hardly help overhearing that the subject of their argument was malaria. The Kansan was insisting that the "malaria season" was all-the-year-round, whereas the Englishman was equally adamant in his contention that the "season was just starting."

Halla and I stared at each other. She jumped up. "I must go and make sure David's mosquito netting is firmly tucked in——"

"It goes on only ten months out of the year." The salesman tapped his pipe stem on the table cloth for emphasis.

The Kansan shook his head. "Nope, all year round." He negligently waved a large hand through the gathering formation of tiny gnats that hovered like a cloud above the table. That morning under our mosquito netting we had found our pillows covered with these little gnats, since the overhead fan in our bedroom merely forced them through the mesh of our netting. I recalled that just that very morning Halla had battled huge water bugs for control of our bathroom. The big ugly insects which resemble giant cockroaches had won.

Halla came back into the room. A moment later, "Hal, have you seen it?" she asked breathlessly.

"Seen what, dear?"

"The little green bug—" she waved her hands. "The one that jumps sideways!"

The three of us stared at her. I wondered if the heat, the

humidity, the water-bug battle and now the talk of malaria had caused her to crack.

I jumped to my feet and pushed a chair toward her. "Why don't you sit down, Halla. I'll get some cool water and——"

She waved me aside and stared fixedly at the table. "There they are right there," she said pointing. "Little green bugs that jump sideways."

To humor her we three men shrugged and glanced down at the table cloth. And then it was our turn to be startled. There actually were little green bugs—an army of them—that hopped sideways to get to where they wanted to go!

We looked at each other and then exploded into roars of laughter. The bearers came rushing out of the service pantry.

One of them, quite worriedly, said: "What ees the mattair, sa'ahb?" and the Englishman pointed to the busy little insects. "These things are playing hopscotch, sideways!"

The bearers looked at the bugs and then eyed us. They resignedly shrugged and returned to the pantry where, we knew, they would ponder the unfathomable ways of the inscrutable "foreigners." After all wasn't it common knowledge throughout East Pakistan that little green bugs always jump sideways!

Halla and I rode in a little "trishaw" which was a tricycle rickshaw propelled by the "rickshaw wallah," a spindly Pakistani who sat on a bike saddle up ahead and vigorously applied leg-muscle power to the pedals.

Behind us rode Mr. Usman Ahmad Ansari, a tall, handsome gray-templed Pakistani official whose gracious hospitality did much to balance the discomforts of the climate.

I halted our tricycle rickshaw and dismounted to get motion-picture footage of the Moslem Pakistani women in their "burkah" veils, garments which entirely cover them from head to toe and through which they see by means of a net insert at eye level. This is worn in the purdah system of the Moslem religion.

Mr. Ansari explained that the burkah veil worn here in East Pakistan differs from those used by women of West Pakistan, a thousand miles away.

"Here, perhaps because of Hindu influence, the burkah veils are in colorful pastel shades of orange, rose-colored, yellow, green," he told us. "In West Pakistan the women prefer either the classic white or else dark, solid tones, like black or navy blue."

We paused and gazed at the passers-by. "Actually the custom of using these veils is dying out," he continued. "By law if a woman wishes it, she can be seen in public without a veil."

At that moment I noticed a figure approaching us. It was a woman who was covered from head to toe by a coarse white garment. The only openings were two ragged holes roughly cut into the material, for her eyes.

"Now there," said Mr. Ansari nodding, "is a typical example of a woman who insists in wearing a burkah although she is quite poor and besides doesn't have to wear it."

"That would be interesting for women in America," Halla whispered.

I pretended to point my camera elsewhere. But as the woman approached I was able to get several sneak shots of her. The costume rather resembled a Ku Klux Klan outfit minus the pointed hood.

Later Halla learned that the gradual disappearance of the veil was causing Pakistani women to abandon another old custom—that of chewing betel nut. This strange habit causes ugly discoloration of teeth and lips. And because the Pakistani women are eager to adopt Western ways of living they are turning from that pastime which dates back to time immemorial and can be compared to dipping snuff in parts of America. Several Pakistani women candidly told Halla that they were quite happy about the disappearance of the betel-nut-chewing habit. "We are now taking up cigarette smoking. We never could smoke behind our veils!"

Wandering and filming through the heat-drenched streets, we grew aware of a feeling of intense, almost feverish activity on the part of the people of Dacca. They all had purpose stamped on their faces, in their carriage. Halla remarked on this to Mr. Ansari.

His head raised, quite proudly. "We are building a new nation," he said. "This has not been an easy thing to do.

"Before the Partition of India into two separate nations in 1947 everyone, not excluding many English and Americans, tried to convince Mohammed Ali Jinnah, the 'father of Pakistan,' that our Moslem nation would perish.

"On the face of it these doubters had considerable material to support their arguments. Look how Pakistan will be divided, they pointed out. East Pakistan, on the Ganges—West Pakistan a thousand miles away, on the Indus River, both separated by India.

"As you know, India and Pakistan do not exactly see eye-to-eye," he said. "It has been only five years since the horror of the communal rioting after the partitioning when millions of people were uprooted."

I recalled the tales I had heard and read of the slaughter of 1946 and 1947 only five years earlier when Indians and Moslems alike put one another to the sword in massacres that defy imagination.

Mr. Ansari continued, "We found ourselves, some 40,000,000 people here in East Pakistan and 30,000,000 in West Pakistan, forced to literally 'start from scratch'! This section of our country produces the finest jute in the world while West Pakistan grows the best cotton, but—" his fine features had twisted in a wry grimace—"all the jute-mill machinery was in India and all the cotton mills were also in India, and we had jute and cotton but no place to process them."

Then he had smiled. The flash of his even white teeth was like the sun breaking through an overcast. "We succeeded in overcoming these handicaps," he said. "We have made a good start toward becoming a prosperous nation. We now have cotton mills and jute mills in five short years although everyone said we couldn't do it." His eyes had wrinkled with a sly expression. "What we're doing reminds me of the story they tell about American aeronautical engineers and the bumblebee.

"As the story goes the learned engineers decided that the bumblebee, aerodynamically speaking, could not possibly fly. According to their calculations its body was too large for the size of its wings and the wings were entirely the wrong shape. Yet the bumblebee, being unable to use a slide rule and unimpressed by mathematical formulas merrily continues to fly—and quite well, to the great discouragement of the engineers! That's how we, too, confounded the experts who said that our country couldn't possibly succeed."

As we resumed our stroll through the streets with their signs in Urdu, Hindi, Bengali, and English and their old-fashioned ornately decorated Victorian-style buildings, Halla with a look of disbelief on her face grasped my arm and pointed. "That store—the sign on it. It says: 'Official Government Opium Store'!"

She was entirely correct. I looked askance at our guide. He

shrugged. "That is our policy," he said. "We feel that it is far wiser for the government to make available to registered addicts heroin, opium, and other narcotics at controlled, low prices, than to foolishly try to ban it like people do elsewhere. By making it legally 'impossible' for an addict to obtain drugs all that happens is that a black market is created; criminals smuggle in narcotics and force the addicts to pay high prices and the addicts turn to crime to get enough money."

He had paused and shrugged. "By making it an inexpensive, rather painless matter for registered addicts our government has taken the profit out of black-marketing. And when crime doesn't pay, crime seems to disappear!"

His explanation seemed logical at first glance. Still the implications, for us, were rather staggering. "But to have legal opium stores," I murmured.

Mr. Ansari frowned. "In the United States you have liquor stores. To Moslems liquor is forbidden, in fact a rather unhealthy, somewhat degrading habit. Liquor acts much like drugs. You Americans have people who become alcoholics, addicts, who cause accidents, commit crimes."

"But you Pakistanis do have liquor stores," I cut in.

"Of course. But only for the convenience of our foreign guests, not Moslems." He thoughtfully regarded us. "But enough of such matters." He smiled at Halla. "How would you like to see young girls who play with cobras!"

"Live cobras?" Halla asked fearfully. Like Ireland, Halla's native Iceland has no snakes. She had never seen one outside of a movie.

"Oh, yes, quite live." He nodded.

Mr. Ansari led us to a side street where a group of girls, about twelve or fourteen years old, sat in a chattering group by a number of large wicker baskets. Mr. Ansari spoke to them and they eagerly nodded their heads.

They took the lids from the baskets and lifted out several big cobras. Halla came close to me and gasped when the cobras raised their heads, spreading their hoods while the girls teased them by holding their hands before the snakes' flickering tongues. When the cobras lunged at their moving fists the girls jerked their hands away a split second before they were bitten. Davey cooed but Halla had to look the other way. Mr. Ansari clapped his hands and told the girls to "pack up." He distributed a few coins.

"I should have explained," he cleared his throat. "These cobras are harmless. They've had their fangs pulled."

I slowly dismounted my camera from the tripod. "I've heard it's possible for cobras to grow new fangs and re-secrete venom."

Mr. Ansari's eyes flickered. "Nothing is impossible, Mr. Linker, in the Orient. But the girls try to notice if a new set of fangs have grown back. Usually they see it in time."

It was the forenoon of the following day when the three of us —Halla, little David, and myself—temporarily abandoned the Circuit House and rode by car with Mr. Ansari to Narayanganj on the Ganges River.

As we rode through the waterlogged countryside we began to notice thick, jungle-like growths of plants which shot up to over twelve feet in height, bearing heavy broad leaves. I asked Mr. Ansari what they were.

"Jute," he smiled. "Those plants are about ready to be cut down and retted."

"Retted?"

"That's the process of soaking the jute plants in water for about six to eight weeks. During this soaking period the bark-like exterior of the plant becomes ready to be separated from the core. The farmers strip this bark from the hard core. In fact if you'll look toward that cove—" he pointed—"you'll see some of our people stripping plants now."

I captured the entire operation on film.

Mr. Ansari continued. "This bark, which is actually jute, is hung to dry along the road on cords strung between trees. As it dries it bleaches. When it has properly bleached it is bundled into huge bales and shipped in barges to the jute mill. The hard core of the plant isn't discarded either. It is used for building purposes, fence-mending, and a dozen and one other things."

"What do they do with the leaves?" Halla asked.

"Nothing. They've no value whatsoever."

At Narayanganj a rather tiny motor launch which would take us on a ten-mile voyage to the Adamjee jute mill was waiting for us.

The loitering clouds of the impending monsoon helped keep the scorching sun from our heads, although the atmosphere itself was so muggy as to almost literally steam. We did not mind it too much. The prospect of a boat ride on the historic Ganges made us feel as though we were "playing hookey" from our motion-picture shooting schedule in order to go picnicking.

When we boarded the launch at Narayanganj, Dacca's "port," Mr. Ansari heightened the illusion of a holiday by announcing that he had brought a hamper of sandwiches since we weren't planning to stay until dinner time at the jute mill.

Little David, then just ten and one-half months old, noticeably perked up when the boatman-navigator started the engine, cast off, and headed the launch downstream. Although the air was super-steam-heated it was a relief to find it in motion over our perspiring faces.

Mr. Ansari explained how the Adamjee mill came into being.

"Before the Partition of 1947 came to pass a successful Calcutta jute-mill owner, a Moslem named Adamjee, decided that he wanted to become a citizen in the new Moslem country-to-be, and open a jute mill there." Mr. Ansari paused.

"He knew that the Hindu Indian mill owners would do everything in their power to retain their monopoly by keeping him from transferring his mill equipment from Calcutta to this area where most of the jute is grown and harvested by Moslem farmers.

"Mr. Adamjee resorted to all kinds of schemes and subterfuge in order to liquidate his Calcutta holdings and raise enough money for his new venture.

"Some of the things which happened were stranger than fiction —truly, Mr. Linker."

"Mr. Adamjee finally succeeded," Ansari continued. "He came to Dacca shortly after Mohammed Ali Jinnah became our first governor-general in mid-August of 1947 and proposed that the new Pakistani Government became a partner with him in the construction of a jute mill. He pledged half of the money and threw into the bargain his many years of experience.

"The jute mill you will shortly see is the result. It represents one of our nation's first attempts at industrial self-assistance."

As we cruised along the Ganges we watched the busy river traffic. There were picturesque, long, half-moon-shaped boats propelled by lateen sails looking like scenes from an Egyptian wall painting, other motor launches, heavily laden barges, and small uncovered ferries—quaint-looking craft laden with passengers who had only their own umbrellas as protection from the elements. The Adamjee jute mill loomed hugely ahead on the water-logged bank of the river. Its low, angular silhouette seemed out of keeping with the primitive, almost wild, lush background.

Mr. Ansari explained that building the mill had been a constant struggle against mud and silt. "In fact it is still going on."

Halla and I saw what he meant. It had cost over $6,000,000 to build the mill. Of that sum a good portion went into the struggle to keep the foundations from disappearing beneath the ooze.

"With all that money to spend I should think Mr. Adamjee would have brought in bulldozers."

"We did that," exclaimed a new voice.

Halla and I turned. A short, stocky man—I judged him to be in his early fifties—came up to us. Mr. Ansari beamed. "Mr. and Mrs. Linker—this is our host, Mr. A. W. Adamjee."

At our introduction to Mr. Adamjee I stammered about not meaning to "be critical."

"Not at all." His sharp, dark eyes twinkled. "It was a logical question. We brought over bulldozers. In fact I'll show you what happened to them!"

He led us to another section where a second mill was in the process of being erected. Pausing, he waved his arm: "There—see how the mechanical giants of Western technology are treated by Ganges mud!"

The scene was dismaying. A little cart loaded with sacks of cement had bogged down in the waterlogged soil. A bulldozer, coming to its rescue, had only succeeded in getting itself buried almost to the top of its metal treads. There were a number of technicians standing about, waving their arms and shouting orders.

But what finally rescued both primitive cart and modern machine was people—Pakistani jute farmers and laborers who grinned and put their collective backs to the task. Ropes were tied to both vehicles in distress and in half an hour they were out.

Mr. Adamjee showed us through the mill itself and explained how the farmers had to be trained to become machine-tool operators.

"It's been hard work but our people are intelligent and eager," Mr. Adamjee said with quiet but positive pride. "Within less than five years these people here have been able to leave their jute farms and become expert machine operators! I think that's pretty good, eh Mr. Linker?"

Halla and I agreed. It was not just good: it was amazing and heartening.

We followed our host through the plant and watched how sheer manpower, three men at a time, was required to carry each 350-pound bale of jute from the storage area into the mill.

The Pakistanis are not large people. And these slender, wiry farmers were typical. Still it was amazing to see three of them lift a tremendous bale with one concerted motion, equally share the load by balancing the weight on their heads, and then casually carry the bale on the tops of their heads into the plant. Halla remarked, "I hope one of the men isn't a fraction of an inch taller than the other two, then all the weight would fall on him."

The operation of converting the raw jute via shredding and weaving machinery into thread which, in turn, was woven into sacking material for coffee bags was a fascinating, hectic, noisy operation.

Almost every operation was done by machine. There were one thousand looms on the floor. Only one task called for hand labor: that of sewing the corners and edges of the bags. We found rows of women and bearded old men who sat in corners and stitched and stitched and stitched. No machine has been found to do this work better.

Mr. Adamjee told us over tea later that the full story of the jute industry could be told only by filming East Pakistan's only seaport, Chittagong, 125 miles down the river. "This place right here near Narayanganj was the only spot on the river with ground that might support a mill. Unfortunately the river here is too shallow for ocean-going vessels," Mr. Adamjee said. "So we have to send our finished product down to Chittagong on barges!"

Mr. Ansari immediately volunteered to provide a government plane for the flight from Dacca to the seaport located on the mouth of the Ganges where it empties into the Bay of Bengal. "We can eat our picnic lunch on the way back to Dacca. We'll leave from the airport there and we should be able to take off this afternoon, fly down to Chittagong, and return by dark!"

When we returned to the launch we were all famished. Halla eagerly opened the food hamper we had brought along and recoiled with sudden horror.

Mr. Ansari and I hastened to her side. She wordlessly pointed into the basket. A swarm of huge, black water bugs had made themselves at home. As we stared they stolidly continued to enjoy our "picnic" sandwiches. Needless to say we did without food all the way back to Dacca.

Our Pakistani pilot turned his head, smiled, and shouted something above the clatter of the two engines on our amphibian. I looked down to where he was pointing and saw that we were circling above the docks of Chittagong. Halla and David had remained behind at the Circuit House to get something to eat. Ansari and I, unfed, were on our way to Chittagong and back that afternoon.

Mr. Ansari leaned toward me and shouted above the drumming engines. "Five years ago we could only accommodate five or six ships here. Now look! There are thirteen ocean-going ships tied up at the docks right now!"

I motioned for the pilot to continue circling while I took many shots from the cabin window.

After a quick conference with Mr. Ansari I decided that we would have time to land and take a quick run into town from the airstrip. It would be a long while before I would have the opportunity of returning to this remote part of a struggling young nation.

Our pilot made a smooth touch-down on the airport runway which, at that time, could accommodate nothing larger than a DC3. Before we left he squinted at the hovering cloud build-up on the horizon. "Don't be too long," he said. "The heavy monsoon is overdue and I shouldn't like to get caught in it!"

"An hour—no more," Mr. Ansari answered.

We obtained a car and rode into the heart of Chittagong. It was rather primitive, almost like a frontier town of the old days of the Wild West. There were few paved streets, several fairly modern buildings—one of which was decorated with a large sign still proclaiming it to be the Bank of India—and a rather unique mosque whose domes and minarets were decorated with broad white, black, and red stripes. "Like Coney Island," I thought.

Traffic consisted primarily of ox-drawn carts with a sprinkling of automobiles and jeeps. Mr. Ansari must have noted the quizzical look on my face because he said: "Right now it does not compare with your seaports of New York, Los Angeles or San Francisco. But give us time, Mr. Linker, give us time. It does serve forty million people just the same!"

Aside from shipping jute and tea, which is another important East Pakistani product, grown in the hill country to the north, Chittagong is also noted as an "elephant training center."

When Mr. Ansari mentioned this I asked to visit one of these training establishments. I felt that footage of elephants being taught to fetch and carry and do the many things which make them invaluable should prove fascinating to my future lecture series and television audiences.

My companion hesitated, eyed the spreading monsoon clouds overhead. "Well, I imagine we'll have time," he dubiously commented.

The training compound proved exciting and colorful. When we arrived there it was just in time to film a five-year-old baby elephant in "class." It still had its baby fuzz on its head. Among the various "lessons" involved were how to kneel and lie down, how to climb part way up a tree, and how to handle poles. There were also instructions on how to pick up objects with its trunk. In fact the trainer was quite proud of the fact that he had taught his little charge to pick up coins. Mr. Ansari tossed a rupee to the ground. The trainer beamed while the little pachyderm, snorting with obvious pleasure, quickly scooped up the coin with the three tiny finger-like protuberances on the tip of its trunk. The trainer held out his hand. His pupil was supposed to deposit the money. The elephant trumpeted (I could have sworn that he laughed) and backed away. There ensued a ludicrous tug of war wherein the elephant stubbornly refused to give up his treasure while the trainer, losing his patience, began to tug—while my camera ground on.

Suddenly aware that there seemed to be very little light left for filming, I glanced up at the sky. The overcast had become a low-hanging blanket. Mr. Ansari beckoned.

"We'd better hurry back to the airfield."

Before we left the compound I looked back. Monsoon or no monsoon, the financial contest between the trainer and his elephant pupil was still going on!

Our pilot was pacing to and fro in front of the amphibian.

When we arrived he wasted no time getting the engines started. "We'll barely make it before the monsoon hits," he said as he taxied to the end of the strip prior to taking off. "There are no radio aids for weather-flying here in Chittagong," he explained.

While Ansari and I fastened our seat belts the pilot gave each engine a quick run-up and then turned the ship's nose into the rising, gusty wind and started his take-off.

No sooner had we lifted from the ground and the pilot got the landing gear retracted when we found ourselves shaken violently by severe updrafts. The next instant we plunged headlong into the churning overcast and it was as though we were suspended in flowing, dark gray, ectoplasm-like matter! We couldn't see a thing ahead. And the clouds had closed in around us so we couldn't see to return either.

My clothing was soaked through and through with perspiration. However I found myself shivering as the air, whistling in through tiny openings in the cabin side windows, brought with it cold moisture. I watched the pilot as he worked elevator and rudder controls, his sharp eyes riveted to the instrument panel. Presently one of his hands left the control wheel and darted amongst several knobs and switches. He noticed me watching.

"I'm going to try to climb above this," he shouted above the roaring engines. The engines seemed to deepen their tone. The ship began to rise. The next instant hail and rain hit us with the suddenness of massed machine-gun fire.

Halla, David, and the Circuit House seemed far away. I stole a glance at Mr. Ansari. He seemed quite worried about our situation. And then I decided to occupy myself in order to take my mind off our predicament.

I recalled how filming the incident with the whale's tongue during the height of the storm off the Iceland coast had made me absolutely forget the heavy seas and the possibility that the little whaling ship might founder. I kept taking pictures now, hoping to forget our danger. The films I made at that time show the beads of sweat rolling down the cheeks of the pilot as he alternately dove the plane and zoomed upward trying to find an opening in the monsoon clouds, and also the rain and hail beating against the front windshield.

Suddenly the clouds parted in front of the streaming windshield.

In the gray, watery twilight gloom I saw that we were now skimming just under the overcast, a scant few hundred feet above the desolate, inundated delta country.

The machine flew more smoothly here. The pilot readjusted his throttles and mopped his brow. He patted the instrument panel. "She's a sturdy one, this one!"

He pointed ahead. "We could land on any of these stretches of water since we're an amphibian. Trouble is we've no food or water with us. No telling how long we'd have to ride at anchor down there. Probably till this weather breaks or someone came along. Perhaps two or three days! Maybe more!"

He grew silent as he scanned his instruments. Ansari and I looked at each other. I cleared my throat. "I wonder how much gas he has on board—how long can we stay up in this monsoon?" My companion shook his head.

I don't know how many strained minutes we skimmed through driving rain just above the surface of the soaked earth. I concentrated on trying to capture the flight on film. And then the pilot uttered a sharp exclamation. He whipped the amphibian into a tight left turn. The low wing of the plane pointed like an arm straight down toward the river. My arms and legs felt leaden. My heart sank.

And then the pilot straightened the ship. The pressure disappeared. Ansari and I leaned forward. The pilot jubilantly pointed ahead. "There right under us. I recognized those buildings. That's the Adamjee jute mill. We'd better land there."

I can't recall when the sight of any landmark ever made me feel so good as did the looming jute mill buildings. Our pilot eased back on the throttles, lowered the flaps and then landed the amphibian on the river.

As we slowly taxied to the mill dock I saw figures emerge and wait for us. Presently we were close enough to recognize the foremost one. It was Mr. Khan the Afghan plant manager we had met earlier.

He shook our hands and bubbled with genuine pleasure. "I didn't expect to see you again so soon——"

His quarters were waiting for us with shelter and food. As we hurried toward the door the pilot paused and looked back over his shoulder at the monsoon clouds. Lightning flickered through the overcast. The distant thunder growled, almost with a note of frustration.

The pilot's dark features lighted up in a grin. He deliberately thumbed his nose at the monsoon-darkened sky and then winked at me—as if to say, "Well they didn't get us that time."

Chapter Nine

Pakistan—The Northwest Frontier Province

THE SULTRY DAY was drawing to a close. Only short hours before Halla, Davey, and I had landed after a wearisome, thousand-mile flight across Indian territory from East Pakistan to Karachi, at that time national capital of West Pakistan.

In our room at the Metropole Hotel, we found ourselves perspiring in the stifling heat. It was July. We had hoped that Karachi, fronting on the Arabian Sea, would be cooler than Dacca or Calcutta. Alas, Dacca had been wet-hot, Karachi was merely dry-hot.

Still we could count our blessings in Karachi. Our room was luxurious when compared with those of the Dacca Circuit House. And the capital itself, bursting with over a million souls, was a real metropolis in contrast with the provincialism of Dacca and Chittagong.

Like the other rooms of the Metropole, our chamber's door and windows opened upon a large rectangular inner courtyard. While I watched, a squad of chattering, turbanned bearers busy themselves arranging chairs in a semicircle in the courtyard, Halla finished the nightly ritual of preparing our eleven-month-old son for bed.

There was an increasingly pressing problem on my mind: money. The $500 retainer promised by the Pakistan Embassy for the film was an elusive will o' the wisp here just as it had been at home, in Honolulu, the Philippines, and Dacca. I had been put off with the assurance that payment would be waiting for me when I arrived in Karachi.

Well, here we were—and still no money.

I was assured by the officials who met us at the airport that I would receive a "cheque" within a fortnight. Meanwhile our funds were down to $10—a single travelers' check. I sighed. We'd have to continue on a shoestring and collect when we got back from Lahore. I would sign "chits" for our meals and such.

The bed looked good despite the heat. The soft voices coming from the courtyard acted as a sort of lullaby. I recall drifting smoothly off to sleep when, abruptly, a blare of noise crashed through our conciousness and brought us erect.

"What on earth is that?" Halla gasped.

I shook my head groggily trying to orient myselt. The clamor grew louder, I recognized it as a blare of slide trombone mixed with trumpets and accompanied by a clashing cymbal and the ruffle of drums.

Little David voiced a mighty howl of indignant protest. I leaped out of bed and rushed to the window. One look was enough. The seats in the courtyard were now occupied by a five-man jazz orchestra. There were gaily colored, illuminated lanterns strung around the courtyard. As I watched the musicians launched into their version of a dance tune while a few couples drifted into sight and began to fox-trot.

Now, with a groan, I remembered the desk clerk who had proudly announced that the Hotel Metropole had a very fine orchestra which played American jazz every night! "Real hot jazz," he had emphasized.

I had assured him that hot jazz was the last thing Halla or myself wanted. But here it was—a wild, thumping variety of sound that reverberated against our skulls and poured through the window.

"This thing is liable to go on all night long," I exclaimed with exasperation.

"Close the door and windows," Halla answered.

While she went to soothe David I tried to soundproof the room by closing everything tightly. The noise was only slightly diminished.

"We'll just have to ignore it," I announced.

Halla did not answer. We both lay there wide awake, staring up at the ceiling. "Thump-bang-blare-clash-thurruppp-dee-dup-dee-dup."

I somehow found myself thinking of the Black Hole of Calcutta where over 150 British men, women, and children had perished of suffocation when they had been imprisoned there in the summer's heat during the Sepoy Rebellion of the mid-nineteenth century. Perspiration drenched me and I found myself almost gasping for breath. My imagination seemed to be running away with me. And then I realized what was happening. By closing all the windows and the door I had turned our hotel room into a Black Hole of Karachi.

I crawled out of the bed and opened the windows again. The night breeze from the Arabian Sea came back in and with it the "real hot jazz." At 3 A.M. it finally ended.

The next morning, feeling as though we had not slept for a week, Halla and I shouldered our gear consisting of camera, tripod, film, David, and his portable stroller filled with nursing bottles, and went about our Karachi filming safari.

Before the Partition the city had been a somewhat off-the-beaten-track community of perhaps half a million population. Now only five years later, we found the capital teeming with activity, from its one million inhabitants. Riding through the thoroughfares and bazaars, we watched the women with their burkah veils intermingled with Europeans and uncovered Indian and Sikh women. From all sides came snatches of half a dozen different dialects as people debated, haggled and gossiped in Urdu, Bengali, Pushtu, Gujrati, Sindi, and Baluchi.

While riding in a horse-drawn, two-wheeled carriage, called a "gharry," on Dundar Road we encountered "Christmas in July." As we passed the imposing Cotton Exchange Building, we heard what seemed to be the jingling sleigh bells of Christmastime.

And then the reason for the jingling came into sight. It was a string of heavily laden carts being pulled at a slow pace by harnessed camels! Around the knobby knees of each camel was affixed a band of sleigh bells. From these came the musical jingle-jangle. Our gharry driver explained in interestingly accented English that the bells were to warn pedestrians out of the way.

About three miles from the heart of the city is Clifton's Beach. Here we found hundreds of men and women lolling on long, wide, flat sands which reminded me of the hard beaches of the State of Maine.

The center of attraction was an ornate pavilion erected by the British during the era of English rule. There were a number of policemen on duty, rather interesting-looking in their immaculate white tunics and red berets.

One of them, a sergeant, obligingly posed for a sequence with his men. He was quite talkative. I remarked on the fact that there were quite a few people present during a "working day" but that comparatively few were actually swimming.

"Most of these people, sar," he said with an impressive sweep of his arm, "are visitors from the North-West Frontier and the desert. They come to see big water, for the first time probably in their lives!"

"Pakistani tourists?"

He nodded.

We saw a number of Moslem women there in their flowing purdah robes. Although we could not see their faces it was evident that they were enjoying the water. They would hike up their skirts just to the ankles and wade into the surf only deep enough to wet their feet. The thought of a bathing suit would have shocked and dismayed them.

Every sea resort has its special attractions and rides. Clifton's Beach has camels. We found that a camel ride appeared to be as appealing to Pakistani vacationers as a roller-coaster ride would be to Americans, although it seemed to us that a camel ride for a desert dweller was really a busman's holiday.

I filmed laughing Pakistani men, women, and children taking their turns, riding the towering, stalking, four-legged "ships of the desert." And I decided I'd like to try one.

Camels are a disdainful lot. When I approached my particular "ship" he casually turned his head and gave me a rather bored appraisal. His skipper uttered a command, pulled on the bridle, and the beast lowered its hulk to the sand so that I could climb on board.

In this strange lowering operation first the camel's front legs fold, leaving the ungainly posterior pointing to the sky. Then the rest of the body sags to the bench.

I gingerly stepped into the peculiar saddle. The attendant uttered another command and I found myself frantically pulling leather as the animal cranked itself to a standing position.

As I rode pitching and tossing on the back of the gawky, ungainly brute I realized why the romanticists call a camel the ship of the desert. The motion in the saddle reminded me of a ship all right, but during a storm.

Although I thought I had prepared myself for dismounting, the sudden drop when my mount folded his front legs and knelt almost sent me flying over his head. When the rear of the camel came to rest I lost no time abandoning ship.

Halla, recording all this on film, thought that the ride was hilarious. Subsequent lecture and television audiences have agreed.

At the time I was wearing a sun helmet which I had purchased in the Karachi bazaar. After successfully disembarking from the camel I took it off to wipe the perspiration from my face. Glancing into the crown of the helmet I saw that the inner lining was beginning to crack open. Showing through the small opening were folded newspapers, obviously used by the hat maker for insulation.

The words were printed in English. I curiously scanned them and then perked up. They were copies of a San Fernando Valley newspaper from the outskirts of Los Angeles where we live. What I was reading was the television program log for August 12, 1949!

From the air the frontier city of Peshawar looked like a dusty collection of low houses of native style interspersed with bulbous mosques and a scattering of "European" structures. The overhead sun blazed mercilessly down on the city. In the near distance loomed the mountain range of the embattled Khyber Pass and, beyond, the Hindu Kush itself—classic invasion route to the Pakistan-Indian subcontinent.

When we drove from the airport into Peshawar I found that like other communities of the North-West Frontier Province, Peshawar is a garrison town. The residents, Moslems almost exclusively, are tall, lean, fierce-eyed Pathans and their language, I later discovered, mainly Pushtu and Afridi.

During the years of British rule of this area the nomadic Pathans who recognized no government or rule save that of the Koran or their tribe, maintained a bushwhacking guerilla-type resistance to the English. The constant clashes, ambushes, and in some cases, large-scale, pitched battles in and around the Khyber Pass were much like the campaign waged by the U. S. Army against the plains Indians during the nineteenth century.

The Pathans in those pre-Partition days were mostly bandits.

Their soil is so arid that cultivation of any sort of crop is hazardous. To augment their "income" they resorted to raiding communities or waylaying travelers and cargo-laden caravans on the lonely, winding passes.

When there was no one else to attack, they would start inter-tribal warfare with other tribes.

Prior to the Partition in 1947 the British stationed between 5000 and 10,000 troops—some English, the rest Madrassi, Bengali or Ghurka—in Peshawar. After Pakistan came into being the new government, with Solomon-like wisdom, created a new regiment which, while using an old and famous name—the Khyber Rifles—was comprised solely of the tribesmen, themselves.

Hostile activities almost immediately ceased since the "bandits" and "soldiers" were now of the same blood. This meant that if the bandits killed a Khyber Rifleman they would probably immediately be involved in a blood feud with the dead soldier's clan.

Despite the heat and dust and the discomfort of our room in Dean's Hotel, a rambling, one-story affair, Peshawar was a colorful and fascinating subject for motion picture photography.

We visited and filmed the winding, shadowy "Street of Story-tellers" where I found venerable bearded prophets and sooth-sayers, typical I imagine, of a hundred centuries in the past, as they regaled fascinated audiences with ancient fables, ancedotes, and tales of battle prowess.

Late one afternoon, as the sun was about to set, we were returning through the crowded bazaars from filming. I had hired a small horse-drawn cart for the afternoon. We three sat on the rear apron of the cart since it had no seats except for the driver. Suddenly I was aware of a strange electric feeling of danger. I couldn't for a moment put my finger on what was causing the feeling. Then I realized that the constant babble of voices and hum of activity which had been with us when we entered the bazaar area had suddenly ceased. I looked around to find that a silent crowd of fierce-looking tribesmen had formed two phalanxes on both sides of our cart as it moved along at a snail's pace. I could see the crowd get larger and ominously enough it consisted only of men. "What's going on?" I whispered to the driver.

"Your lady's dress, sahib," he whispered back.

And then I realized that to these strict tribesmen in an area where about 98 per cent of the women were in purdah robes by orders of their menfolks, my blond wife's summer dress, held up by only two thin shoulder straps was the height of indecency. Her shoulders were actually bare!! Halla whispered, "I'm frightened, Hal." She was sure that just one shouted criticism from a religious fanatic in the crowd would set the mob on us. I reached down and unfastened one of the heavy legs of the tripod I carried. It was made of stout wood and had a two-inch steel spike in its end. Any weapon would be better than nothing, I felt. I had left the little .25-caliber pistol in the hotel, since I had anticipated no trouble within the city limits of Peshawar. Then I realized that this slight tripod weapon would be useless against a mob. I unbuttoned my own shirt, took it off and wrapped it about Halla's shoulders. "Whip up the horse," I whispered to the driver. But as we started to pull away from the crowd several of the men began to run to keep up—then they gradually dropped back, muttering. Dean's Hotel never looked as good as it did when we finally got back.

The commandant at the fort, which was originally built by the Sikhs after they had conquered the area in the eighteenth century, invited us to film the Khyber Rifles during a typical parade.

Knowing that the soldiers were themselves tribesmen, barely five years removed from having been "enemies of authority," we half-expected to find the parade a sort of parody. Imagine our astonishment when we saw rows of tall, uniformed men, their equipment brilliant with legendary spit-and-polish, as they marched past the commandant and his staff with precise steps.

Their uniforms consisted of rather long gray tunics, loose trousers fastened at the ankles, and red berets. Their weapons shone and as they strode, with typical British cadence and arm-swinging, before my camera, their company and platoon commanders crackled sharp "Eyes Right" and as one the soldiers smartly tendered me the military honor.

After that the formations of soldiers staged a "pukka drill" of marching and countermarching. I remarked to one of the reviewing Pakistani officers that these uniformed Pathans would do credit to any professional army.

"They should," he said in crisp British accent. "See that major out there leading them?"

I nodded.

"He's a regular British Army officer, assigned to help train them."

The Pakistani fingered his mustache and smiled. "A few years back, before the Partition, he led English and Indian troops against these very same chaps—when they were wild tribesmen!"

Halla was intrigued. "How do you account for their abrupt change?" she asked.

The officer's chest visibly swelled. "Because they are now part of us—Pakistani citizens!"

However I found that there was still enough potential danger lurking from the as yet unsubdued Pathans.

One night I was summoned by the manager of the hotel to the lobby. There I found a "civilian" waiting for me.

He was himself a Pathan—representing the Pakistani government in a minor capacity. He drew me to one side and in a manner which reminded me of a cloak-and-dagger motion picture whispered that I was invited to visit the village of Kohat "right in the shadow of the Khyber Pass."

"The Khan, ruler of the village, will show you something very interesting," he promised.

"What?" I asked.

"I cannot tell you now." He peered about the small lobby. "But you come. Only you, however. Do not bring your wife or child! And no matter what, do not tell the soldiers or police!"

Early the following morning I told Halla that I would be gone for several hours and that I had been asked to come alone.

"Please be careful," was all she said.

It took me a while to find a taxi and driver who would take me to Kohat. But finally I was on my way. And as we drove over the dusty road, occasionally passing cold-eyed tribesmen dressed in white or dark-colored tunics, I began to wonder what I was getting myself into. His insistence that I leave Halla and David behind me was strange enough, I thought. But his fierce demand that I refrain from telling the authorities where I was going began to worry me.

The rugged mountains towered above us when we drove into the single street of the "village." A group of lean, gleaming-eyed, swarthy men gathered around the taxi, each had a rifle slung over his shoulder.

I got out, carrying my camera. It was hot and I was perspiring but as I mopped my brow and tried to smile a greeting to the silent onlookers I was conscious of a slight chill.

My "friend" appeared. With him came a tall, mustached young

man of about thirty or so whose carriage radiated "authority." This turned out to be the Khan—the ruler of the tribe which inhabited Kohat. The Khan spoke very little English. He wore a caracul lambskin "jinnah" cap.

He led us to one of the mud-walled huts. There I found several men and boys squatting over crude red-hot forges. There was a great deal of banging and clattering of hammers upon white hot metal held on anvils by tongs.

I looked at the Khan. "Are they making horseshoes?" I asked.

The Pathan who had invited me here smiled. "Look again," he urged.

I went closer. One of the workmen put down his hammer and reached off to his side. The next instant I found myself staring at a revolver, a facsimile of the British Army .455 Webley.

Now I realized the need for secrecy—the hush-hush attitude on the part of my "hosts." The entire village of Kohat, under the very noses of Pakistani authority, was an arms-manufacturing center. While in this amazing place I filmed men and boys busily engaged in turning out somewhat crude but efficient revolvers, .303 Enfield rifles, and even submachine guns!

Later, back in Peshawar, I was told by an army colonel that the government was quite aware of this clandestine arms factory.

"Those guns don't last very long," he said. "The barrels quickly wear out and they are not at all accurate. You see, intertribal warfare and feuding goes on regardless of what we do or say. And since the tribesmen are determined to have guns we close one eye and let them have access to those of their own manufacture rather than force them to raid our outposts and steal weapons or else 'trade' with people who live on the other side of Afghanistan!"

"You mean the Russians?" I asked.

He shrugged and let the matter drop.

It was this same colonel who arranged for us to visit Fort Salop, an outpost near the Khyber Pass itself, some forty miles from Peshawar. This time the invitation included Halla and David.

Fort Salop looked like a strong-point straight out of the pages of *Lives of a Bengal Lancer*. Smartly uniformed soldiers rendered a rifle salute as we drove in and were greeted by the commanding officer, a young colonel about thirty-five years old.

He told us we would be treated to a demonstration of the Khattuck dances.

At Chittagong, East Pakistan, with baby elephant at elephant training school.

Young girls brought cobras into Dacca, East Pakistan, to show how they could avoid the lunges of the snakes.

On the Ganges River on the way to the Adamjee Jute Mill, East Pakistan.

East Pakistan. Woman worker in jute mill at Narangjanj.

On the Ganges, East Pakistan.

Making illegal arms in village of Kohat near Khyber Pass, West Pakistan.

Village of Kohat, guarded by illegal rifles and submachine guns (near the Khyber Pass).

Saber dancer at Fort Salop, Northwest Frontier Provinces, West Pakistan.

Davey's first birthday in Israel. Jewish religious candle in cupcake at Tel Aviv.

Halla and David in Tel Aviv, Israel.

Little Davey when he finished his first trip around the world.

President Batista, still in power in Cuba, takes a liking to David.

Street fiesta in Santiago, Cuba. This festival was especially put on for our cameras during the Fidel Castro uprising there.

Davey's second birthday cake. Two candles in a box of cookies at Santiago because of martial law shutdown of city. Headlines of the day's newspapers tell of those killed in Castro's attack on the Moncada barracks.

Dancers in Cuban night club.

With Sergeant Jesus Maria Garcia as we leave Santiago, Cuba, after revolution. Note submachine gun carried by heavy-set man at left.

I had to dress in sixteenth-century costume to film the Brussels "Omme-gang" procession.

Vigelund statues in Oslo, Norway.

Davey at the controls of a
DC-6B over the Pacific en
route to Japan.

Young Japanese "Maiko" Geisha who acts and dances in our film of Japan. Kyoto, Japan.

Cormorant fishermen at Gifu, Japan, on the Nagara River.

Pearl divers of Japan.

Blowing conch shells at Japanese festival at Haranomachi.

The Hairy Ainu of Japan. Man is bearded, unlike the Japanese. Woman is tattooed around her lips in a special way.

Shinto priest.

"Here—in the fort?" I asked.

He nodded and smiled. "Why not. The tribal dancers are our soldiers. We let them do this every once in a while—to let off steam!"

It was then that I heard a sudden beating of drums and the weird sound of flutes. The next instant a long line of fierce-looking tribesmen, bareheaded and clad in typical long white tunics and baggy white trousers, danced toward us in single file. The Khattuck dance seemed grueling. The men whirl, snap their heads, and twist and twirl. The pounding beats of the drums are wild and sent shivers up and down our spines. As the dancers came close to us we saw that their eyes were glazed. It was as though they had put themselves into a trance. Twist and twirl, snap their heads, on and on it continued for an hour.

Presently the music stopped. The dancers assembled in a large circle. There was a momentary pause.

"Now you'll see the saber dance," the commandant said.

The drums and flutes started again. One man, brandishing a long, gleaming cavalry sword, dashed headlong at the "orchestra," which consisted of two drummers and two men blowing flutes, and made a threatening pass with the heavy blade.

The sword-bearer repeated this strange performance once more, as though warning the musicians to do their best "or else." The latter imperturbably went on with their playing while the dancer began to gyrate, viciously twisting the saber through the air and slashing it from side to side. Each time he slashed to his left he pulled his left arm out of the way at the last second. We noticed that while he manipulated the heavy sword with his right hand he held a small cloth or handkerchief in his left hand. We learned that part of the dance consisted of seeing how close he could come to just missing his left hand with the whirling sword blade!

When the time came for us to return to Peshawar it was growing dark. If we had any notions that the Khyber Pass country had become completely peaceful it was dispelled when the commandant insisted on assigning two fully armed soldiers to us as body-guards for the return to Peshawar.

"As long as the soldiers accompany you there's little likelihood that any bandits will molest you," the commandant explained. "They wouldn't want to hurt one of the soldiers and start a blood feud!"

When the two troopers, smartly uniformed, rifles slung, and bandoliers crisscrossing their tunics, appeared, I took a second close look at them. It was incredible, I told myself. Only a short while before they had leaped and whirled out there in the blazing afternoon sun, wildly slashing swords to the beat of drum and shrill of flute. Now they were impassive-faced soldiers once more, escorting us safely back to Peshawar.

After the wild all-night drive from Peshawar to Rawalpindi which I described at the very beginning of our story, the three of us almost dead from lack of sleep and heat exhaustion, finally boarded a battered DC3 which flew us from Rawalpindi and the wild reaches of the North-West Frontier Province to Lahore, Pakistan's second largest city and center of culture and learning.

On landing at Lahore (we were the only passengers deplaning, the rest were proceeding to Karachi) we were told that a bus would shortly be along to take us to a hotel.

After an interminable wait a decrepit old rattletrap bus of questionable vintage—perhaps pre-World War I—wheezed its way to the terminal building. Halla and I stared at the steaming vehicle and then looked at one another.

"Hal, do you think it will be able to make it to the hotel?" she asked.

"Don't joke, Halla," I said. "I've got my fingers crossed."

The driver frowned. "This ver' good bus, sah'b!"

"Kismet," I muttered. We loaded our gear, David, crib, and dwindling supply of baby food, etc., on board. We were the only passengers. The engine started with a raucous roar of protest and we creaked and rattled our way down the rough road. The vehicle jounced and swayed.

Davey and Halla looked as if they could use a nice bath and some rest in a cool place.

I was about to utter some words of consolation when our bus came to a jarring halt. The driver frantically shifted gears and raced the engine but the contraption refused to budge. At first we thought we had become imbedded in a soft spot. We quickly learned that the rear axle had snapped and there we were, stranded in the middle of nowhere.

When we finally were able to get another vehicle more than an hour later, we were driven to the only hotel in operation at that time, named Faletti's, only to be told that it was completely filled.

Officialdom in Karachi had told me to call on "the government" anytime we were in difficulty.

And if ever a "feller needed a friend" it was us in Lahore. I finally reached someone in the local Government Tourist Office who understood my predicament. He told us to wait. They would send transportation to take us to an army barracks where we could "temporarily bed down."

After another doleful wait a rather youthful officer arrived with an army half-ton truck. We were jounced across Lahore to a rather foreboding, fortress-like structure which must have dated back to 1890.

After entering the barracks, if we had any doubts whether or not it was only for the military they were quickly dispelled. As we made our way down a corridor, Halla with David in her arms, and myself bringing up in the rear, we encountered six men who were wrapped in towels, but just *barely* wrapped, and obviously heading for the showers.

Tired and disconsolate as we were the situation was a bit amusing. Halla took it in her stride. But the officers were startled out of their wits. To find themselves confronted by a woman, a blond foreigner to boot, carrying an infant, in territory sacred to military males—incredible!

When we were ushered into a high-ceilinged room we learned that we were supposed to have our own towels, sheets and pillow cases with us. Although straw-filled mattresses were provided it was customary for itinerant travelers, such as ourselves, to bring all bedding with them wherever they went, we were told.

While I stood there, trying to solve this latest problem I heard Halla begin to sob. Poor girl, I berated myself, the all-night drive, subsequent flight and the inconvenience had finally worn her down. But it was not that at all.

She was sitting on a chair holding little David in her lap. While I had been talking to our guide she had begun to change our son's diapers. "Look, Hal," she sobbed. "Davey's burning with fever and covered from head to toe with a horrible rash!"

I stared at Davey's mottled skin and I visualized all sorts of horrible oriental diseases it could be. Then I grabbed the arm of the officer who had brought us. "We've got to get help. Is there an American consul in Lahore?"

He noded. "I'll take you to the telephone. It's downstairs."

The people at the consulate were sympathetic. They told me to go at once to the United Christian Hospital, an American-supported establishment on the outskirts of Lahore.

When we arrived we found the buildings old but sparkling clean. Two American doctors, one a former missionary M.D. in China, the other a young, comparative newcomer, ran the establishment, which was supported by private donations from the United States, mostly from private citizens of Grand Rapids, Michigan.

The senior physician, Dr. Edwards, examined our son and diagnosed the ailment as a type of dysentery plus severe heat rash. He assigned Davey and Halla to a room. Halla with Davey in her arms, followed one of the nurses and then I heavily sat down to catch my breath and try to get up enough strength with which to return to the barracks.

The doctor eyed me professionally and then remarked: "And I think you'd better stay here too, Mr. Linker. You need some rest, or I wouldn't be surprised if you crack up." I decided to remain there too.

Our three-day sojourn in the hospital was like a reprieve. While Davey recuperated and Halla rested I got to know the two medics —particularly the younger one, Dr. Ralph Blocksma. He was a Grand Rapids plastic surgeon who had grown tired of his practice in the States and had elected to come to Lahore with his wife and three children. He had heard of the great need for doctors in Pakistan and had volunteered to serve for several years.

He told me that he had enjoyed an extensive and lucrative plastic surgery practice at home. "But I wanted to get away from the routine of fixing noses, changing facial contours, things like that," he said.

And then he eyed me smilingly, "So I closed down my practice thinking I'd get back into general medicine, and what d'you suppose I discovered?"

I shook my head. "Can't imagine, Doctor."

He smiled. "There seems to be an old Moslem custom here in Pakistan wherein a husband who finds his wife unfaithful or who *thinks* she has been unfaithful remedies the situation by cutting off her nose!"

Seeing the incredulous expression on my face he nodded. "It's a

124

fact. When I arrived I found many poor girls, their lives virtually ruined, walking around noseless behind their burkah veils! So I've been doing mostly plastic surgery, patching noses, giving a lot of women a second chance!" He sighed and lit a cigarette.

"Just goes to show you. As the prophets would say—what must be must be. I was cut out to be a plastic surgeon, a nose-fixer, by golly. So here I am—halfway around the world, away from Grand Rapids, Michigan, still fixing noses!" He waved his arms in mock futility and grinned.

The sight of Karachi Airport again beneath the wings of our transport perked us up. Not that we regretted anything about our expedition to the North-Western Frontier Province and our subsequent stay in Lahore. Far from it.

I knew that every moment of discomfort we had experienced had been far outweighed by our experiences, the people we had encountered and the motion-picture film I had obtained for my travel-lecture series.

We had made many friends in Peshawar and Lahore. We had visited and filmed the incredibly beautiful Gardens of Shalimar, built by the great Mogul Shah Jahan, the ruler who erected the Taj Mahal in Agra. We had also explored the Badshahi Royal Mosque, one of the largest in the world.

But our Pakistan adventure was due to terminate. We were weary and thankful to land and return to our room at the Metropole Hotel.

As our stay in Karachi drew to a close I found myself again appealing to the government for the promised but still elusive $500 retainer fee. By now our need for the money was acute. We had accumulated a number of bills which had to be paid before we could leave. And since our flight from Karachi to Israel via Philippine Airlines would take place within a few days, I found myself in a rather desperate position. "Tomorrow" was always the answer.

During the last few days here we met the famed Begum Liaquat Ali Khan, wife of the man who had been appointed first Prime Minister of Pakistan after it gained its independence.

Because of his progressive attitude he had been called Pakistan's Abraham Lincoln. The fact that he had been assassinated while in office lent further impetus to the comparison.

The Begum, a handsome, flashing-eyed woman, had been vigorously carrying on her husband's policies. She had also created the Pakistan Women's Army and Navy Reserve—the equivalent of the U. S. WACS and WAVES. She arranged a parade of her organization for our cameras.

Our last day in Karachi was a Saturday. I kept phoning the government office at almost hourly intervals. Our airliner was scheduled to take off from Karachi for Lydda in Israel at three the following morning!!

The lesser bureaucrats I spoke to were vague. They would "relay my message." They would do this, that, a thousand and one things.

Finally I blew up. I called the Ministry of Information late in the afternoon and handed them an ultimatum. They would either immediately send the money due me to the Metropole or I would cancel our agreement and double the price we had agreed on for the film!

My threat worked. Within the hour arrangements were made for the American Express agency to pay me the funds from their government holdings and I was able to pay off the obligation which had accumulated. (Incidentally, a few months later I completed the film to the great satisfaction of the Embassy of Pakistan. It was called "This is Pakistan" and they ordered twenty copies of the production for distribution throughout the United States.)

The Metropole Hotel management informed us that at 10 P.M. there would be a special exhibition of Pakistani dancing which I could film in a private dining room of the hotel. The only hitch was that men attending were merely required to wear ties and jackets but women were expected to appear in formal dress.

I was able to borrow a tie from the hotel manager. But Halla was stumped until I suggested that she wear her Icelandic national costume which consists of a long ankle-length skirt with a decorative "apron," a beaten-gold bodice, and a tiny, rather saucy little cap that sits on the side of the head and has a tassel which comes down through a silver tube. She had it along for her return to Iceland.

"Oh Hal," she exclaimed. "An Icelandic costume—here in Pakistan!"

"Why not!" I countered. "It will be no more out of place than the saris some of the women will be wearing!"

126

After some persuasion she finally agreed. When we made our entry her blond beauty and unusual costume captured everyone's attention. A hum of conversation arose.

I whispered into her ear: "They're all probably wondering what sort of a costume you are wearing: where you come from?"

"Their attention makes me blush," she replied.

A tall European, a man about forty-five years of age, rose from his table across the room, crossed the floor where the Pakistani dances would take place and bowed. "Am I mistaken or are you wearing an Icelandic national costume!"

Halla and I were amazed that he was able to recognize it. We invited him to join us and he immediately switched to Icelandic and launched into an animated discussion with Halla. It turned out that he was a Dane who had spent many happy years in Iceland.

He flashed a smile at me: "Now I live here in Karachi. I did not realize how much I miss Iceland and the Scandinavian countries until I saw your wife in this costume. It made me so homesick, all of a sudden!"

At 3 A.M., our bills all paid, we left for Israel, only six hours away by plane but a world apart in many ways.

Chapter Ten

From Israel to Cuba

THE SETTING SUN momentarily splashed the Mediterranean with gold as Halla and I lounged on the balcony of our room at the Gat Rimon Hotel on Hayarkon Street, in Tel Aviv. It was relaxing listening to the gypsy dinner music being played by the hotel orchestra, two floors below.

"Ah, Tel Aviv," Halla murmured. "What a wonderful place!"

I could understand why. The streets were sparkling clean, the buildings modern, and the people walked with familiar purpose in the warm but not stifling late afternoon.

"It's like being back in the Western world." I said.

I took her in my arms and we danced to the romantic music.

Halla glanced back into the room where our son slept soundly. Behind us lay the heat, humidity, and frustration of India and Pakistan. A Tel Aviv doctor who had studied in Vienna had, on our arrival, quickly administered new antibiotics which were slaying the oriental dysentery in our son's little body. At the United Christian Hospital, the old-China-hand chief doctor had prescribed the remedy he had always used in China—plain castor oil!

One of the modern laundromats, at that very moment, was efficiently lifting the burden of the hand washing of diapers from my wife's shoulders. For six weeks, with only one respite at the United Christian Hospital, Halla had done Davey's diapers by hand daily. The disposable ones we had taken along had been quickly used up the first three weeks of our trip.

Ahead stretched the adventure of Israel, the old-new republic barely the size of Massachusetts, a fascinating mixture of biblical antiquity with the bustle of the mid-twentieth century.

With the exception of Jerusalem itself there was probably no city in Israel at the time of our visit (1952) which pointed up the difference between old and new as did the contrast between Tel Aviv and its now-attached former Arab city of Joffa (both had been combined as Tel Aviv-Jaffa).

Tel Aviv was sparklingly modern—having been only begun about forty years earlier as a suburb of Jaffa; now the tail was wagging the dog and Jaffa was a suburb of Tel Aviv. Jaffa still had its former Moslem air with mosques and minarets and only an occasional new building. Tel Aviv was obviously a new and planned city with broad avenues and up-to-date business and residential sections.

At the time of our visit Israel was still in the vacuum of an uneasy truce with its neighboring Arab nations. When we arrived in Jerusalem, capital of the new republic, the sight of the barbed-wire-infested no man's land, of ruined rubbled area separating "new" Jerusalem from the old city under Jordan control, reminded us that this ancient land, birthplace of Jesus Christ, Prince of Peace, was still in the shadowy valley of mankind's conflict.

When we were there the days were sunny and peaceful. Still, standing by the barbed-wire barrier near the Jaffa Gate which separates the old and new cities, Halla and I felt a distinct chill at the sight of ravaged bullet- and shell-pocked buildings.

From the top of the King David Hotel we could gaze across No Man's Land and see the Jordan lookout posts, manned by soldiers and equipped with aimed, loaded automatic weapons.

"Please hide your camera when you film," the hotel manager begged us. "They'll fire on you if they see you taking pictures."

I carefully did so.

Streaming to and from each "frontier" was a steady column of people wearing costumes both old and new. They went about their affairs, seemingly oblivious of the two, opposing, armed-to-the-teeth hostile forces a stone's throw away.

Following a visit to Haifa, Nazareth, Caesarea, and the ancient Roman resort of Tiberias, built two thousand years ago on the shore of the Sea of Galilee, 300 feet below sea level, we returned to Tel Aviv.

It was David's first birthday, July 27, 1952, and time to leave Israel for Rome.

When I searched for a birthday cake I drew a blank. Shopkeepers gave me a surprised look and told me that Israel was still in a state of war. Strict rationing was in order. Cakes were forbidden as luxuries for peacetime only. The only candles permitted were big ones for religious purposes.

When I returned to the hotel the manager, a former Hungarian, noticed my discouragement. When I explained the birthday-cake problem he grinned.

"Don't you worry, Mr. Linker. You go up to your room. We'll manage to get some sort of birthday cake for your little boy!"

"But the rationing," I said. "I couldn't even buy a small candle——"

He put his finger to his lips. "Just leave it to me!"

Ten minutes later there was a knock on the door. When I opened it there stood the manager holding a large plate. In the middle of the plate was a small cupcake. Thrust into its center was a lighted Jewish religious candle—which towered about five or six inches high!

"Happy birthday, little David," he announced, advancing into our room and placing the "cake" on a table. Davey cooed at the light and enjoyed the cake as much as if we had bought the finest one in all the world.

At twelve noon that day we boarded a plane at Lydda Airport and six hours later found our airliner touching down at Rome's Ciampino Airport. It was early evening when we got to our hotel and, consequently, still David's birthday which, by now had been spent in two nations. Since he spent the morning of his first birthday in Israel and the evening in Rome we like to say that this makes him non-sectarian.

Looking back over our son's travel and birthday log we note that since we are traveling every summer he has spent each July 27 in a different country.

His second birthday was celebrated at Santiago, Cuba, to the accompaniment of distant machine-gun fire! The third celebration and incidentally the first to be dignified by a proper cake, was in Belgium, while the fourth observance took place on the other side of the globe, in Japan.

By all odds the most bizarre was his fifth, for which we had a party on a Congo River diesel ship during our five-day river journey from Stanleyville to Leopoldville in the Belgian Congo.

The most glamorous birthday, his sixth, took place in Honolulu

130

where Miss Aloha of 1957 personally presented him with a candle-decorated cake. The following year saw David playing host to Turkish and American youngsters at his seventh birthday party at the Hilton Hotel in Istanbul, Turkey.

Lima, capital of Peru, was the background for his eighth observance following our return from a grueling trip to the headwaters of the Amazon River.

And as you read this account David will already have celebrated his ninth birthday in Vaduz, capital of the principality of Liechtenstein, a tiny nation of 15,000 souls situated on the east bank of the Rhine River between Austria and Switzerland.

After a two-day stay in Rome we flew on to London where we boarded a plane for Iceland. My purpose was two-fold: to display our son before his grandparents and other Viking relatives and to again show my hour-and-a-half-long Iceland color film to lecture audiences in that country. When we arrived in Iceland, Davey was one year and two weeks old. And since his travels had started from Iceland the year before, he had now completed a trip around the world.

At the outset I was a bit apprehensive about the audience acceptance of my film. After all, my narration was in English. Still the response was enthusiastic and that summer I gave twenty-five showings throughout the country. The fees I pocketed, while not large, were a monetary "transfusion" which enabled Halla and myself to return to the States with money left over.

It was early fall when we landed at Idlewild in New York. A welcome batch of lecture engagements meant that we would have to "barnstorm" almost immediately and we made our way across the United States to Los Angeles giving travel lectures. It was not until late October that we finally were able to unlock the door of our Hollywood apartment. Meanwhile, little David's fame began to spread.

The first indication that his travels were newsworthy came when Chicago reporters, tipped off by the lecture-hall management, came backstage to interview the tiny, globe-encircling, year-old Marco Polo.

Baltimore newspapermen reacted the same way. They were interested in Halla and Hal Linker but the star was David.

This phenomenon was repeated in Des Moines, Iowa and in a dozen different cities. David grew as used to crowding reporters and flashing photo bulbs as he did to travel by plane, train, rickshaw, or camel.

The winter of 1952 and spring of 1953 saw us shuttling back and forth across the continent. It was not exactly a placid existence. We lived out of suitcases, playing one-night stands in between either air or surface travel.

But on the other hand our greatest mutual compensation was in the fact that the three of us were always together. Halla saw eye to eye with me on the desirability of our not being separated by time and space. And I am happy and proud to say that this closely knit family partnership, or corporation, is to this day paying us rich dividends in unmatchable happiness.

In between lecture engagements I continued to think about using my travel series for television. With this aim I approached a prominent television personality who was conducting a program featuring personal-adventure films over a Los Angeles television channel. He invited me to appear as his guest, with my whaling expedition film. The fee he offered was very small but I accepted. He then asked that Halla appear in her Icelandic national costume with me and was flabbergasted when I told him that an extra talent like hers would require additional payment. He insisted that he always got the wife free, but I was adamant—and finally he agreed to pay an extra $25 for her appearance.

The warm audience response for that show convinced us that television would accept an authentic family travel-adventure program, as did the several additional shows I later gave for the same producer.

Each season in the travel-lecture field we had to produce a new film to stay with the competition, and so—casting about for a next summer's filming "target" for a new lecture—I hit upon Cuba. This time we felt we would be absolutely on our own. There was no arrangement with the Cuban government, airline, or anyone. The lectures and sporadic television appearances had provided us with enough working capital to see us through for a month or so.

We organized ourselves for travel with a minimum of fuss and excess baggage clutter. David was almost two years old, a surprisingly agile walker and weaned from the bottle.

We boarded a Mexicana de Aviación DC6B at Los Angeles International Airport for a non-stop flight to Mexico City. There we took the connecting flight to Cuba, landing en route at Mérida in the Mexican State of Yucatán, famous for its Mayan ruins at Chichén-Itzá and Uxmal.

When we arrived in Havana on June 26 we went immediately to the famous Hotel Nacional where, much to our pleasant surprise, the hotel's publicity director, Miss Nena Alemán, arranged for us to be their guests as soon as she learned about our visit. Almost from the moment we arrived we set about taking films in the city.

The hotel's publicity department told the newspapers about the "Norteamericano movie-making family." Interviews with Halla and myself, pictures of David, were published.

This turned out to be a blessing because the Cuban government became aware of our presence—and the reason for our being there. I was pleasantly surprised to receive a telephone call from Ed Chester, the personal secretary to President Batista.

"Would you like to meet the President?"

Would we!

The courteous voice on the other end of the line then told me that a presidential limousine would come by shortly to take us to Batista's residence.

We were excited as, decked out in our best despite the heat, we swept through the lobby and approached the long, sleek official limousine which awaited us by the portico of the hotel's driveway.

Waiting in the car with its police-uniformed chauffeur was Señor Ernesto de la Fé, Minister of Information in the government. After introducing himself he helped Halla and David into the limousine and I joined him as he entered.

Halla's blue eyes sparkled with delight.

"This is so exciting," she whispered to me. As the car started I glanced down on the floor in front of Señor de la Fé. There, snub-nosed and dully a-gleam with sinister purpose, reposed a Thompson submachine gun.

I sank down next to Halla. "Yes—it's pretty darned exciting, all right!"

Halla saw my look and glanced down too. I saw her start.

As the driver put the car into motion I began to think of all the rumors I had heard. "Just an old Cuban custom, I guess." I muttered to Halla.

Major General Fulgencio Batista y Zaldívar had begun his climb to the Presidency on September 4, 1933, as a simple sergeant in the

133

Cuban Army. He had led the revolution which threw out the hated dictator Machado and then after taking over the reins of government, was now accused by many of having himself become a dictator. After several years as President he had stepped out of office and then had returned in 1952 to take over the government again in a "military coup" from President Prío Socorras.

His residence was a rambling *finca* or ranch called "Kuquine" just outside of Havana, with meticulous landscaping, beautiful royal palms—and interestingly enough, no visible uniformed guards.

The then ruler of Cuba personally greeted us. He was an intense, stocky, strong-shouldered man whose face was quite Indian-looking, a man who seemed as if he could always get his way. Still the warmth of his greeting and his genuine pleasure at meeting little David made us instantly feel at home. He explained that he had four sons himself, the youngest only about five months old, the oldest about fifteen years.

He led us into his study where we were introduced to several people who were members of his inner cabinet. While we settled ourselves his wife Marta joined us. She was a striking brunette in her late thirties. We later learned she was his second wife.

Batista's hospitality was exemplary. To others he was a ruthless, dictatorial ruler. We saw none of this as his guests that night.

His interest in our travels was acute. When he learned that Halla and David accompanied me wherever I went he turned to his wife and snapped his fingers: "That's a wonderful idea—traveling all the time, isn't it, Marta!" (Little did he know that he would some day be sent involuntarily traveling by Fidel Castro.)

When we had originally accepted the invitation to visit the President, Mr. Chester had suggested that I bring along one of my films. I offered to show the color film I had made of Iceland.

Batista, his family, and cabinet members watched my motion pictures with rapt attention. I delivered my narration in Spanish—dug from my memory of college study. Fortunately it was one of my best subjects and I am told that I do quite well in that language even now.

It must have gone over well because Batista that night offered us official government transportation to any place we would wish to film in Cuba. I later learned that my sequences on the fishing industry in Iceland had interested him in buying Icelandic fish.

He assigned us an official guide, an army sergeant named Jesús

134

María García who would accompany us wherever we went, whether by official police-driven automobile or aboard a Cuban Air Force C-47 transport. That first name of his was a stumbling block. We frankly couldn't force ourselves to call out "Jesús!" when we needed him—so he became "Sargento" or "Señor García."

We covered the length and breadth of the island by car and plane. Sergeant García was an engaging, walking encyclopedia of information about his "beloved Cuba." In time Halla and I even grew accustomed to García's ever-present .45 Colt automatic.

Toward the end of July we returned from filming expeditions to the little town of Trinidad, the Isle of Pines, Camaguey, and Piñar del Río. President Batista himself suggested that we should fly to Santiago for the unique and colorful *fiesta* which takes place annually on the twenty-fifth and twenty-sixth of the month.

Halla and I vividly recall the President's suggestion and the circumstances surrounding it. At the time we were again at his residence. After issuing orders for our airlift to Santiago he turned to little David. "And for you, tiny world traveler, here is a token for your coming birthday, a souvenir of your visit!"

And with that he placed an amethyst ring bearing both his and David's initials on it, on David's thumb. It was a duplicate in miniature of the President's own ring and the ring was then too large for the boy's tiny fingers. We still have this ring today.

Sergeant García accompanied us, as usual, on our flight to Santiago. We took up quarters in an air-conditioned motel-like establishment called the Rancho Club overlooking Santiago itself. Not far from where we were was the Moncada military barracks. In fact we could see the buildings from the patio of the motel. Sergeant García stayed at Moncada. I emphasize this because of what took place shortly after our arrival.

The townspeople had been told that I was present, as a special "presidential guest," to film the fiesta street dancing. The evening of July 25 seemed peaceful enough with some preliminary costume parades. I was assured by the mayor that the fiesta, involving costumed *comparsa* dancers and street musicians "would start on schedule" the following day.

We awakened early the following morning in our air-conditioned, almost soundproof motel room. Our most pressing problems were, at the time, twofold: to obtain the footage of the fiesta dances and a cake for David's second birthday which would be July 27, the next day.

Going to the window I raised the blinds and peered out. A riot of color greeted my eyes. Filming would be good. I happened to glance toward the Moncada barracks and saw puffs of smoke. "Looks like the soldiers are burning trash," I casually remarked to Halla.

Stepping outside, prior to walking to the patio to order our breakfast, I paused when I heard an odd sound coming from the barracks. Halla and David were just behind me when I stopped short to listen.

"What is it, Hal?"

I shook my head. The sound was familiar—too familiar. I had occupied a more-than-ringside seat at too many Pacific Island invasions to mistake the sound of machine-gun fire and exploding grenades!

Halla peered over my shoulder. "Sounds like firecrackers. Is the celebration starting early, Hal?"

"I'm afraid its something more than firecrackers, my dear!"

We stepped up on the patio and found attendants and a handful of guests speaking in whispers. When our waiter, a badly shaken individual, came to our table for our order I nodded toward the source of the gunfire. "Are the soldiers maneuvering—practicing?"

"Oh no, Señor Linker. It is the revolution. The rebels have attacked early this morning," his eye brows raised. "*Muchos muertos —mucho* dead, *mucho* hurt!"

Halla visibly blanched. I pointed out to her (with a certain amount of bravado which I most certainly did not feel inside) that the shooting was at a distance. Furthermore we, as American tourists, were certainly not involved. "Don't worry about it, dear," I concluded.

Our waiter arrived with the first course of our breakfast. I began to toy with some fruit when the thought struck me: why not use my telephoto lens and obtain some footage of the fighting!

I jumped up, mounted my camera on its tripod, affixed the big lens, and had just started to press my finger to the shutter trigger when it dawned on me that I was being foolhardy. I was not here to take pictures of a revolution. People seeing me and knowing that we had come here as a guest of the government might assume that I was a Batista man. At the moment, with the strong

136

possibility that Santiago was probably full of trigger-happy soldiers and rebels, all I might wind up doing would be to become a typical "innocent bystander."

I quietly dismounted the camera and sat down to my breakfast. It was a strained atmosphere. We spoke very little as we ate and listened to the distant gunfire.

From where we sat we could look down toward Santiago's streets and also over to the single row of motel-like entrances to the Rancho Club rooms.

As I lifted a cup of coffee to my lips I heard a roaring engine and then watched a jeep come tearing up the private road and come to a tire-screeching halt right in front of our room. The vehicle was crammed with half a dozen men clad in a wild variety of civilian dress. Two of them wore khaki trousers with white Cuban *guayabera* shirts hanging over them. They were all uniform in one respect however—each man carried a submachine gun.

I literally froze, cup suspended in midair, while this wild-eyed group of militant beatniks made a beeline for the door to what I was sure was our room in the long row of identical entrances.

Halla, noticing the expression on my face, leaned forward. "Is anything wrong?"

I shook my head and watched the strangers go to the door of the room adjoining ours. They began to pound with the butts of their weapons. Perspiration broke out on my forehead. I was sure they had heard about me or seen me filming, and were mistakenly knocking on the door next to ours. Perhaps Sergeant García had been tortured and had told them where the "American cameraman who knew Batista" was staying. While the unfortunate occupant of the next room confronted these men I quietly got to my feet, picked up my camera, took it into the bar, hid it behind two cases of Bacardi rum, as I recollect.

Rejoining my family I sat down, aware that the machine-gunners and the individual, whom I could only assume they took to be me, were still engaged in loud conversation.

Halla watched me. "Hal, what's wrong?"

I shook my head. "Just continue with your breakfast, dear—as though nothing unusual were happening." Somehow I had lost my appetite but I forced myself to take additional mouthfuls of the scrambled eggs we had ordered.

At that moment the group looked up in our direction. The

armed men left the man they had been talking to and dashed up the path to the patio where we sat, rushing directly towards our table. My heart sank. I had visions of their shooting first and asking questions afterward.

They streamed past us and crowded into the bar. I started to rise. Maybe they'd seen me hide the camera there. But instead I heard the desperate-looking tommy-gunners shout "*Cerveza fría— pronto.*" All they wanted was cold beer, right away! It turned out that they were soldiers from the Moncada barracks who had been out on the town the previous night on leaves of absence and had just been rounded up to help fight the rebels. They had stopped here to pick up their colonel, who had been spending the night in the motel room right next to ours. Until I learned this from our waiter (who had prudently disappeared until the ragamuffin group identified themselves) I'm sure I aged perceptibly.

The attack on the barracks, which was beaten off, had killed over forty men on both sides and a total of eighty-seven were to die after the ensuing chase that day. The ringleader of the attack was captured and through Batista's clemeny was merely exiled instead of being executed. There is a sequel to this story, too.

At the time, however, we knew nothing of what was to come and were merely worried about being caught up in the martial law which was immediately declared for Santiago. All shops were closed and all public gatherings were canceled. It was Davey's birthday, however, so we borrowed a big box of assorted cookies from the motel and found two candles in the kitchen. With the candles in the cookies we managed once more to improvise a sort of birthday cake.

The following day, worried about having no fiesta for my film of Cuba I arranged to see the mayor of Santiago and the colonel who had been placed in charge of the city under the martial-law proclamation. Passing by taxi through the silent and almost deserted streets was an eerie experience. In the city offices the two men listened with obvious amazement as I made my request. I was asking them to put on the Santiago fiesta especially for me, with a few dancing groups, so that I could show American audiences what a *fiesta* in Cuba looked like. "Impossible," they said immediately. "Martial law has been declared, groups of more than five persons are prohibited—No, no it can't be done." But I was persistent. Did they want Cuba shown to the world with no summer fiesta? No, they didn't, especially the mayor for whom the Santiago fiesta was a matter of personal pride. A long distance call was made to Havana and I saw a look of amazement on the face of the colonel, when he turned to me and said, "Tomorrow at 4:30 be at this corner," and on a map he pointed out a street crossing in the heart of town. "We will block off several streets and arrange to have several *comparsa* groups show you what a fiesta here is like." And so it was that I got my Santiago fiesta films after all.

The sequel to the story that I mentioned above? Well, the date of the night attack on the Moncada Barracks which we witnessed was July 26, 1953. The leader of the attack who was later captured and exiled instead of being shot was the then almost unknown revolutionary named Fidel Castro. Batista lived to regret his clemency and that day became the rallying date for Castro's 26th of July movement.

Two days later Sergeant García rejoined us. He had been out chasing the rebels after having been caught up in the original attack. When we finally boarded the plane for Havana all seemed normal, except for an occasional machine-gunner at the airport.

Chapter Eleven

Belgium to Japan

HALLA WAS BECOMING an old hand at this business of professional, global gypsying and David was shooting up like a sapling.

The highlight of 1954 was the three-months journey which took us by car, train, plane and canal boat through all of Belgium.

We were made the guests of the Belgian government by the distinguished and courtly Arthur Haulot, head of the Belgian Government Tourist Office. We found Belgium an enchanting potpourri of beauty and culture; with its stone magnificence of medieval Gothic and the contrasting pace of present-day commerce and industry. Ghent, Bruges, Liége, Louvain, Antwerp, Ostend, Dinant, and Brussels all were filmed. It seemed to us though, that over the country is an under-the-surface remembrance of past conflicts. We encountered the memories of war in the battlefield of Waterloo virtually on the threshold of Brussels; and in the reminiscences of Antwerp citizens who still spoke with bitterness of the Nazi World War II V-2 "buzz bombs." The Mardasson Memorial to the American GI defenders of Bastogne in the Ardennes, scene of Von Rundstedt's "bulge" attack, and the scattered Allied cemeteries of World War I like those near Sanctuary Woods, reminded us of the many wars fought on Belgian soil.

Yet the Belgians proved to be cheerful hosts. Driving through either the Flemish-speaking northern and western area or the distinctly French southern and eastern districts, we constantly met friendly people wherever we stopped.

Our driver, a short, stocky Government Tourist Office chauffeur (he was a one-time wrestling champion, we later discovered) was an ambulating Baedeker of fact, some of which was even true, we learned.

As he drove along the narrow roads, through crooked towns and on city streets and occasional highways he showed an utter disregard for caution. Time and again Halla and I winced as he bore down upon obstacles and people and slackened his pace not at all when he missed them by a hair's breadth.

And when these crises arose (which meant practically all the time) he was generally handling the steering wheel with one tremendous fist and gesturing with the other at the same time turning his head to pay more attention to us than the road ahead or the oncoming collision.

Once, when he took a curve on two wheels with tires shrieking and with David and Halla hanging on for dear life, I leaned forward and tentatively suggested: "Aren't you going a bit too fast?"

"Don't worry, m'sieu," he shrugged. "I have good reflexes!" Well, there is a saying that God takes care of fools and drunks—and evidently frustrated race drivers who have "good reflexes."

I particularly recall that specific incident because that time he brought the car to a skidding, jouncing halt, stalling the engine during the process. "*Voilà*," he exclaimed, pointing to a sign on the outskirts of a town. "This place is named after you, M'sieu Linker!" I stared at the sign. Sure enough, the picturesquely quaint little town founded in the fifteenth century, bore the name Hal. I remarked that it was nice of the Belgians to name that town after me five hundred years ago, knowing I would visit there some day!

Our guide grinned. "Later," he nodded over his shoulder. "I take you to another town—this one named Linker!

Halla's eyes twinkled. "Why didn't you tell me that your ancestors once lived here!"

"They didn't," I murmured. But near Antwerp we came to the newly constructed suburb across the Scheldt River—with the name Linker-Oever which I learned means "Over on the Left Bank." The town's name was in Flemish which, as our guide remarked, is actually Dutch spoken with a slightly different accent, the difference between Dutch and Flemish being something like that between English English and American English.

We lunched in the village of "My" and then had tea in "Silly" before dining in the town of "Boom." "Erps Qwerps," the name of still another town, made us laugh.

Later we wandered through the village of "Sinsin" (which I insist apparently has twice as much "sin" as any other town) before driving to Hoboken, the community from whence came the name of New Jersey's bustling city.

Brussels itself was the high point of our Flemish venture. We steeped ourselves in the seventeenth-century atmosphere of the Belgian capital's Grand'Place and filmed the Town Hall and the striking Church of St. Gudule, which resembles Notre Dame de Paris. I even ate sea snails sold by a street corner vendor so Halla could film it for my lecture film.

Our visit was timed to coincide with the staging of the colorful pageant known as the *Ommegang*. Held in the authentic confines of the Grand'Place the celebration is a re-enactment of the historic visit, in 1535, of Emperor Charles V and his sister, Marie of Hungary.

Visitors from all over the world converge on Brussels for this event. The sight of the participants clad in authentic sixteenth-century costumes is unforgettable. It is a fascinating, living lesson in medieval history with its colorful pomp and circumstance.

Even the music, performed with authentic instruments, was typical of the melodies in vogue during the time of Charles V. With the background setting of the Grand'Place's ancient architecture, our modern world of electronics and jets disappeared. We had the feeling of having been transplanted, by some sort of time machine, back to the sixteenth century.

This illusion was heightened for me when I procured a costume and actually joined the pageant.

It was not vanity nor a hitherto stifled streak of exhibitionism which prompted my move. I needed close-up shots of the people in the pageant for my film. The Brussels authorities had erected photographers' scaffolds at strategic sites for this purpose. However, these platforms were set rather far back from the actual pageant. To obtain close-up detail I found that I would have to use telephoto lenses on my cameras—a highly unsatisfactory arrangement for me.

Jean Gyory of the Belgian Tourist Office explained their motive in keeping photographers at a distance. They strive for authenticity in the Ommegang, and the appearance of motion-picture and still cameramen in their modern dress amidst the pageant would be an incongruous note.

I pleaded for special dispensation. I offered to participate in the pageant. The major-domos in charge of the pageant huddled with Gyory.

"Granted," said a patriarch clad in the flowing crimson and black robes of a sixteenth-century burgher. "Provided you wear a medieval costume and try to conceal that camera of yours!"

Halla and David were entranced onlookers in the costume room while I was bedecked in a velvet costume consisting of a soft-crowned, feather-decorated, drooping-brimmed hat, a short jacket with puffed sleeves and exaggerated shoulders, knee-length pantaloons, long hose, and buckled shoes.

Although the outfit drew me in at odd places on my anatomy it was not uncomfortable. When I was finished being dressed I asked: "How do I look?"

"Well, Hal, I don't think it will start a new trend in men's clothing." Halla laughed.

The color film I made of Belgium that summer was the finest I had made to date. Upon our return I quickly obtained two contracts to make sound short subjects of Belgium—one for the Belgian government and one for Sabena—and our financial condition from that moment on started its upward climb. The lecture-season bookings had come in from all over the country and the end of that season was a landmark, since my records could be written in black for the first time since our marriage. In addition, a fortunate contact with Cran Chamberlin, producer of the "You Asked For It" television program, had resulted in several assignments to make film sequences for him while on our travels. This, too, bulwarked our finances.

The late spring of 1955 found the three of us winging via the Great Circle route from Vancouver, British Columbia, to make a film in Japan.

This aerial pathway which straddles the Arctic Circle is a short-cut, by some 800 miles, between America's Pacific Coast and Japan, as compared with the classic, mid-Pacific Honolulu-Wake Island route.

Our Canadian Pacific airliner touched down for fuel at Cold Bay in the remote Aleutians before skirting the Bering Strait and then turning south by west with the Iron Curtain of Siberia lying in the haze beyond and below our right wing.

Our skipper spoke of that Iron Curtain. He told us that some-

143

times Russian Air Force MIG jet fighters inspect passing Canadian and American airliners from a distance.

"It's always an uncomfortable feeling when those chaps suddenly appear and just sit out there, giving us the once over!" he remarked.

"What happens when they show up?"

He shrugged. "They'll fly along for a while and then go back to wherever they happen to be based. With their speeds it's as though they materialize and then disappear like ghosts!"

We learned from him that the Iron Curtain is absolutely silent, from the aspect of radio communication. The airliners maintain constant radio checks with ground installations in western Canada and Alaska. For a certain interval, after leaving the Aleutian chain, aircraft are beyond the range of North American radio stations until they near Japan.

"When we hear from the Japanese bases it's like seeing a friendly light in the distance," the captain told us. "The stations in Siberia —and there are plenty—never transmit a word."

"But they know you're flying this route," I remarked.

"Oh yes. They have us on radar constantly. We know we're being watched every second." The captain grinned. "It's rather like walking down the center of a lonely street, conscious that suspicious people are watching you from darkened rooms!" In the far distance to the left the red flares of a series of active volcanoes flickered in the night.

My first visit to Japan had been after V-J Day when our navy ship, the APA 70—the *Carteret*—put into Sasebo to board U.S.-bound troops. At that time Tokyo was still a shambles as the result of the devastating B-29 fire-bomb raids which some military authorities believe actually were as effective as the A-bombing of Hiroshima and Nagasaki. I hadn't gotten to Tokyo that time.

Then in 1949, during my pre-Halla filming days, I had spent two weeks in Japan on the way around the world. The war scars were still partly visible then, although not as much as in 1945. But in 1955 when we arrived at the Japanese capital the sprawling city with a population of almost 9,000,000 people bore hardly a trace of the war years.

I felt myself more than adequately prepared to cope with Japan. During the war, prior to my becoming a Navy Amphibious Forces' intelligence officer and fleet photographer, I had studied the Japanese language for thirteen months at the Navy's Japanese-

144

language school at Boulder, Colorado. And although my command of Japanese was not exactly fluent I still could remember enough to more than get by.

Halla's and David's introduction to Tokyo was somewhat hair-raising, and I shared their anxiety, during our drive in a Toyopet taxi from Haneda Airport to the famous Imperial Hotel just across from the Imperial Palace grounds in downtown Tokyo.

Traffic in that Japanese capital is a seething, furious, churning speedway race of every conceivable type of vehicle. Some world travelers pin the accolade of the planet's worst traffic conditions on Mexico City, Paris, or Rome. In our opinion Tokyo makes the rest resemble quiet village lanes. Moving to the left, as in the British Commonwealth, Tokyo's cars, buses, trucks, and three-wheeled delivery contraptions race one another without heed for disaster. Time and again, between the airport and the hotel, our cab driver deliberately aimed between trucks, buses, or streetcars that closed in upon us from opposing directions. Even our experiences with the driver with "good reflexes" in Belgium hadn't prepared us for this.

Later on, remarking upon the mad Tokyo traffic to a Japanese friend, we heard him explain smilingly, "Most of our drivers think they're in a race. In fact we have a nickname for our taxi drivers."

"What is it?" Halla asked.

His smile widened. "We call 'em Kamikazes—suicide bombers."

From then on whenever we entered a taxi in Tokyo I gave the driver our destination, then we leaned back and closed our eyes until we arrived. Like the ostrich, I felt it was better not to see the danger.

Tokyo is a tremendous city of steel, stone, cement, and glass; however, much of the rest of Japan is still quiet, peaceful, and typically old-time Japanese.

Everywhere we went we found the Japanese people to be courteous, genuinely friendly, and gracious hosts regardless of whether they were simple farm folk, hotel people, travel officials, or police.

When we visited Hiroshima we learned that the survivors of the atom-bomb attack could speak of their frightful experience without rancor. Looking back upon our 1955 visit it is difficult for us to reconcile our experiences with the Japanese people of that time

145

with the student and leftist rioting against President Eisenhower in Tokyo in 1960.

Purposely straying from the beaten paths in order to obtain a complete motion picture record, we quickly learned that the "tourist" routing shows only a tiny façade of this nation and its peoples.

The three of us crisscrossed the Japanese islands, running the gamut from fine European-style accommodations to beautifully landscaped Japanese inns in the hinterlands, where Americans were, for the local residents, quite a novelty. We even tried the communal baths where everyone bathes together.

My ability to make myself understood in Japanese made me an even greater curiosity to these friendly people. Everywhere we went, whether by electrified railway coaches, tiny taxi cabs or rickshaws, communicating with them in their own language brought forth even greater warmth than usual.

Had it not been for the Japanese which I spoke we would not have been able to visit an exclusive Kyoto geisha house and film the solemnity of the tea ceremony as well as elaborate enrobing and stylized dancing by the doll-like geisha girls clad in valuable kimonos.

Even more absorbing as subjects for filming were the Kabuki plays in which all women's roles are played by men.

Nara, with its park-like lawns and tame deer, was particularly fascinating for David. As far as he was concerned he would just as soon have settled down there to play with his "Bambis."

Miyajima, the "Shrine Island" about twelve miles southwest of Hiroshima was like stepping back into the golden, artistic age of Japan.

The shrines at Miyajima are numerous. And the main shrine, connected with satellite structures, is built upon pilings in the lake so that at high tide the Shrine Gate, brilliantly vermilion, seems to float. My film of this shrine at high tide, during a gorgeous sunset, has brought applause from audiences throughout the United States.

During the closing weeks of our Japanese expedition, after having traveled about 5000 miles through the islands, recording the pearl divers, the Sumo wrestlers, and the festivals and pageants, we went to film the cormorant fishing in the Nagara River at Gifu. And it was here that I ran into the only mild annoyance of the entire trip.

We were staying, by preference, at a Japanese inn. We had grown to love the Japanese-style buildings whose clean, functional lines predate occidental "modern" architecture by dozens of centuries.

It is the custom in Japanese hotels and homes to remove one's footwear prior to entering, whether shoes or sandals. The footgear I normally wear is sturdy and heavy, designed to take the scuffing, wading, or the dozen-and-one requirements which surround the activities of a motion-picture cameraman. We had returned from filming the long-billed birds that swim down the river at night to retrieve *ayu*, a sort of trout, for their masters. At the inn, I removed my shoes prior to entering. The next morning they were gone!

The hotel manager was aghast. This had never happened before at the inn. Nor even in all of Gifu to his knowledge.

I was, however, perturbed for a different and more practical reason. For the Japanese it was a matter of "face." For me it meant that I would either have to film in my bare feet until a spare pair could be shipped down from our hotel in Tokyo or else "shop" Gifu's shoe stores for substitute foot gear.

It was a strange shopping expedition I embarked upon: padding in my stockinged feet from store to store to seek anything that would fit. I found that Japanese feet are much smaller than my normal occidental size 10½. I finally had to compromise on a pair of canvas sneakers which were actually two sizes too short and narrow. A judicious penknife slash fore and aft made them fit, after a fashion.

For the remainder of our stay in Gifu I pad-padded about with my big toes and the other edge of my soles protruding! As for the fate of my missing shoes: that remained unsolved. Even the efficient police who suspiciously scanned the feet of every passing large-sized native could not come up with a single clue.

Possibly our most unusual experience in Japan was our visit to the northern Island of Hokkaido, homeland of the "Hairy Ainus." These are believed to be the aboriginal inhabitants of Japan. The original Ainus, we discovered, were of the Caucasian race which occupied the islands long before the arrival of the Japanese themselves.

They resemble Siberians, and many of them have blue or gray eyes. A vacationing Japanese anthropologist whom we met at the

Noboribetsu Hotel near the Ainu town of Shiraoi told us that comparatively few survivors of the original Ainu population remain in Hokkaido.

Most of the men and women we saw and filmed had distinctly oriental features. "This," explained our friend, "is because they intermarried with Japanese during the past thousand years. Even so, an Ainu man, regardless of the Japanese blood in his veins, can usually still grow a full beard, something a pure-blooded Japanese cannot do!" He had grinned, "That accounts for our nickname for them, the Hairy Ainus."

A number of Ainu women, clinging to an ancient, tribal custom, had mustache-like designs tattooed around their mouths. Although this practice has been outlawed by the Japanese government the older women still sport this unique defacement.

It was odd to confront these people whose eyes had typically oriental "folds" and discover that these eyes were often as blue as the Viking eyes of my beautiful Icelandic wife. In fact I took a close-up of Halla alongside a heavily bearded Ainu to show the similarity of their eye coloration.

"It seems strange to find remnants of Caucasian people here, living in Hokkaido," I remarked to the anthropologist.

"True," he replied. "Yet we have found strong evidence that the Caucasians originally inhabited not only these islands but the Chinese mainland as well. Take the Mongols. It is not generally known but Genghis Khan, the thirteenth-century Mongolian conqueror, had gray eyes and, supposedly, auburn hair! In fact his tribe was known as the 'Bourtai' or 'Bourchikan' which meant 'the gray-eyed.'"

Aside from the presence of blue- and gray-eyed natives Hokkaido had something else which reminded Halla and me of her Iceland home. We found vast hot springs and boiling pools of mud, just as in Iceland, only a quarter of a mile from the Noboribetsu Hotel itself.

Upon my return to Los Angeles, a heavily booked lecture season plus orders for several additional short subjects, still further brought our finances to where we occasionally could even save something. After all, Davey was growing. He had celebrated his fourth birthday in Japan and both Halla and I wanted him to go to college. He was an American citizen through me, in spite of having been born in Iceland. But since he had been born "outside the Territorial

Limits of the United States" we knew the U. S. Constitution prohibited him from becoming President. But nothing could keep him from being a university president or a senator or a member of the Cabinet. So we kept saving.

Chapter Twelve

Africa and the King with Four Hundred Wives

EVER SINCE I first began to read and grew aware of the outer world, Africa had been a source of fascination. I knew the saga of Stanley and Livingstone. Edgar Rice Burroughs' original Tarzan novels became prized possessions.

However, during my adolescent days the thought of visiting Africa always meant lengthy and expensive safaris through mysterious jungles teeming with lurking, bloodthirsty savages and man-eating carnivores. After all, I had seen the film *Trader Horn* with Harry Carey; I knew what Africa was like!

Long before World War II I learned better. Still, the thought of filming the Belgian Congo, which I chose for our 1956 filming, posed a number of problems. These revolved around the practicality of venturing there with a young wife and small child. But during the winter of 1955–56, while dashing to lecture at New York's Town Hall, the National Geographic Society, the Chicago Geographical Society and audiences at San Francisco's Town Hall, I had decided to fulfill our ambitions and go to that fabulous country in Central Africa which my recent readings had taught me was much changed since the olden days.

I sounded out the Belgian Congo Tourist Office. Would they be interested in a Linker-filmed study of the Belgian Congo? Their answer was an enthusiastic yes.

Thus it was that in May we found ourselves taking off from Idlewild International Airport bound for Brussels, first stop on our journey to Africa.

We had taken along the film made during our 1954 tour of Belgium. The presentation had been so successful with American audiences that I had arranged for a showing of the picture to Belgian audiences at the Brussels Palais des Beaux Arts.

My lecture, "Belgium Through the Eyes of an American," attracted the Brussels press to the special premiere. The audience was made up of ordinary Belgians with a smattering of tourist bureau, airline, and newspaper representatives. They gave the film and accompanying narration in French a heart-warming ovation. The published reviews, the following day enthusiastically pointed out that "an American has been able to see more in our country than we ourselves do!"

Two days later, still glowing from our fine reviews, we boarded a DC6B bound for Leopoldville, capital of the Belgian Congo, some thirteen hours by air from Brussels. At Rome we refueled.

When we landed at Kano, Nigeria, our next stop, it was almost midnight. Our feelings on setting foot for the first time on African soil were a mixture of awe and excitement. During our travels we had been to many strange and picturesque areas of the world. But Africa—this was something else. Before we had landed at Kano we had been almost exhausted after the long flight. Now, seeing the natives swarming around the plane, listening to their strange language and smelling the scent of unfamiliar plants and flowers we suddenly found our hearts beating faster.

We remained there only an hour while native airport employees, supervised by European airline officials, refueled our huge, four-engined transport.

The flight from Kano to Leopoldville paced the dawn. It was broad daylight when we circled over the Congo River, dividing line between the then Belgian Congo and French Equatorial Africa, now called the Republic of the Congo.

Leopoldville itself was astonishing. The pattern of paved thoroughfares and modern buildings seemed incongruous in the heart of what was once called Darkest Africa.

As our plane banked into its final turn, prior to landing, we flew over Brazzaville, capital of the neighboring French colony. We glided down over the Congo River and could easily see the seething rapids

Even from our plane the turbulent rushing water looked menacing. Later, standing on the bank of the river, we learned how menacing these rapids are. The Congo River has been forced by natural narrows to form a ten-mile-wide lake just above the rapids.

The constant flow of water from the lake is compressed in the rapids which lead to the Atlantic Ocean, approximately 100 miles south and west of Leopoldville. When we stood on the banks near the rapids we were conscious of the shaking of the earth as the frightening mass of water with twisting froth-covered waves two and three stories high smashed its way toward the distant ocean.

We had been told that the rapids are absolutely unnavigable. Standing there and seeing them, showed us why. It was a roaring maelstrom. Several men had tried to conquer these rapids in boats, and lost their lives.

Leopoldville had been founded at the point above the rapids where the river becomes usable. Upstream from Leopoldville, the river is navigable for 1200 miles to Stanleyville, the city named after Henry Stanley, the British journalist who tracked down Dr. Livingstone and found him living peacefully in a native Congo village during the 1870s. Stanley himself had also founded Leopoldville, named after his sponsor in his African explorations, the King of Belgium.

When Stanley first arrived here he had decided that the site of the present city, approximately 1000 feet in altitude, provided a climate "almost passable for Europeans." The place where river transport became possible was turned into a transshipping point for the supplies brought by natives and muleback from the Atlantic coast. There finally emerged this modern metropolis which boasts fifteen-story apartment houses, literally spotless streets, electrified public transportation and a population of 25,000 Europeans who then were living in peaceful coexistence with 300,000 natives.

We gazed in amazement through the windows of the chauffeur-driven limousine which whisked us through Leopoldville along wide, park-like thoroughfares and then penetrated the flow of bicycle and automobile traffic between modern stone-steel-and-glass edifices. The tree-shaded sidewalk cafés we saw were empty— we learned that they start filling up at 5 P.M.

Our driver was a husky native Congolese. A few years before he had lived in a tiny village near Matadi. Now he drove with the dexterity of an American cab driver. Yet the tattoo marks of his tribe were clearly visible: a decorative scar which dropped from his curly hairline on his forehead to the tip of his nose.

Our host was a fascinating, roly poly, gray-haired, fifty-five-year-old Lebanese cosmopolite named Maurice Alhadeff. A man of many talents and culture he was acting consul of Israel in the Congo. This was a sideline to his main occupation which was managing a vast business enterprise which covered all of the Belgian Congo, and had interests in neighboring French Equatorial Africa as well as the adjoining, Belgian-supervised United Nations trust territory of Ruanda-Urundi, mountainous homeland of the colorful warrior giants, the Watusi.

We discovered that M. Alhadeff was a dynamo beneath his casual attitude. In addition to his business and consular activities, either of which could constitute a full-time occupation, he also devoted time and considerable money to his hobby of being a patron of native art and artists.

Our meeting with this interesting person had taken place in the Regina Hotel, our Leopoldville headquarters, several evenings before. He had introduced himself to us, explaining who he was and telling us that he had read with great interest of our arrival in Leopoldville. Like all the residents of that amazing metropolis he referred to it by the nickname Leo.

His attitude had been friendly without being intrusive and his interest in us as a traveling, working family threesome so genuine that before long Halla, David, and I felt as though we had known him for years.

He had offered to "show us Leo" if we would not think him too presumptuous. "I know you are fascinated with the Belgian Congo, otherwise you would not be here," he said. "And since Americans fascinate me——"

We eagerly took up his invitation. And this tour of the city was the result. Actually it was a tour of two cities. Like other Congo communities Leo, at the time of our visit, was two separate towns —the more concentrated modern area for Europeans and the sprawling suburbia for natives, with its one-family concrete homes in profusion.

In the course of our drive I found myself complaining that I was having difficulties obtaining the necessary credentials and co-operation from Governor-General Leo Petillon, administrator of the vast Belgian Congo. "I can't even get an appointment with the man."

M. Alhadeff nodded. "His Excellency is a cautious man—especially when it comes to dealing with foreign journalists and correspondents!"

His essentially correct and fluent English carried a heavy French accent. He said: "weeth" and "zhoor-nah-LEESTS!"

"But I'm neither," I protested. "We're here to film the country and its people purely for educating and entertaining audiences throughout the U.S.A.!"

I warmed up to my mission: "You'd be amazed how much interest in the Belgian Congo my films and lectures will generate back home. Surely General Petillon must realize that——"

He smiled. "Granted, Mr. Linker. But His Excellency must convince himself of your good intentions and that you are not here to stir up trouble. He must go slowly. He is sitting on a keg of dynamite!"

Halla and I looked at each other. We were aware that in many other European African possessions and territories white authority and black populations were locked in growing conflict.

South Africa was a widening chasm of interracial strife and the grim object lesson of Mau Mau terrorism was still vivid in the minds of the British in Kenya.

"But we Americans have always been under the impression that Belgian rule here and in Ruanda-Urundi was enlightened, beneficial for the natives."

"Of course, of course." Our host leaned forward to the driver. "*Restez-la*, Kafa," he murmured, pointing to the curb.

The Congolese nodded and we came to a halt. "Something I wish you to see," M. Alhadeff said. He produced and lit a long cigarette.

"You were saying that the Belgians treat the natives well—" I refused to be sidetracked.

"Extremely so. They are developing heavy industry, building airports, weaving a network of communications." He waved his hand. "They, the authorities, are in a program of erecting nice homes for the natives."

"Then why——"

"The native Congolese may soon want some form of independence. They want to govern themselves. Across the Congo in Brazzaville the natives have just been given the vote and have elected a native mayor."

Halla frowned. "But is it not true that the Belgian government has stated that it will eventually grant them their freedom?"

"*Oui*—yes. But they are impatient." His eyes crinkled at us.

"Show me a growing child who does not eventually become impatient with a father."

Above traffic I heard a strange, approaching chuff-chuff. M. Alhadeff's face lighted. "It comes: that which I want you to see."

He led the way out of his limousine. We stood on the broad street. Other cars had stopped and people also looked upward, toward the oncoming sound.

Halla and I were mystified. Everyone was looking with an expression of what seemed to be pride, as though whatever it was that made the queer noise, was a matter of great importance to both whites and blacks, including ebony policemen with their white sun helmets.

David suddenly pointed: "Look—a helicopter!"

The machine swooped down on us and floated by. A fine spray of white smoke descended in its wake.

M. Alhadeff beamed. "*Voilà.* You see—we spray the whole city regularly with DDT—to keep the harmful flies and mosquitoes down."

He ushered us back into the limousine. Other people, we noted, were going on their rounds. The policeman had resumed his post. We passed a white uniformed native who was tending a pump forcing white fumes into a sewer.

"We even fumigate the sewers quite regularly," he added as Kufa turned a corner. "Leo is a cleaner city than many in Europe and, I daresay, even the United States."

We were leaving the European section with its glittering *décor* and sumptuous homes and penetrating the native quarters. The market squares were colorful and jammed with shoppers. And the odors were unique, to say the least. Occasionally we passed scenes of clearance projects: large bulldozers, most of them controlled by natives, engaged in leveling areas.

"New housing projects for natives," Alhadeff remarked. "Leopoldville, the entire Congo is building, building, building——"

During the next two weeks of "marking time" I filmed old and new Leopoldville from one end to the other. I even persuaded the Belgian head of the Police Department to let me film a formal parade of the red-fezzed, blue-uniformed, rifle-carrying native gendarmes.

The men were the acme of spit-and-polish and marched with precision. The Leopoldville Fire Department also put on a display for us: row after row of helmeted, leather-coated men swinging by my camera.

The composition of both the police and fire departments told us much about Belgium's ultimate objective: self-government for the native Congolese. The only white officers were those in the highest command. At that time, four years before the independent Congo came into being, not only the firefighters and police but the Army as well were 99 per cent purely native! But complete independence for the natives was only a hazy, dimly-seen-in-the-future plan.

It was a pleasant interlude but I had a schedule to follow and the necessary "co-operation" from the Governor General's office was still ungranted.

To spur this help, which we sorely needed if we were to visit remote areas and be assisted by the local Belgian administrators, I decided to have a showing of my color film of Belgium, the one the Belgians had liked so much. Perhaps the Congo officials would come to see it and would like my work. The newspapers helped us obtain a hall for the showing. The audience was happily large and enthusiastic. Although the Governor himself did not attend there were other officials of his department present. My films of their home country made them nostalgic—and fascinated the native Congolese in the audience.

The newspaper reviews were raves—but the best payment of all was a message to appear at the Governor-General's office for discussions.

One of his assistants greeted Halla and me with a beaming smile. "I thought your picture about Belgium simply wonderful," he said.

We expressed our thanks.

He cleared his throat and rustled some papers. "But about your request for credentials and co-operation here in the Belgian Congo—" His brow furrowed.

Halla and I looked at each other. I began to feel a sinking sensation in the pit of my stomach.

"We have decided to issue you documents—" He held up an important-looking envelope—"as *Code Trois*—Code Three."

I swallowed. "Most kind of you, sir. What does Code Three mean?"

His eyes twinkled. "Nothing much—except that you are the official guest of the Government of the Belgian Congo. The last group to receive Code Trois happened to be comprised of His Majesty, King Baudoin of Belgium, and the royal party!"

Luluabourg, capital of the Congo's South Central Kasai Province, was a fairly short DC4 hop from Leopoldville. Set against a background of flat country we found that the capital of Kasai Province owes its existence primarily to the big army camp nearby.

The city itself, with population of 2100 Europeans and 40,000 natives, is comparatively new.

Our visit to the military base at Luluabourg gave us an opportunity to see how the Belgian authorities were preparing the native Congolese for the time when they would take over the reins of government.

The "fort" itself sprawled over several acres. We visited the immaculate homes maintained for the white Belgian officers who were stationed here on detached service for the prime purpose of teaching the people how to soldier in the atomic age.

The non-coms and enlisted men, all native, also lived in neat, comfortable homes and barracks. Many of the men, serving their six-year enlistment, brought their wives and children. The military command maintained large community kitchens where the women prepared their food.

Our host was a distinguished colonel who wore many ribbons for service in Europe during World War II. He personally escorted us through his post and proudly staged a regimental parade and pass-by for my insatiable camera.

As the companies marched by, with rank upon rank precision, their boots stamping the ground with a rhythmic cadence, the colonel remarked: "Practically every one of these men comes from the bush country. When they enlisted many of them had never worn shoes or even seen an automobile. None of them could read or write. Now look at them: they are being taught not only how to defend their country but they go to classes to become literate!"

We visited their quarters, met their wives and watched the women at their housework. The colonel explained that the Congolese troops were not merely for parades. "We constantly put them through field problems and see to it that they are familiar

157

with every type of military weapon. It's a rather small force, as modern military establishments go, but it's a crack mobile unit—ready to take on an invading enemy twice its size, if need be!" Little did he know then that a few short years later, in 1960, these same troops would turn for a time into rioters the moment the strict Belgian military authority was removed.

M. de Mayeur, the Belgian administrator at Luluabourg, told us that no visit to the Belgian Congo would be complete without paying a call on His Majesty Bope Mabinshe, chief of the Bakuba people of Kasai Province.

"His residence is at the village of Mushenge, a rather difficult drive. He is a friendly old despot and loves to have visitors!"

And then the administrator smiled at Halla and added: "Besides, he is the only man I know who has four hundred wives!"

Halla and I were both flabbergasted. "You can't be serious!" she exclaimed.

He laughed. "I am—and it is perfectly true. We're rather proud of the old boy. After all not many countries can boast of a man who can handle four hundred women."

I looked at Halla. "Maybe King Mabinshe has the right idea."

She smiled. "The way prices are nowadays I doubt that many men could afford *four* wives, let alone four hundred."

Aladdin had his magic lamp. We had the equally magic Code Three credentials which conjured up at a moment's notice a government car and a Bakuba driver who spoke no English and only a little French.

The road leading from Luluabourg to Mushenge was unpaved. We traveled over almost table-flat country, paced by the clouds of dust raised by the wheels of our car. An overnight stop was made at Mweka at the only hotel—one with six rooms.

Mushenge itself was a collection of bamboo and thatched huts. We were met by a young sun-helmeted Belgian administrator, wearing khaki shorts, who had been informed about our magic Code Trois and was anxious to do anything we might ask. He showed us the Bakuba skill and artistry with wood carving and their ability to weave a special velvet-like cloth known as *velour de Kasai*.

He explained that unfortunately the wood-carving artists of Mushenge, being members of the rather tremendous royal household, were permitted only to carve renditions either of their living

"Lukengo"—King Bope Mabinshe—or of his regal predecessors. If that tired them they were free to carve ceremonial drums but nothing else.

We learned that the King would receive us in his royal pavilion. In addition he would honor us by wearing his full regal regalia. It took two full hours of labor to bedeck His Majesty with the complete costume of his exalted office—an act ordinarily reserved for only the most important state occasions!

When we stepped from our car near the royal pavilion we were greeted by a pair of elderly, barefooted Bakuba nobles—slender, grave-looking individuals who wore only skirtlike blue garments that hung from their waists almost to the ground. Tiny raffia skull caps, secured by long hairpins with tiny bells on the end, completed their costumes.

We were escorted through several reed fences and outer buildings to the inner courtyard. As we stood by the rustic residence, blinking in the sunlight, we heard women's sonorous voices chanting a greeting to the sovereign accompanied by a muffled thumping which we later learned was the sound of empty gourds pounded on the ground in homage to the King. Two blue-skirted courtiers appeared, carefully sharing the burden of an ornately carved stool.

And then His Majesty King Bope Mabinshe, slowly emerged. He was an elderly, massive person weighing about 275 pounds, with pleasant features. When we saw his regalia we realized the extent of his welcome. Although his torso was bared like the rest of the Bakuba, we noticed, just beneath the hem of his dusty-rose-colored "shirt" that each of his thick legs were encircled by dozens of rings of burnished copper.

His Majesty walked slowly, with difficulty. Each leg carried over sixty pounds of the ornamental copper.

His Majesty's face lit up with a fleeting smile of welcome as the three of us were presented to him. My camera gear intrigued him and then David's cowboy outfit caught his eye. In faltering French I explained about small American boys and their love of six-shooters and the Wild West. He nodded but I am not at all sure he understood. When he looked at Halla his eyes beamed. He commented lengthily in Bakuba. I noticed that the Belgian administrator looked uncomfortable.

His Majesty motioned to his courtiers. Two of them instantly brought over the carved stool and helped the royal body lower itself. The rest of the courtiers immediately sat down in a semi-circle and went into their roles as imperial counselors.

King Mabinshe began a speech. We noticed that whenever he paused his listeners would clap their hands three times in unison.

"What does that signify?" I asked our guide.

"He is discussing matters of state. When he makes a decision he waits for his council's opinion. If they clap their hands it means they agree; no clapping means they disagree!"

I began to record the meeting on film. Everything the King discussed that day seemed to have the wholehearted approval of his counselors. Not once did they fail to strike their palms in agreement.

When the pertinent business of government was concluded the King asked questions, through our interpreter, about America. Halla touched my arm and whispered: "Ask him if he really has four hundred wives."

Her question evoked a broad grin. His relayed answer, accompanied by a shrug of his massive shoulders, was that he had at least that many in the royal household.

"They aren't actual 'wives,'" he went on. "I only have seventy or eighty 'real' wives. The rest are 'honorary.' Different tribes sent women to my household. It is considered a privilege. Once here they stay." He leaned forward and his grin broadened. "Besides I inherited a number of them from my father. They accumulate. *Que voulez-vous?*"

He added something else with a stomach-quivering laugh echoed by his retinue. Again I noticed the discomfort of our guide. When I pressed for an interpretation he mumbled: "Later."

"Well, ask him if we can visit the wives' quarters so I can do some filming—"

King Mabinshe pursed his lips. He turned to his counsel and embarked on a long harangue. When he finished they slowly responded by bringing their palms together once, twice and then again.

The King's "harem" was located in an entirely different enclosure, guarded by several elderly, spear-carrying men. We entered to find that many of the women were engaged in weaving the rather beautifully designed *velour de Kasai* on large looms. Children, ranging from crawling infants to pre-teen-age, wandered about in droves.

The wives themselves wore nothing from the waist up. They ranged in age from sixteen to about eighty. Halla pointed out that many of them wore ceremonial scars across their breasts and abdomens. Others had tattoo marks. Several were quite handsome, by European standards.

Our appearance in their enclosure caused quite a stir. Europeans are not common in Mushenge, let alone in the royal concubines' quarters. Most of the young and middle-aged "wives" abandoned their tasks and stared at us with round-eyed amazement. The children especially were fascinated by David, who was perfectly at ease. In fact so much so that he began to demonstrate his ability as a quick-draw artist with his brace of cap pistols! Halla stopped near a hut for a moment to replenish her lipstick and within moments all the girls and women had crowded around giggling and imitating her. The ones near her relayed to those in the rear who couldn't see the exact motions of my wife, obviously thinking this was the most hilarious thing they had seen all year. I realized that if things were reversed and one of these Bakuba women stood in the middle of Fifth Avenue and put on her ceremonial facial paint, the reaction of the New Yorkers might be comparable.

We had to make a formal farewell appearance before King Mabinshe before driving back to Luluabourg. We told His Majesty through our interpreter that we appreciated having been shown his domain.

He smiled and nodded several times and then uttered a command to his aides. They helped him to his feet. The King beamed at Halla and addressed me at some length, with a sly grin on his face.

Our guide blushed. But this time he could not wriggle out of the translation. "His Majesty wants to know how much you'd want for—for—" He glanced at my wife.

"For me?" Halla gasped.

The guide nodded.

David frowned. Wearing a grimly determined expression he drew both cap pistols and placed himself in front of his mother. I knew the King was joking—but was he?

"Tell His Majesty that I am honored by his interest. But under the circumstances——"

Our interpreter launched into a quick explanation. King Mabinshe shrugged and answered. He paused, peered at our grim-faced little gunman. His Majesty puckered his features in a mock scowl, pointed a pudgy forefinger like a pistol, and made a clicking sound with his tongue.

The King laughed and then, assisted by his retinue, slowly retired to his private quarters.

As we got into our car to start for Luluabourg I asked our driver what the King said when I had turned him down.

"Oh, he said his offer stands, should you ever change your mind."

I settled back and looked at Halla.

She caught my glance. "What are you grinning about, Hal?"

"I was wondering how many cowrie shells and wood carvings you'd fetch——."

David interrupted by pointing to the road ahead. "Mommy, daddy—lookit all those flames!"

Our driver slowed down and pointed to our left. "It's a brush fire," he exclaimed.

We saw an awesome cloud of dark smoke on the horizon. A lick of flame showed at the base. "Do the natives start these fires?" I asked.

"Sometimes. But now it's summer. Dry. No rain. They begin—" he gestured—"by themselves."

"Spontaneous combustion."

The smoke and flame seemed to come closer. I speculated on the possibility of a shot. "I should get some footage of this," I muttered. I grabbed my camera and got out of the car. The driver looked anxious.

"Please do not be too long, Mr. Linker. Sometimes the wind can shift and the fire can trap people on the road."

I glued my eye to the view-finder and began to record the new nearby column of smoke and crackling flame. And then abruptly I realized that the fire had changed its direction. It was coming toward us. I took some last scenes twenty feet away from the roaring flames and then charged back to the car.

"Let's go," I yelled.

The driver put the car into low gear and we shot ahead. Flames lapped at the edge of the road. Behind us tongues of flame leaped across and began to ignite brush on the opposite side. There was a frightening moment of searing heat—and then we were out of danger.

162

Chapter Thirteen

Congo Witch Dancers and Famous Watusis

A DISTANT, SUDDEN THROBBING of drums told me that the witch doctor's dance was about to begin. I glanced at the inscrutable Mai Munene, chief of the tribe which bore the same name—a man wearing a fantastic costume of sea shells. He stood like a graven image, a feathered headdress crowning his head. Bandoliers of sea shells crossed his chest and even covered his crimson skirt. On one shoulder was an ocelot skin over which was suspended a small war ax. In his left hand he held a scepter of office with a horsehair tuft at its end. A band of white paint outlined his mouth in honor of our visit.

M. Robert Verly, a Belgian artist, tapped my shoulder.

"I trust your camera is ready: they'll be here at any moment!"

I nodded and made last minute adjustments. The village, not far from Tshikapa, seemed remote in time and space.

For the first time during our trip to this African wonderland I had to film alone. Halla and David had remained in our hotel in Tshikapa. Women were not permitted to see the witch doctor's action and "M'sieu" Verly, who suggested I visit the Mai Munene village to film this dance, was emphatic when he stated that the taboo extended to white as well as black females.

The drumming grew louder. And then we heard weird, ferocious shouts.

"The dance is intended to frighten demons from the village," Verly whispered.

The witch doctors abruptly rounded a hut and came into view. One dancer wore a tight-fitting raffia costume which covered him from head to toe like a gaudily colored suit of chain mail. Two grotesquely decorated eyepieces enabled the performer to see.

Immediately behind him leaped another witch doctor whose costume consisted of a tremendous wooden mask which covered him from his head to just below the waist. It was daubed with huge staring eyes and splashes of brilliant crimson, alternating with streaks of white.

They advanced with violent gyrations, the first one brandishing a weapon that slashed and chopped against the invisible "demons." A loud roar went up from the surrounding audience of Mai Munene tribesmen. The drumming grew louder and more frenzied as the men of the village joined in the stage, gyrating dance. As I recorded this performance on film I felt chills chase up and down my spine despite the fact that the equatorial sun was blazing hot.

When Verly had originally arranged for my visit to the village I had argued that surely Halla's presence, as an American, would not disturb the natives.

"After all, since you yourself are here on an official mission for the Belgian government you could explain to this chief that my wife's appearance would do no harm!" I had argued.

His answer in Tshikapa had been: "Impossible, Mr. Linker. Not even a patrol of troops could guarantee her safety! When you see the dance you will understand."

Now, surrounded by the gesticulating, leaping, shouting performers I understood only too well. Their eyes glared at us and yet seemed to look through and beyond the two white men standing in their presence as though we were phantoms.

When the witch doctors finally leaped and whirled away to end the dance I dismantled my equipment and thanked the chief for his courtesy.

Verly translated for me. The dignitary eyed us as though aware, for the first time since the ceremony that we were still in his presence. We shook hands, the special Congo chieftain way—a strange sort of double-grip ceremony (which Verly had made me practice before we started for the village) and departed.

En route to Tshikapa Verly said: "You've made history, Mr. Linker."

"How so?" I looked at him with surprise.

"To the best of my knowledge this is the first time the witch dance of the Mai Munene has ever been photographed."

164

"M'sieu" Verly proved to be an invaluable source of information for us during our stay in the areas around both Tshikapa and Bakwanga.

The slender forty-year-old Belgian had been commissioned by Brussels to study native art and to encourage tribal wood carving and painting.

"They are quick to pick up many of the bad aspects of European ways and forget their own artistic heritage," he told us one evening when we visited him and his wife and small son in Tshikapa.

Halla frowned. "What will happen if these people get their independence?"

Verly shrugged. "That is far in the future. It will be twenty-five to fifty years before we can give them self-rule." Little did he know then how close were the unforseeable riots and self-rule of 1960.

Verly remarked that the United States had an important interest in one of the products of the Congo. "You mean industrial diamonds?" I asked. The Congo produces over 80 per cent of the world's supply.

He shook his head. "Radioactive pitchblende. For nuclear use. There are deposits here from which your country gets tremendous amounts of uranium."

Halla and I both stared at him. "Where are those deposits?"

He shook his head. "I cannot say."

I later learned that much of the radioactive pitchblende comes from the rolling bushland country of Shinkolobwe, near Elisabethville. However, the amount of the critical material produced and the method and route of transporting it to the United States at the time of our visit in 1956 was top secret.

Diamond mining in the Tshikapa district involved fleets of dump trucks being loaded with diamond-bearing soil by steam shovels. The excavated earth is later sifted onto large grease-covered tables that enable the workers to pick out diamonds.

To obtain the full story of the Congo's diamond industry we made a quick flying trip to Bakwanga, a modern facility controlled by the colossal Belgian company called the Union Diamantière.

Here, unlike the steam-shovel operation around Tshikapa, we found a four-story-high continuous-shovel arrangement which fed gigantic gulps of earth to a conveyor belt that in turn carried the raw material to the mill. There, large centrifuges separated mud,

165

water, and stones from the diamond-bearing soil. Inside the mill we were thrilled when we were shown two buckets completely filled with the precious gems.

Unlike those of South Africa's Kimberley, the precious stones produced here are primarily intended for industrial use. Occasionally, however, they do run across gem stones. And while our Belgian hosts were generous and friendly, we quickly learned at Bakwanga that there were no samples being given away that day.

One of the most interesting tribes we met near Luluabourg was the Bapende, whose women wear a strange hair-do involving the use of mud, rancid palm oil, and red clay. The faces of these belles are tattooed, not only for tribal identification but also for beauty.

When we visited one of their villages the effect of the tattooed-faced women smiling a welcome with teeth filed to a point (for more beauty) was overwhelming.

Elisabethville or "E'ville," as the Belgians like to call it, sprang up like Topsy in rather desolate Katanga province because of copper mining. In the southeastern corner of the Congo, it was founded several generations ago by the powerful Union Minière.

Second in size to Leopoldville, E'ville in 1956 had about 10,000 Europeans and a native population of some 110,000.

There was a fine first-class hotel, the Leopold II, with an excellent restaurant where Davey could indulge in his Belgian-developed liking for *escargots*—snails.

With our Code Trois melting all barriers we were able to gain permission from the powerful Union Minière to thoroughly inspect the copper-mining industry, an important reason for the Congo's prosperity.

An offshoot of the tremendous Societé Générale de Belgique, the Union in 1956 held over 13,000 square miles of mining-concession territory.

The city came into being about 1891 when geologic explorations indicated that the almost unpopulated plateau possessed untold mineral wealth. In 1910 the present city was officially named by King Albert I after Princess Elisabeth of Belgium. The natives, however, insist on calling it Lumumbashi—the name of the river which provides it with water.

The Union Minière at the time of our visit was a bewildering industrial complex. A "benevolent" concern with strict governmental supervision from Brussels, the Union also had created a variety of subsidiary companies that furnished electricity, flour, housing, and chemicals as sidelines to the copper-mining operation.

We visited the huge smelter whose chimneys loom above the city. The mountain of black slag alongside the factory reminded us of the bleak Welsh mining districts we had visited.

Elisabethville is situated on a plateau at an altitude of almost 5000 feet and we found the late afternoon and evenings quite brisk, even though we were not too many degrees south of the equator. Since we had brought only warm-weather clothing with us to the Congo we had to shop for a sweater for Halla. We mentioned this to a newspaperman who interviewed us the next day and he had a fine headline for his story. It read: GIRL FROM ICELAND IS COLD IN THE CONGO!

One of the most intriguing aspects of the community life here was the school established by the Union for the wives of native workers. While the men were on duty in the mines and mills their wives attended classes where they were taught modern methods of housekeeping.

Halla was particularly fascinated by the sight of the tribal women learning to cope with sewing, modern plumbing, the use of European type kitchen utensils for cooking. These courses were to prepare them for the time their men would "step up" in their jobs.

In other buildings of the schools maintained by the Union we saw the children of these women being taught to read and write. Mothers and children both went to school at the same time. The teachers, for the most part, were young and attractive Belgian women who had come to E'ville under a three-year teaching contract.

Our DC4 which took us from E'ville northward was a magic carpet that deposited us in the tiny UN trust territory of Ruanda-Urundi, domain of the famous giant Watusi.

Usumbura, the capital, was a mixture of towering, slender, black-skinned Watusi, stocky Bantus, Europeans, and a vast number of Moslems from Pakistan and India.

After establishing our "base" at the Hotel Paguidas, a four-story affair embellished with huge bay windows, we investigated Usumbura and found ourselves strongly reminded of Pakistan. There was the same, somewhat unfinished "frontier" aspect. Compared with the modern, throbbing activity of Leopoldville, Usumbura seemed like a village, although a picturesque and pleasant one.

Street signs and shop windows bore inscriptions in Arabic. We saw Moslems identical with those we encountered in the Middle East; a mosque of the Ismaili sect of the Moslem religion (which the Aga Khan heads) stood in a side street. Some of the women wore saris, reminding us that their parents were Moslems from pre-Partition India.

It might be well to explain at this point that the trusteeship of Ruanda-Urundi comprises two separate countries, each with its own ruler. Ruanda is in the north and here in the more fertile areas live most of the pure blooded Watusi. To the south is Urundi with many of the Watusi who have mixed blood from their Bantu neighbors. Most of this section is barren, hilly wasteland.

The towering Watusi, rulers of Ruanda-Urandi, comprise only one tenth of the population. Most of the natives of Ruanda-Urundi today are stocky Bantus of the Negro race. The Watusi themselves are a tall, handsome, dark-skinned people whose finely formed features are Caucasian rather than negroid. Anthropologists do not classify the Watusi as Negroes in spite of their color. They are separately listed as "Hamites," descendants of the tribe of Ham.

Among these people six-footers are considered small. The average Watusi we encountered loomed well over six feet seven inches tall. Many towered over seven feet. And although Halla, David, and I felt like Gullivers in the Land of the Brobdingnagians I could not help but reflect on what a field day the talent scout for the Harlem Globetrotters' basketball club would have recruiting amongst the Watusi!

These people strikingly resemble those depicted on paintings in ancient Egyptian tombs. They are thought to have originally migrated from the Nile country—a belief substantiated to a great degree by their cattle with immense horns shaped like the musical lyre of ancient Egypt. Hathor, the cow-god of the Egyptians is shown wearing such horns on ancient tomb paintings and in gold statuettes in the world's museums.

Usumbura itself is located on the shore of Lake Tanganyika. We drove along the winding road pacing the shore, passing terraced farms and large herds of the big-horned Ankole cattle. Small steamers plowed through the waters. The lake looked invitingly cool.

When Halla and David suggested that we stop for a swim our guide shook his head. "Impossible," he said. "The water is full of flukes—little parasites that attack the liver."

He motioned ahead. "Up north, at Lake Kivu, there is a safe place to swim!"

As we drove we found ourselves gradually climbing. And before long we were at 4500 feet and despite the equatorial sun comfortably cool.

Our destination was the town of Astrida, where we would be presented to the Mwami, or King, of Ruanda and with luck see one of the colorful Watusi dances made famous by the motion picture *King Solomon's Mines*.

At Astrida our Code Trois again worked its magic and our Belgian guide was able to arrange an audience for us with His Majesty, Charles Leon Rudahigwa Matura III, King of Ruanda. The Mwami wore European clothes—sports clothing, as a matter of fact. When we were ushered into his royal presence he leaned forward with interest on his delicate features and made us welcome in French.

The King was extremely interested in the way our compact little family managed to travel the world, combining work with adventure. He was absorbed by the fact that I, an American, had married an Icelander and that our son had, thus far, covered more of the known globe in his short lifetime that millions of adults.

I asked if it would be possible to film the famous Watusi dances. The King smiled and rose to his feet. The sight of His Majesty rearing to his full height of seven feet was breath-taking.

"We would be delighted to have you film our dancers," he said.

The following day the Royal Dance Troupe of the Mwami made their appearance on a clear grassy field I had chosen. Tall as the King himself, they wore headdresses of long strands of raffia that gave them the appearance of wearing lions' manes.

Their upper torsos were bare save for crisscrossed bands looped across their chests. Crimson and white kiltlike skirts covered their hips, descending to the calves of their slender, muscular legs. Barefoot, their only other adornment consisted of anklets of bells.

The musicians arranged themselves in a compact group and

began to play a weird, somewhat querulous rhythm on drums accompanied by melodies carried by cowhide horns.

The King explained that originally the dancers were pages in the court, then they became fighters, the warriors of the Watusi. Because of that warlike heritage the dances primarily re-enacted tales of battle exploits or hunting prowess. The long sticks they carried were symbolic spears and bows.

The music, at first low and questioning, brought the long, mane-tossing line of Watusi into sight. They would perform a hesitant series of steps, pause, look about as though scouting for possible enemies, and then proceed to come closer in that strange, almost mincing fashion.

Then the flutes ceased and the beat of the deep-throated, high-standing drums became louder and more thrilling as the Watusi came closer to where I filmed. The drummers began to increase their tempo and the dancers suddenly charged directly toward us.

Just as it seemed that the thundering, onrushing wave of leaping, shouting, gesticulating warriors would inundate us they paused and then began a graceful, arm-swaying dance that was almost like a ballet.

Their faces wore a smile, almost of sensual pleasure mixed with a strange adoration as they twisted their supple torsos, tossed their heads so that the shoulder-length headdresses swished across their faces, and stamped their feet, making the anklet bells jingle in time to the accompanying music.

The King told us that the singularly rapt expressions indicated their devotion to him and their happiness at being able to serve in his retinue. The effect was so spectacular that later, when our television travel program "Wonders of the World" came into being we used the film of that dance, complete with the sound of the drums and bells, as the opening theme for every program.

As an extra attraction the Mwami gave a signal and two groups of men entered bearing two long thin poles fixed upright on bases. The men wore spotlessly white shorts and undershirts and were barefoot. The two standing pieces were placed about ten feet apart and a bamboo rod was suspended between them on pegs extending from the poles. I suddenly realized that this was a high-jumping device just like those used in regular competition. The King informed me that his high jumpers would now perform for me and that they would jump over the bar when it was seven feet high. At that time the Olympic record was less than that height for high jumping and I was anxious to see how they could jump higher than that famous standard of athletic prowess.

As I fixed my camera into position to be ready for the event, six of the athletes staggered in, bearing a strange burden which they deposited at the foot of the high-jump bar. It looked like a stone, but closer inspection showed me that it was a solidified anthill, a *termitière*. Then I learned that the jumpers would step on this hard anthill as a take-off for their jump over the bar. When I carefully measured the anthill I found that it was eleven inches high, which means that the jumpers were taking off from a point almost one foot above the ground; thus the secret of the great heights attained by the Watusi high jumpers was explained. I filmed the jumping event but I carefully included a scene showing how I measured the height of the "step," so that Olympic athletes throughout the world wouldn't be frustrated to hear of the great heights the Watusi could clear.

From Astrida we went south to Urundi. We had been told that the dancers of Ruanda we had filmed in Astrida were literally "old hands" at performing before cameras.

"But the dancers of Urundi have never, to my knowledge, been filmed," our Belgian guide informed us.

We therefore headed southward, passing increasingly large herds of the cattle with lyre-shaped horns. Although the cattle are numerous (our guide estimated that at least a million of them roamed Ruanda-Urundi) they are not raised for domestic purposes. They are Watusi status symbols. The more cattle a Watusi owns the greater his prestige in his community.

"But don't they ever use these animals for food, or their hides for leather?" Halla asked.

"When they die of natural causes," our guide rejoined.

He also told us of another Watusi custom concerning these animals. When a Watusi wishes to make another person obligated to him he presents that person with one or more cows or bulls. Since the animals cannot be slaughtered the recipient of the "gift cow" finds himself in the position of owning an expensive "white elephant," if you'll excuse the expression!

And because the presentation of the gift requires a reciprocal action the unhappy new owner is now in debt to the donor.

"Generally speaking, those who receive these animals for presents have to reciprocate by working for the person who gave them the animal."

"You mean they work without pay?"

He nodded.

"And meanwhile have to worry about taking care of the gift cattle?" Halla chimed in.

Our guide shrugged. "That's how it goes here in Ruanda-Urundi!"

As we moved southward the land became more desolate. Our car came to a halt by a smooth-sided stone pyramid on the top of a little hill. The guide opened the door and pointed to the 15-foot-high structure which seemed incongruous in this desolate area.

"This is the monument which marks the source of the Nile!" he announced. A plaque, set into one side of the pyramid, bore the inscribed names of the various explorers who had undertaken to find the source of the Nile during past decades and the claimed discoverer in 1937, Dr. Burkhart-Waldecker.

At the foot of the hill, some one hundred feet below the pyramid where we stood, a tiny stream gushed out. This spring is joined by others as it goes north and this process is repeated until, eventually, it becomes the Nile, sweeping across eastern Africa through Egypt.

It was a solemn occasion. I recalled how Napoleon had told his troops as they stood before the Pyramids of Egypt 2000 miles north, "Forty centuries looked down upon us."

We had with us a bottle filled with coffee. On an impulse I went to the car, obtained the bottle, and slid down the hill to the stream.

"What are you going to do with that?" Halla asked.

"If someday they complain at Cairo that the Nile is more coffee-colored than usual," I called back, "you can blame me!" And with that I ceremoniously emptied the bottle of coffee into the source of the Nile.

Chapter Fourteen

Simba! The Search for Lions

His Majesty Mwambutsu, the Mwami of Urundi, honored us by displaying his newest possession, a gleaming, chromed Cadillac parked in the driveway of the palace at Kitega. As he extolled the virtues of his imperial "coach" I carefully studied the rather youthful ruler who had been educated in Europe.

Like most of his subjects here in Urundi the Mwami was not a pure-blooded Watusi. According to legend his ancestors had looked more kindly upon "fraternization" with the conquered Bantus than did their Ruanda brethren.

The King's stature was "only" five feet, ten inches—a pygmy in comparison with his northern cousin. Surrounded as we were by members of his court who were of the same general dimensions, Halla and I did not feel quite so overwhelmed as we did in Astrida.

The influence of his European education was clearly shown by his clothing, speech, and mannerisms. The Mwami was not only fond of fast, high-performance automobiles, but considered himself quite the ladies' man. He was extremely attentive to Halla. For a while I had the uncomfortable sensation of being the "invisible man" insofar as the royal personage was concerned.

Halla, her charming but level-headed self, helped steer the conversation to our objective: filming the Urundi version of Watusi "Ntore" dancing.

"Of course," he replied. He spoke one short sentence to his retainers and things began to happen.

From an over-all aspect the Ntore dancers here were similar to those of Ruanda. However there were marked differences in costume. The Urundi dancers wore shorter headdresses fabricated of white colobus monkey fur. Narrow beaded straps crisscrossed their muscular chests like cartridge bandoliers and their costumes were fabricated of leopard skins. In addition these swaying, gyrating performers carried two raffia-decorated "symbolic" spears.

While I filmed, His Majesty kept up a rapid-fire explanation of the different dances, all of which basically re-enact historic legends or battles. The opening performance was "The Wielder of Thunderbolts," followed by "The Blessed Airborne" and a final terpsichorean feat called, simply, "Thanks." When I finished filming these I learned the thrilling news that this was the first time these dancers had ever been filmed. So this was our second exclusive filming coup in the Congo.

Afterward we learned that this art of dancing, called Ntore for both Ruanda and Urundi, dates back to remote antiquity. Originally the Ntore dancers were the elite of Watusi nobility. Boys were selected from "first families" for training in Ntore dancing. Not only did they receive their special education in the choreography but were also taught proper court manners, "refined" speech, and the politics, law, and military science of the day. Also in between dance sessions the Ntore were called upon to not only act as bodyguards for the Mwamis but frequently to enter battle as elite troops. In the pre-European era Ntore dancers performed with battle shields, lances, bows and swords.

However for several generations prior to the coming of the white man the art of Ntore almost disappeared. Court intrigues plus almost incessant warfare between ruling Watusi factions caused the art to fall into disuse.

Belgians, interested in preserving native art, discovered that a few of the Ntore dancers still survived. The Europeans, enthralled by the stirring, savage pageantry of the dances, encouraged the Mwamis to revive the art without, however, either its military or political undertones.

At the time of our visit Ntore dancing was at the apex of its renaissance. During the filming of the dances both in Urundi and Ruanda and later, while visiting the schools where the young boys who hope to be chosen as dancers received their long coaching, we were constantly reminded of our Leopoldville friend, M. Alhadeff and his enthusiastic insistence that "Congolese and Ruanda-Urundi art and culture are as valuable to the world as minerals and gems!"

Although the air in the shade was delightfully cool we were all hot and perspiring when we paused at the mission of the Belgian White Fathers of the Congo while enroute to Usumbura.

A delightful establishment solidly built of brick the mission was a place of learning for not only Watusi but Bantus as well. The three gentle Belgian priests there ranged in age from one who was in his early sixties down through a forty-year-old, heavily bearded father to a soft spoken neophyte of twenty-five. They were dedicating their entire lives to their flock.

We forgot the heat while the oldest father proudly showed us the classrooms and buildings and the work of the students who were being taught to read and write and grow aware of the tremendous, modern outside world.

The "pride" of the three White Fathers was a handsome young Watusi who had only recently become a neophyte.

He was being groomed for the not-too-distant future when he would take over the mission and continue the work begun almost a century before by the White Fathers of the Congo.

The patriarchal-looking oldest priest spoke of the work accomplished by his order as well as by other European and American missions. "Although these people are still living virtually in a Stone Age frame of mind many are intelligent and adaptable," he said, during a simple but refreshing luncheon.

"How do they accept Christianity?" Halla asked.

He shrugged. "Better than you'd suppose. The thought of peaceful coexistence appeals. Primarily, I daresay, because the African blacks have always been victimized and persecuted, if not by marauding Arab slave traders, then by invading, more powerful, warlike tribes."

"Isn't there opposition from the old tribal religions—the medicine men?" I interrupted.

He nodded. "But we overcome tribal taboo and the so-called witch doctor by using the greater miracles of faith, tolerance, and modern knowledge of medicine, agriculture, and science.

"Many of them have proved their intelligence by learning, in so short a time, how to manipulate the white man's tools—cars, trucks, heavy mining equipment—" A grimace crossed his face. "And, of course, the white man's implements of destruction: military weapons."

He sighed. I stole a glance at the two younger fathers and the

175

Watusi neophyte. They sat watching him with the rapt, devoted attention of children seated before a beloved parent.

"However, we missionaries have been working to—" his eyes twinkled—"how can I put it to an American—to uplift their spiritual status so that they can have the internal equipment with which to handle the external tools and thus cope with this tremendous, changing world!"

For a moment there was a short silence broken only by the distant chanting, from the adjoining classrooms, of native pupils learning their alphabet.

"In some ways," the father resumed, "they are like the white man! Look at us. We fly higher and swifter than eagles. We project our voices and images across mountain and flatland with the speed of light. We have unlocked the secrets of the atom—and yet we have not conquered ourselves. We are still ready to make war."

He suddenly looked at his watch and rose to his feet. "It is getting late and I must make my rounds."

His method of locomotion was unique. Carefully tucking the loose ends of his clothing around his ample frame he donned a pair of goggles, mounted a motorcycle, and kicked the engine into raucous life.

He waved to us and then tore out of the mission, leaning well over to one side with true racing verve, and disappeared in a cloud of dust down the road.

Although our objective after leaving Usumbura was the Albert National Park game preserve, we were able to first visit beautiful Lake Kivu in the Kivu-Ituri district. The road wound and doubled upon itself as it climbed up the mountains and rivers before dipping down to the Lua River which forms the frontier between the "kingdoms" of Ruanda and Urundi.

As we climbed we passed coffee, cotton, and cinchona tree plantations. We stayed at government-maintained travelers' rest houses where each night the roaring fire in the fireplace was a welcome delight. Finally we wound down into a narrow plain bordering the Ruzizi River.

A turn across an iron bridge across the Ruzizi and we were in the little bit of Europe known as Bukavu, headquarters of the district. Previously named Costermansville, the small city, nestling on a peninsula which juts out from the Southern shore of Lake

Kivu, at the time of our visit boasted a population of 3600 Europeans and 26,000 natives.

Our magic Code Trois got us luxurious accommodations at the Royal Residence Hotel.

We had been told by M. Alhadeff and Belgian officials that the Kivu was "probably one of the most spectacular and beautiful areas to be found throughout the African continent."

Halla, David, and I agreed the morning following our arrival in Bukavu when we boarded a cabin cruiser for an exhiliarating cruise to the north shore town of Goma. As we cruised over the dark blue waters we could see the active volcanoes of Nyiragongo and Nyamlagira towering beyond the north shore.

One of the officers of the cruiser told us that the volcanoes are not only "spectacular, particularly at night when their cones burn like gargantuan red traffic lights, but help keep the lake water around Goma free of parasites, therefore safe for bathing and water sports."

It seems that eruptions (Nyiragongo's last convulsion was in 1951) sent avalanches of molten lava down ancient channels to the water. The lava "sanitized" the lake around Goma, effectively destroying the parasites that infest the southern shore and other bodies of Congo water.

"Goma is our swimming resort," the officer said. And when we docked at Goma we saw a replica of a typical sea shore resort with people swimming, boating, and indulging in water skiing.

Our Goma headquarters was a picturesque establishment grandiloquently named the Hotel des Grands Lacs. The first night of our stay it was rather chilly and I donned a jacket for the occasion. But on entering the dining room I encountered a typical member of that strange race of people known as maîtres d'hôtel.

The gentleman in question politely seated Halla and David and then eyed my sport shirt under my jacket with frosty disapproval.

"Here, m'sieu, one cannot dine without the cravat!"

"You mean—I must wear a tie?"

He nodded.

"In the middle of Africa?"

He drew himself up. "Even so, m'sieu!"

Like everyone I have speculated on the outcome of a collision between the ultimate forces of rest and motion. I produced the Code Trois. The maître d'hôtel merely shook his head. Defeated

I went to the room and managed to find a wilted tie. Thus properly adorned I returned to the dining room. Although the color and design (not to mention the fact that it had been crushed by other articles in our baggage) clashed horribly with my jacket the dining-room guardian of protocol instantly thawed.

He ceremoniously ushered me to the table, clapped his hands, and almost immediately set into motion one of the finest gustatory experiences we have ever encountered during our trip through the Congo.

Driving north from Goma to Albert National Park we saw that twin, active craters were part of the Virunga Peaks, a chain of eight volcanoes extending from Lake Kivu to Uganda. The brooding area, desolate and devastated of foliage by past lava flows, reminded Halla of parts of her native Iceland.

The towering volcanoes themselves reared into a sullen, overcast sky and our guide told us that giant gorillas live in bamboo forests on the slopes of the 14,000-foot volcanoes.

David thoughtfully checked the cap-loads of his pistols.

"I don't believe I'd care to meet a gorilla face to face," Halla remarked.

The guide looked surprised. "They are perfectly harmless—as long as one doesn't bother them," he said.

He told us that an American was actually responsible for the preservation of the gorillas and other game life in Albert National Forest. "Your Carl Akeley, the sculptor-naturalist-explorer, nagged the Belgian government into creating a sanctuary for the wild life here," our guide said. "He died of fever in 1926 and is buried in the village of Mikeno at the foot of the volcano."

Similar in design to our own National Parks, the Albert Game Preserve, created some forty years ago, is Africa primeval as it existed before the coming of the white man. Approximately 125 miles long and about 35 miles in width, the territory is unfenced and neither whites nor natives may live there permanently. Weapons are forbidden within the park and that includes even spears. A tremendous variety of animal life, carnivorous and herbivorous, thrives and multiplies. It is their domain and the two-legged animal known as Homo sapiens can only visit their domain at his peril.

The approach to the park's Rwindi Camp, a government maintained collection of round, native huts with thatched roofs, plus some cottages, was by way of a steaming hot-springs area called "May Ya Moto" (yes, Halla felt right at home here, too) meaning, literally, "hot water."

Rwindi, we found, was 'restricted.' The authorities restricted visitors to a stay of not more than three days. We could, I suppose, have used our almost infallible Code Trois (which had only failed us with the maître d'hôtel) to extend our stay but we decided not to.

From the moment we arrived we found a native ranger assigned to act as our guide, companion, protector, and general assistant. He was a friendly, although serious young chap clad in a khaki uniform and a green fez. Although he could not speak a word of English I was able to manage with my French.

Halla nicknamed him our "shadow." For that he was. From the morning when we awakened until we returned to our hut each night he never left our side.

There are two specific roads within the park which are open to visitors. One, the Rwindi circuit, is about 35 miles in length, going in one direction. The other, the Rutshuru, a few miles longer wanders to an opposite termination point.

Our ranger was specific about our sticking to these roads.

"It is forbidden by the government to wander off the beaten paths," he explained. "It would disturb the animals. Then also it is dangerous—for you."

I was not entirely happy with this arrangement. It was my ambition to film lions and the huge African elephants.

But I remembered what had happened in northern Finland when I left the beaten path and almost got myself blown up by those abandoned German land mines, and I made no attempt to wander off. I had been warned that some tourists who hadn't listened to their guide-rangers had been mauled by lions, so I must confess to a feeling of excitement when we set out for our first "hunt" with camera and film.

We drove on the dirt road across the vast stretch of plain covered by thornbush or clumps of euphorbia interspersed with stands of tropical trees. The area was classical African veldt for those whose acquaintanceship with the Dark Continent comes from motion-picture adventure features.

At first the flat country, stretching away to the horizon seemed deserted. And then we began to spot antelope, water buck, cob's buck, topi, and impala. We stopped the car and I used a telephoto lens to get footage of those animals and of warthogs and hyenas grazing not far from the road.

The hyenas looked mean enough. But I was particularly wary of the warthogs. Like American razorbacks they are vicious and their incredibly sharp tusks can shred leather.

During this filming the ranger only permitted me to stand by the side of the car. I also noticed that he instructed our driver to keep the engine idling. Halla and I "got the message." If the four-legged natives grew hostile our car would be ready for a quick get-away!

When we reached the Semliki River we found a congregation of hippopotami lolling in the water below the road. The ranger informed us that it would be quite safe to go to the edge of the embankment to get close-ups.

"They can't charge uphill," he grinned. "Besides, they're getting used to people."

These animals cannot be considered attractive by any stretch of the imagination, but as we watched the ungainly creatures, Halla made a very cogent remark. She said, "Did you ever stop to think, Hal, that to a hippopotamus another hippopotamus may be beautiful?"

There were baby hippos galore—many of them sprawled half in the water, half on their mothers' backs. Occasionally mother would open one eye, cast a curious glance our way and then close it again.

Just when it seemed that the water-loving creatures (hippopotamus means "river horse" in classic Greek) would never "emote" for my voracious camera a pair of males started an argument. Halla laughed and called it a "fight in slow motion." Even so the quarrel stirred the entire pack into action. With more reluctance than annoyance the huge animals took deep breaths and then submerged en masse. It was getting late, so we turned back.

The established routine at Rwindi strictly required that we return to camp before dark. When I pointed out that we had not encountered any elephants or lions the ranger agreeably remarked, "Perhaps tomorrow, m'sieu."

At that we were thankful to be done with travel over dusty, rutted roads. When we returned to the camp our native-style hut afforded us the luxury of a cold shower and changes into clean clothing before adjourning to the dining room near by.

All I can say about the cuisine at Rwindi was that it was adequate. Our attention was drawn away from the food, anyway, by the hordes of tiny tree frogs no bigger than a nickel which hopped everywhere over the dining-room floor.

As for our accommodations, although the huts had running cold water, the general feeling was that of semi-roughing it on a safari. Inside the huts it was necessary to sleep under mosquito netting, not because of the mosquitos, since there were none at that altitude, but because of the lizards which were constantly falling out of the roof thatching.

That night at Rwindi in the heart of the game preserve of Albert National Park seemed to be intensely dark. Beyond the few lights kept going by a camp generator the blackness was like an impenetrable wall. We took a short stroll down the camp "street" but when we reached the boundary and stepped beyond the reach of the last, solitary electric bulb it was like taking a step into the inscrutable unknown. The silence was absolute. Above, the black sky was dappled by a billion scintillating stars. At that moment the everyday world, as we knew it, seemed as remote as Mars or Venus.

We retired quite early. While Halla and David fell asleep I burned a bit of midnight oil, going over the notes I had accumulated of the footage I had already taken. Somehow my eyes grew leaden. I remember being barely able to turn off the light and dropping off to sleep. Suddenly, abruptly, I found myself sitting upright, wide awake in the dark.

And then I heard it: a maniacal, high-pitched, screaming laugh that seemed to come from all quarters of the compass. Then some sharp howls and yapping barks. Halla awoke and reached over to grip my hand. I could feel her tremble. "What on earth is that, Hal?"

I opened the door and poked my head into the night air. A shadowy figure popped into view. It gave me a nasty start. But the next instant I sighed with silent relief. It was the ranger.

"Noisy, isn't it," I tried to be casual.

He nodded. "Oui, m'sieu——"

The maniacal laugh came again. "What is that?" I asked pointing toward the darkness.

"Hyenas," he replied.

Of course. Laughing hyenas. But what a laugh; what a horrible sound. I could not help shuddering.

He waved. "Also jackals—and *autre*—other *animaux*."

Of course. What else could I expect. This was their home. We were the intruders, the visitors. I gained a new respect for big-game hunters who went far afield on safari, deep into the heart of the jungles. "Do these animals—*animaux*—ever come here—into the camp itself?"

He shook his head. "Sometime, perhaps. But they do not stay. They don't like our smell."

"I see." I nodded. "*Eh bien, bon soir.*"

He touched his fez. "*Bon soir, m'sieu!*"

I returned to Halla. "It's all right, dear," I told her getting back into bed. "They're merely hyenas and jackals. We're perfectly safe, though. They don't like our smell!"

The brilliant sun and invigorating air the next morning made the terrors of the night seem ridiculous. We all three had ravenous appetites as we hurried to the dining room for a quick breakfast. Our ranger was already standing by the car, saluting us with a smile and reminding us that we were due to take the Rutshuru 41-mile circuit within twenty minutes. The sun was just rising.

We found a middle-aged couple seated at the next table. The man was dressed in a bush jacket and British walking shorts. His companion was a youngish, pleasant-faced woman who looked up when we entered and smilingly nodded in greeting.

"Good morning," I said. "*Bon jour—*" and helped seat Halla and David.

I remember discussing the animal chorus of the night before with Halla and our son. He took us to task for not having awakened him so he could hear the hyenas also.

Just then the distinguished-looking gray-haired man from the next table rose and came to our table. "Please excuse me," he said. "But I could not help overhearing you speaking English. Are you, by any chance, from the States?"

"Why yes——"

A smile broke over his lean, craggy features. "We're also Americans," he said. "I'm Dr. James Chapin and this is my wife——"

It was my turn to be utterly amazed. The year before, while lecturing in Detroit, I had mentioned to George Pierrot of the Detroit Institute of Arts, that we were going to visit the Congo. At the time he asked us to be "sure to look up my friends Dr. and

Mrs. James P. Chapin. He's the famed American ornithologist whose research in the Belgian Congo is known the world over! You'll find him not only splendid company but a gold mine of information about Africa. He's spent practically his entire life there." I had tried to reach him at his farm near Bukavu, only to be told that he was out traveling somewhere, and now here he was at the next table.

We joined them and I remarked on the long arm of coincidence, giving him Mr. Pierrot's regards. "We were going to drop by your place on the way back, as a matter of fact——"

Dr. Chapin chuckled. "What luck. Now that we've met here you won't have to waste time." He paused and filled his pipe. "First visit to the game preserve?"

We nodded.

"Sleep well?" Puff—puff—with a quizzical glance over his pipe bowl.

Halla and I could not keep a straight face. The Chapins joined our laughter. "We overheard you telling your little boy about the animal concert," Mrs. Chapin said. "If it's any consolation practically every newcomer has the same experience."

I mentioned that it was my hope to film some of the mighty African elephants. "Yesterday I didn't have much luck, though."

Dr. Chapin shrugged. "It's spotty, all right. Sometimes one can wander all day and never see hide nor hair. Then again you can be driving along, come around a bend and there'll be a whole herd of 'em!" He puffed away with a reflective expression. "Don't worry, today may be your lucky day."

We *were* lucky that day. An hour after leaving camp (but not until I took some footage of the good doctor and his wife) we almost collided with a tremendous herd of the towering tuskers!

These creatures are larger and much wilder than their Indian cousins. Although the herd we encountered was some one hundred feet from the road our ranger would not let me stray farther than six feet from the car. I noticed that he ordered the engine kept idling just in case one of the jumbos happened to take a sudden dislike and charge us. The car we had was actually a rather ancient and tired station wagon. I wondered if the car could have generated enough speed to "out-drag" the beast, had one of those bulls decided to come our way.

Fortunately the elephantine curiosity was passive rather than

183

belligerent. They have very poor eyesight and rely on sound and smell. We parted company with them the best of casual acquaintances, to the relief of Halla and the disappointment of David who insisted we should have brought "peanuts for the el-funts!"

It was a good day. As we continued along the Semliki Plains our ranger ordered the driver to put on the brakes. He pointed to the brush and whispered excitedly, "Simba—simba!"

For a moment we stared blankly at him. "Simba, m'sieu," he jabbered. "Lions!"

"Lions!" Sure enough there they were—nine of them, a "pride." The animals moved slowly through the underbrush hardly more than thirty yards from where we had stopped.

I clambered to the top of the wagon and began to film them with the telephoto lens. I realized, as I exposed film, that my good fortune was running over. Normally it was hard enough obtaining a good shot of one lion in Albert Park; here I had many of them posing for me. One of the lions paused and looked me over. His huge eyes blinked and then his tremendous jaw opened in a yawn of sheer boredom. I thought for a moment, "Say, I've seen this animal before," and then I realized it was a case of mistaken identity. I had just been seeing too many MGM movies lately.

Chapter Fifteen

The Vanishing
Duck-lipped Women

As WE WAITED in the center of the tiny hamlet of Bunia, north of Rwindi, our Belgian guide held a pow-wow with the Babira chief a short distance away.

Our objective here was to obtain footage of the legendary "Duck-lipped" women. Like so many other Americans I had always thought that the native females who wore the grotesque lip-stretching wooden plugs were called "Ubangi."

Our guide had set us straight during the drive to Bunia. "The Ubangi live in certain parts of French Equatorial Africa," he said. "The 'Duck-lipped' Congolese belong to the Babira tribe. The name Ubangi was given to them, I believe, by an American who picked the name at random from a map. He was a circus propagandist."

"Press agent," I amended.

He nodded. "That's it. Descriptive. At any rate these women have mistakenly been called Ubangi ever since. We call them *'femmes à plateaux.'* "

Now the guide and the chief, obviously in agreement, returned to our side. The chief summoned an aide and sent him off at a trot.

"He's going to bring the women here," our guide whispered.

Halla gazed at the encircling ring of curious Babira.

"I don't see any of them in *this* group," she remarked.

"The custom is dying out," the Belgian answered. "We made it illegal about forty years ago. Only about thirteen remain and the youngest is fifty-five." He pointed over our shoulder. "Here they come now."

We turned. A group of females, led by the chief's envoy, slowly approached us. In the forefront walked a woman who seemed much older than fifty-five. They came to a halt and stood there, darting curious glances at Halla and David and myself. The women all wore sad expressions. In view of the huge, saucer-like plug which had converted their upper lips to something resembling the duck-like bill of a platypus I could readily understand why they whispered amongst themselves, giggled, and nervously drew lines on the earth with their bare toes.

Halla's expression was a mixture of curiosity and repugnance. "It's such a horrible thing to do," she said. "Why?"

"The custom originated over a century ago as a means of protection against the Arab slave raiders," the guide answered. "When they attacked a village the girls and women would remove the plugs which had stretched their lips. The effect revolted even the Arabs. In that way the women retained their freedom."

I had begun my filming. After a pan shot of the entire group I moved in for close-ups. The oldest woman's wooden lip plug was enormous, being almost as large as a plate and about half an inch thick. Some of the other plugs, although not as large, were ornately decorated by patterns of beadwork. As I filmed, the women shyly stared into the lens as though not quite sure whether the "evil spirit" lurking in the whirring mechanism might not leap out and put a hex upon them.

Behind me I could hear Halla muttering over and over: "I can't believe it. I just can't believe it!"

While I paused to rewind the spring of my camera I mentioned that the women probably lived in constant torment because of the disfigurement.

The guide shrugged. "On the contrary. As time wore on the custom became a desirable thing. The plugs were considered marks of beauty. The girls used to compete with each other to see who could stretch their lips so as to wear the largest and most decorated discs. As the years wore on the males fell in with the notion that these duck-bills were things of joy and beauty to contemplate!"

"Incredible," breathed Halla.

As I began to resume my filming I muttered, "Well, anyway, I bet I know where the English got their saying 'Always keep a stiff upper lip'!"

186

"Now here ees an okapi. Ver' eenteresting ahnimol—no?"

The okapi was, indeed, interesting but equally as interesting was the speaker, Captain De Medina, our host and overseer of Epulu Camp, a collection of huts, tents, and corrals located within a clearing in the dense, lush Ituri Forest.

When we had reached the small village of Irumu we had been told by a White Father of the Congo, a missionary priest, who happened to be at Irumu's hotel at the time, just what to expect at the unique forest which begins fifty or so miles west of Irumu.

"It is the domain of animals and pygmies and virtually uninhabited save for Captain De Medina's camp at Epulu."

"Captain De Medina?" Halla asked.

The good father laughed. "A world-famous character," he said. "He's a Portuguese soldier-of-fortune who lives with the Pygmies and animals in the forest. He keeps the zoos of the world supplied with all sorts of creatures. Particularly the okapi." He had paused and ruffled David's hair. "Ever see an okapi, *mon petit?*"

David, his eyes showing his interest, shook his head while gazing up at this genial, modern version of Friar Tuck.

"Then there's no use even trying to describe it—or Captain De Medina. You must see for yourselves. I insist!"

We headed for Epulu the following morning passing en route native banana and manioc plantations. In the distance we had beheld what seemed to be a solid green mass. Our road abruptly curved and plunged directly toward that dense escarpment. It turned out to be the forest itself—a growth of tremendous, luxuriantly foliaged trees some of which towered well over eighty feet high.

The hard-packed earth road plunged through the forest. From all sides came a thousand and one sounds of animal life. Soon we stood in Epulu Camp itself, our rapt attention equally divided between the weird looking okapi and Captain De Medina, a short, rotund man clad in a wilted, perspiration-stained semi-military outfit consisting of bush jacket, shorts, and a military-looking cap.

"For long time, maybe 150 years, Europeans think okapi deedn't exeest," De Medina said. "Natives tell the explorers about okapi. Explorers theenk natives crrazy or dronk." His chubby face crinkled with laughter while his belly shook. "A few explorers see okapi—tell people in Paris, Brussels, London—people theenk explorers dronk or crrrazy—" He pointed to the animal in the corral of woven tree branches. "About hondred years ago first one bring to Europe and everywan see stories true."

Gazing at the animal I could readily see why the creature's reality was so hard to believe. The size of a donkey, the improbable beast had a head like a giraffe on the supple neck of a camel and sported the striped hind quarters of a zebra.

As we stared, the creature aimed its muzzle toward a low-hanging branch. Its mouth opened and at least two feet of tongue uncoiled to wrap itself around the branch. There was a sharp cracking noise. The tongue had torn the branch loose and crammed it into the animal's mouth. The okapi began to contentedly munch. It had a tongue something like an anteater.

Our intriguing host proudly guided us through the remainder of his encampment, showing off specimens of cape buffalo, a caged lion he had named Simba, and small and large antelope, the latter called bongo. These, we learned, were destined for zoos in Europe and the Americas.

The highlight of Epulu Camp was the elephant-training "school" where the huge African beasts were being trained to fetch and carry, haul and move.

The African pachyderms are larger than their Indian cousins. For many years they were considered impossible to tame. For that reason a number of so-called historians have questioned the truth of Hannibal's claim to have used African elephants when the Carthaginian general crossed the Alps to attack ancient Rome.

Captain De Medina assured us that Hannibal had, indeed, used the ancestors of the elephants in Epulu. "Carthaginians were Africans," he reminded us. "Afterr Rrrome conquered Carthage, people forgot how to tame and trrrain elephants. Zen Belgians come here and bring Indian mahouts. Now natives learn 'ow to train and African elephants ver' good workers. Rrregard!"

We "regarded" the huge African elephants pulling carts, hauling logs and carrying out a dozen and one different tasks assigned them by their native mahouts. It was then I asked De Medina about his friends the pygmies.

In common with a vast majority I had the belief that the pygmies were mysterious, aloof, and "dangerous" people. When I mentioned this to De Medina he gave forth with one of his body-quivering laughs.

"I show you pygmies," he said. "They ver' friendly!"

We followed him along a narrow path that wound through the dimly lit trunks of towering trees. As we walked in single file, David behind De Medina, Halla following, and I bringing up the rear with my camera and tripod on one shoulder, I kept eyeing the shadows on either side and hoping that the pygmies were as friendly as the captain insisted.

The village was approximately a mile from Epulu Camp.

Suddenly De Medina turned to say something to us and instead rushed over to David and started to pick something from his clothing. Halla, being nearest to our son hurried over to see what was happening and De Medina glanced at her for a moment and then began to pick something from her bush jacket. Much to our horror we saw that there were red "army" ants over half an inch in length, which were causing obvious distress on the part of our guide. There were ten or fifteen on both Halla and David, which he picked off gingerly and crushed. When we could find no more of these insects De Medina breathed a sigh of relief and taking us by the arm hurried us away from that spot.

"We are verree locky, thees ees only advance party of red ant army," he said. And then went on to explain that the bite of the red ant can be extremely painful and that even the pygmies fear them. Armies of red ants periodically sweep over vast areas of the forest destroying everything in their path. Halla and David had apparently brushed against a log being explored by the advance party and from that moment on we carefully followed Captain De Medina's warning to watch where we were stepping and to be careful not to brush against any trees, brush or fallen logs, lest we get some additional red ant "hitchhikers."

When we first arrived, the cluster of tiny, four-foot-high thatched huts seemed deserted. And then the "little people" materialized from all sides.

Tiny people, their complexion was a lighter brown than we had anticipated. According to De Medina they are not classified as negroes. In fact anthropologists believe that they were the original inhabitants of the Congo area before the Bantu negroes arrived.

Our host explained that the Bantus regard them as "our pygmies." The wee folk, averaging between three feet, eight inches, and four feet in height, are primarily nomadic, forest-dwelling hunters. Evidently there is an "arrangement" between them and the Negro tribes whereby the pygmies hunt game and swap their

189

"kills" with the Negroes for fruits, vegetables, and other farm products.

De Medina told us that the arrangement is actually a sort of truce. "The pygmies were never actually conquered," he explained. "To say that the pygmies and surrounding Negro tribes 'like' each othair would be wrrrong. The Negroes do not like the pygmies. They are even a leetle afraind of zem. But uner the Belgian rule—" he shrugged—"they get along."

The pygmies stood about us, staring at Halla, David, and my camera. After having felt like Lilliputians among the towering Watusi we now enjoyed the benefit of stalking like giants among these bright-eyed, fully grown men and women, many of whom were no taller than David.

We had heard that Captain De Medina was carrying on a perpetual "love affair" with the Congo in general and the Ituri Forest in particular. The high regard of the tiny people for the merry, rotund captain was obvious. He guided us into their cramped quarters. The women, interrupted by our arrival, returned to their family duties. They had been in the process of preparing a supper delicacy —boiled peanuts.

At De Medina's urging the pygmies showed us how they constructed their huts by the simple process of thrusting freshly cut saplings into the earth, tying the tops together, and covering the entire affair with banana leaves.

The chief insisted that we partake of their supper. Fortunately all we had to do was to taste the peanut stew. After that they gave us a demonstration of dancing and singing.

As the entire village danced by us we could see that many of the girls and women had pierced ear lobes in which tiny wood plugs were inserted and that many others had pierced their upper lips and inserted twigs, or had pierced the septums of their noses and inserted small sticks. Since there was no danger of Arab slave traders any more, we could only suppose that it was this season's fashion.

I had heard of the pygmy prowess as archers. When I asked De Medina if I could film a demonstration of their marksmanship he beamed. "They'd like nawthing bettair!"

Their bows and arrows were in proportion to their stature. They showed us two different types of arrow—one with a large, flat arrowhead for normal game and birds, the other with no arrowhead

but with a hard point which was tipped with "Ingongo" poison—
the famous, secret, deadly potion of the pygmies.

De Medina, acting as an interpreter, explained that they used
the poisoned arrows for the largest game, up to and including
elephants. They would stalk their prey, sometimes for days on end,
and shoot the poison into the beast, following it until it collapsed.

The archers put up a target consisting of the stem of a banana
tree approximately six inches in diameter. Backing off some twenty-
five paces (about seventy-five feet) a group, including boys, took
turns firing shafts at the stem. De Medina commented that this
was roughly how they killed an elephant—"by shooting at its legs."

As I filmed I noticed their unerring accuracy (not one arrow
missed) and also the rapidity with which they sent shaft after shaft
into the target.

They then fastened a large leaf to a tree trunk and set up a
firing line almost a hundred feet away. The top archer put on a
display which literally lifted the hackles of my hair. After watching
three arrows form a hit pattern which could be covered with my
fist I realized why the Negroes have a healthy respect for the
diminutive but potent little forest nomads.

De Medina put it neatly when, with a serious expression, he
said: "I'm always glad dey shoot for me and not at me."

Time was drawing to a close for our Belgian Congo safari. The
next scheduled destination was Egypt but first we would sail the
mighty Congo River from Stanleyville to Leopoldville, a trip that
would occupy five days and nights of our African adventure.

En route to Stanleyville to take the boat we paused at Paulis,
capital of the Mangbetu tribe, considered the most intelligent of
the Congolese. These handsome people were reluctant to relin-
quish the custom of binding the skulls of their infants to elongate
the heads—a sort of "beauty" mark which seems to have had its
origin in ancient Egypt. At the time of our visit the practice was
still apparent although the Belgians had outlawed it, as they had
the "Ubangi" lip plugs.

However, the women still bore decorative tribal tattooes on their
faces and wore over their buttocks, as part of their costume, a
strange woven pad called a *negbe* which, when they decided to
sit down, automatically fell into place as a chair pad.

A close-mouthed clan, the Mangbetu were nevertheless more

than willing to stage their wild, colorful, spear-and-shield-brandishing torchlit dances at night for my camera.

In direct contrast were the cheerful, smiling Wagenia who eke out their living by catching fish with basket-like traps in the boiling, unnavigable, menacing rapids a few miles above Stanleyville.

The swirling, turbulent rush of water marks the northeasterly termination of the one thousand-odd navigable miles of Congo River water stretching to Leopoldville, where the other stretch of rapids closes the rest of the waterway to ship traffic.

We had sufficient time before the departure of our ship, a diesel-powered packet named the *Baron Liebrecht*, to film the doughty Wagenia fishermen.

Although the Wagenia rapids are not as fearsome as those between Leopoldville and the Atlantic seaboard they were formidable enough. The tribesmen, we learned, string their fish traps (which resemble woven "horns of plenty") to spindly networks of poles driven into rocks during the dry season when the river partially subsides.

After the water rises and the rapids boil with thunderous sheets of flying spray the intrepid fishermen daily climb over this scaffolding into the spume and mist to collect their catches. A unique tribe, the Wagenia people virtually "live" in the water.

A Belgian official who accompanied us from nearby Stanleyville to the village told us that the Wagenias regard other Congolese as "landlubbers."

At his suggestion we took a ride with some of the Wagenias in one of their dugout canoes. We noticed that their paddles had sharp, metal, spear-shaped tips. I remarked that they looked like "fat spears."

"That is what they are," he replied. "They will be handy if we meet any crocodiles, since the paddle is also a spear!"

Stanleyville, which lies almost in the geographic "center" of the African continent, was at the time of our visit a lusty boom town, with a population of 4000 Europeans and some 70,000 natives. Before boarding the *Baron Liebrecht* for our long river journey we rode through the thriving city, admiring the numerous, well-stocked stores and luxurious homes which front on the river.

Our ship was scheduled to depart July 25. And since we would not dock at Leopoldville until July 30, it meant that we would

Dance of the Watusi warriors at Astrida, Ruanda-Urundi.

Old-style hairdo on Watusi man. Ruanda-Urundi.

Wagenia fishermen setting their fish traps on the Congo River.

At monument marking source of Nile. Ruanda-Urundi.

Watusi woman of Ruanda-Urundi on the right; the other two women of mixed Bantu blood.

The vanishing duck-lipped women, with wooden lip plugs.

Halla and David ride with the Wagenia fishermen on the Congo River.

The mysterious Congo witch dancers, chasing demons from village of Mai Munene.

The Chief of the Mai Munene wearing his everyday robes. His lips have been painted white in honor of our arrival.

Night dance of the Mangbetu. Paulis, Congo.

Halla at 5 feet, 5 inches towers over fully grown Pygmy couple. Ituri Forest, Congo.

The Watusi warriors of Urundi dance in their leopard-skin costumes which differ greatly from those worn in Ruanda.

The King with 400 wives has a meeting with his advisers.

Congo Mangbetu girls wearing special pad called *Negbe* on which they sit. Hairdo is on bound head. This is the tribe which binds the heads of the children to make them elongated, a custom dating back to Egyptian times.

In a Leopoldville night club—the Congo.

Davey has his birthday cake on the Congo River.

Firemen of Leopoldville.

Halla and David ride in Egypt.

Inside the tomb of Ramses VI at the Valley of the Kings near Luxor, Egypt.

Guide Rangi and David greet by touching noses. Rotorua, New Zealand.

David and Halla with the Maori of New Zealand.

Halla and David with the rare kiwi birds. Auckland, New Zealand.

Kava ceremony, near Pago Pago, American Samoa.

Police at Apia,
Western Samoa.

Filming the dances of Ta-
hiti. Papeete.

Sunset at Tahiti. Moorea in the distance.

A Fiji policeman.

celebrate David's birthday, July 27, approximately at the midway point of our river journey.

With this in mind we went to a Belgian bakery in Stanleyville and arranged for a huge cake with which we could celebrate on shipboard.

The steward of the vessel was agreeable to keeping the cake in refrigeration. With that problem solved we stowed our gear in our cabin, one of twenty on the ship, and settled down for the voyage. The cabins, at that time reserved for the use of European passengers, were separated by bathrooms containing hot and cold running water and shower facilities. Native passengers had their own quarters in another section of the vessel. The ship itself carried no cargo but it pushed several laden barges lashed to the completely flat bow.

The voyage itself reminded me of descriptions of Mark Twain's Mississippi River trips as the *Baron Liebrecht* maintained a zigzag course, following the ever-changing channels and avoiding sand bars. On either side of the foremost barge young Congolese sailors were seated. They constantly took soundings with long bamboo poles. Directly in front of them on stands stood microphones, and whenever they touched bottom they chanted a warning which was carried to loud-speakers in the navigating bridge about one hundred yards behind them.

Our ship was commanded by two captains. One had the responsibility during the daylight hours while the other took over after sundown. Why this should be so was never fully explained.

When I asked the younger captain (he was in his thirties, the other was about ten years his senior) why two masters with apparently equal authority were required he merely shrugged and changed the subject.

Halla remarked that we certainly should enjoy the trip. "With two captains we're twice as safe," she insisted.

The voyage was a happy, lazy affair which saw us passing through some of the most primitive scenery in Africa.

In the pre-diesel days the journey, in wood-burning packets similar to the old-fashioned Mississippi stern-paddle-wheelers used to take from ten to twelve days. We were told that the old-timer ships could only sail for a hundred miles or so before putting in to shore for fresh supplies of firewood. This had encouraged natives to create riverside settlements for the sole purpose of selling wood to the river boats.

We saw several of these little settlements. They were "wilting on the vine," however, because only a few of the old wood-burners are left.

During our trip the *Baron Liebrecht* made only five scheduled stops. At one town, during an hour pause, the residents offered the passengers as a delicacy, shoulder of crocodile. The native passengers aboard considered this an epicurean treat.

Frequently, as we traveled along without stopping, natives would come out from shore furiously paddling dugout canoes, shaping a course that intercepted our ship. We were cruising at about twelve knots. They would cast lines aboard which were secured by the crew and would then be towed along by the ship while they offered fruits, vegetables, and fish for sale to the native passengers who either could not afford or else disliked European cuisine.

July twenty-seventh, our second day on the river was the happy occasion of our son's fifth birthday. There were several Belgian children aboard as fellow passengers and they joined our celebration. Their eyes widened almost to the size of the cake when it was brought forth from the ship's refrigerator.

The celebration was marked by our arrival at Coquilhatville, the halfway point of our journey. Since the ship was scheduled to anchor for several hours we took advantage of the stop to drive a mile out of town to a stone monument which marks the equator itself.

While I filmed Halla and David examining the monument, my wife reminded me that our visit marked the third time we had crossed that imaginary line since embarking on our African adventure. She enumerated the occasions: the first time had been during our flight from Europe to Leopoldville, the second when we had journeyed from Ruanda-Urundi to the game preserve and the Ituri Forest. I told her that we would cross it yet a fourth time before we left Africa: "After we take off for Egypt."

Davey remarked that he had heard of a boy who was very much afraid of the equator because he had heard that it was a "menagerie lion" running around the earth.

At the town of Bolobo we saw a swarm of native canoes bearing exquisitely carved ivory invading our ship. Halla and I (and not a few of the Belgian passengers) were like children in a candy factory. Our impulse was to go absolutely hog wild and load ourselves with mountains of ivory carvings, bracelets, statuettes, etc. It took rather stern self-discipline to force ourselves to make judicious purchases. To this day, though, we regret that we did not buy more at the time.

Finally on the fifth day we entered the Stanley Pool and arrived again at Leopoldville.

Our itinerary called for us to return by plane to Stanleyville where we could connect with the Belgian-flag airline that would fly us directly to Cairo.

Flying back to Stanleyville in a DC4 we retraced our river journey in a matter of hours instead of days, and after landing drove to our hotel, the Equateur, where we expected to be accommodated in an air-conditioned room we had reserved before leaving on our river trip.

To my chagrin I learned that the hotel management had "forgotten." The air-conditioned rooms were sold out. All that remained were a few stuffy cubicles.

That night, since we had to leave the window open or else suffocate, the three of us provided an appetizing change of diet for Stanleyville's voracious mosquitoes. When we awakened, all of us were covered with bites. And because malaria was a real danger there, despite the most stringent precautions of the Belgian government, I felt I had sufficient cause for worry. The Aralen tablets we took in malaria areas were only supposed to lessen an attack if you came down with it, not prevent it.

We were particularly concerned about our son. His face, arms, and legs were a mass of welts. But we were now ready to leave the Congo and in the preparation for the departure we all forgot these worries.

On the big Sabena DC6B we chatted with the stewardess and copilot and retraced for them on a map our 10,000-mile, three-month-long travels through the Belgian Congo. The copilot was particularly impressed. He sadly related that although, as an airline crew member, he had landed frequently in either Stanleyville or Leopoldville to "overnight" before returning to Belgium, he had yet to actually see anything of the country.

It was much later, during the night in fact, that I was awakened by the stewardess. She whispered that the captain wanted to see me up front.

Halla and David were sound asleep in the dark cabin. Other passengers were shapeless, slumbering shadows in their seats. As I followed the stewardess forward I glanced through the windows. The outside was pitch black. Only the speckling of stars gave me a clue as to where the horizon was.

The captain's face was faintly illuminated by the dim glow of the huge and complicated instrument panel. The copilot nodded to me and introduced me. After an exchange of pleasantries the captain got down to business.

"I must warn you, M'sieu Linker, that things are quite critical in Cairo. President Nasser has just seized the Suez Canal."

"So I understand," I mumbled, still half asleep. "I read about it in Stanleyville."

"In fact, by the time we arrive at Cairo, a state of war may exist between Britain and the Nasser government."

His words jolted me into complete wakefulness.

He frowned at the instruments and made a quick adjustment of the propeller-control knobs.

"If serious trouble breaks out we will, of course, divert to an emergency airport. Otherwise we will land there." He looked at me. "Should the radio operators at Cairo answer me in a hostile manner I advise you, for your family's sake, to remain in the plane while we refuel."

"Then—then you think it's really bad, Captain?"

He shrugged. "It isn't good, M'sieu Linker."

Chapter Sixteen

King Tut's Tomb

THE SUN LIFTED ITSELF over the arid flatland of the Red Sea off to our right and pierced our night-widened eyes with painful intensity.

Ten thousand feet below, the parched reach of the Sudan was still covered by predawn darkness. The crew in the cockpit put on sunglasses. The captain beckoned to me. He took a pair of spare earphones from a hook and made motions for me to put them on. I adjusted them. A thin, taut voice speaking with clipped British accents that still could not hide a feeling of urgency was broadcasting a news bulletin.

It was a short-wave BBC newscast. Static put garbled punctuation into the sentences. ". . . The situation in Suez is worsening . . . Nasser indicates he will use force, if necessary, to retain his hold. . . . However it is hoped that the special August 16 emergency conference will . . ." The voice faded in a roar of electrical interference.

I soundlessly returned the earphones. The captain leaned toward me. "It depends on how the Egyptians reply when I call them," he sighed. "It could be all right; then again we may have to start evacuating Europeans from Egypt."

For a moment it was quiet in that cockpit save for the droning and drumming of the engines and props. "If the plane is sold out and if we have to evacuate I'll still make room for you and your family. Even if you all have to crowd in here, in the cockpit, and even if it *is* against regulations!"

I thought of Halla and David, still asleep in the passenger cabin aft. Ever since she had been a schoolgirl in Iceland she had dreamed of visiting Egypt, climbing the pyramids, meeting the eternal Sphinx. If the looming crisis forced us to remain on the plane it would be a heartbreak for her. In addition, I had been able to make arrangements in Leopoldville to produce a film for Sabena, in Egypt. We would now probably have to forego making that film.

The door leading to the cockpit opened. There was the aroma of coffee and eggs. The pretty, bright-eyed stewardess tapped me on the shoulder. "We are ready to serve breakfast, m'sieu," she smiled.

Somehow that announcement dispelled my gloom. Regardless of what lay in store the airline would continue to function as though everything was normal.

I followed her to find Halla and David wide-awake and ravenously hungry. The meal was delicious. For a while I debated whether or not to tell Halla about the Cairo situation. If nothing happened I would have spared her needless worry. And then I chided myself. Although she had implicit confidence in my judgment and decisions it was only proper that she should know exactly what the odds were.

During coffee I gave her a quiet briefing. She calmly listened. When I finished she smiled and clasped my hand. "Well, Halminn, let's not worry about it. If it's all right for us to stay in Cairo, we'll stay. If the airline people think we had better fly on with them to Europe—" she shrugged—"we'll go to Europe—and maybe return to Egypt when things calm down!"

A short while later I sensed a different note in the sound of the engines. The huge plane began a wide, sweeping turn. We peered through the window and saw that we were passing over the sprawling outskirts of Cairo.

As the landing gear extended itself and the large flaps were lowered I felt a sort of tenseness that was not too remote from the sensations I used to experience during the war prior to an island invasion. The ship settled toward the runway. The houses and streets we skimmed over seemed quiet.

We made a feather-smooth landing. The plane proceeded to taxi toward the terminal buildings. The stewardess made an announcement first in Flemish, then French, and finally English. All passengers were to remain in the plane until further notice.

There was a crowd of people at the terminal watching us. Several heavily armed, uniformed soldiers stood nearby. I felt a surge of apprehension. The captain, followed by the copilot, emerged from the cockpit and hurried down the aisle toward the cabin door. As he passed he paused and murmured: "Today they were friendly on the radio, m'sieu— Keep your fingers crossed!"

Halla and I both crossed our fingers. Within a short while he returned, this time accompanied by the airline operations manager.

The latter was a young stolid individual named Schoonheit whose quiet and precise manner of speaking immediately reassured us. "We feel sure nothing serious will happen until after the scheduled conference on August 16. After that—" He shrugged.

"Not war?" I asked.

"Possibly."

"Well I should be able to get my films and be out of here by the fifteenth," I said.

"In that case, M'sieu Linker, I am certain your visit here will be quite in order." He paused and frowned. "However, to play safe I will arrange for you to work with the Egyptian Tourist Office. They have special guards—Tourist Police, they call them. I will ask them to assign a guard to you!"

"But if you don't think there'll be trouble——"

"Ah—there is always the possible fanatic to consider—like in 1952. Many people were killed in the anti-European riots and Shepheard's Hotel was burned to the ground."

Head Constable Ahmed Gamal Eldin Kamel of the Tourist Police was a handsome, nattily uniformed young man. He assured us that tourists were highly "desirable" insofar as his government was concerned.

"Most of the 'trouble' is newspaper propaganda," he told us while a driver whisked us from the Metropole Hotel, our Cairo headquarters, out through the oven-like heat of the city. "Actually this matter of the Suez Canal—it will be discussed—calmly, in civilized fashion."

The air was almost unbearably hot. Halla, David, and I constantly kept mopping our brows. "I'm glad to hear you say that, Constable——"

"Things," he exclaimed, "are really peaceful here."

At precisely that moment we turned onto a wide boulevard. Straddling the traffic was a huge statue of an Egyptian soldier armed with a submachine gun and hand grenade. Nearby was a tremendous painting of a tank and stationed at frequent intervals, along the bridges over the Nile, were soldiers armed with rifles and automatic weapons.

Halla and I stared at our constable to see if he was joking. His face was serious. "We wish to encourage tourists," he said, evidently oblivious of the warlike panoply on all sides.

During the next several days, as we visited and filmed the Sphinx, the Pyramids, the citadel built by Sultan Saladin of twelfth-century Crusade fame, we found our constable an invaluable companion. There were some who eyed my cameras with suspicion, but a word from the constable was like a verbal Code Trois.

In the evenings, while relaxing from our daily sightseeing and filming jaunts, we would visit with members of the European colony. Many of the English were apprehensive. They remembered only too vividly the rioting of four years before. Our friend, the Belgian airline station manager, dropped by to tell us that air traffic into Cairo was a two-way affair.

"Tourists are still coming in while Europeans stationed here send their families home," he remarked. "It is a cockeyed situation!"

Although the Tourist Office people were extremely co-operative and our constable more than obliging I still had a slightly uneasy feeling. I wanted to finish the Egyptian segment as quickly as possible and leave before the August 16 conference took place.

Despite the sweetness and light exuded by the constable, Nasser's broadcast harangues, booming and reverberating from street corner loud-speakers, got on our nerves.

The English and French press were full of foreboding and apprehension. And although I could not read the Egyptian-language publications, their flamboyant headlines, flattering pictures of Nasser, and equally unflattering cartoons of British, French, Israeli, and American statesmen were unmistakable.

People in Cairo's streets, while not exactly hostile, still did not eye us with anything that resembled warmth and affection. Halla put it neatly when she remarked: "Although I do not understand their language, I 'get the message.'"

Our itinerary called for an overnight train ride along the Nile to the ancient cities of Luxor and Karnak. However before undertaking that journey I expressed a desire to visit and film Cairo's native bazaars.

The constable's face turned grave. For a moment I thought he would object. Then he nodded. "Very well—after lunch—today."

While we waited we speculated over his odd hesitation. "Maybe he thinks it would be too dangerous for us," Halla remarked.

I shook my head. "The new Nasser government is sensitive. They're probably fearful that my camera might catch some untidy nooks and corners of the bazaar!"

When the constable came by to pick us up I realized that Halla's guess was more accurate. For the first time he was armed with a large, holstered .38-caliber revolver.

We drove deep into Old Cairo's winding streets until the car could progress no more. Then, shouldering camera tripod, I brought up at the rear of our little procession as our somewhat apprehensive guardian led us through teeming, narrow alleys jammed with people and hole-in-the-wall shops.

The lounging, swarthy men regarded us with a mixture of curiosity and hostility. The slender, half-veiled women stabbed at my wife's uncovered blond beauty with burning, dark eyes.

Everywhere we stopped to film, a crowd collected. Mindful of our experience in the native bazaar at Peshawar I kept a sharp eye on the expressions of the surrounding natives, particularly the fezzed or turbanned men. But our constable, I noticed, kept referring loudly with constant, ingratiating smiles, to the fact that we were Americans.

That seemed to be a magic talisman, because the atmosphere definitely grew relaxed each time. We were able to obtain more than enough footage of people haggling with merchants and shop-keepers over every conceivable item, not to mention close-up shots of cross-legged coppersmiths hammering out intricate and beautiful items of copperware.

As the afternoon wore on our constable grew more cheerful. In fact he was quite enthusiastic about our bazaar expedition and began to come up with all sorts of suggestions about where to go and what to film. I reminded him that our train was scheduled to leave the next day.

His face gloomed again and then he grinned and smacked a fist into a palm. "We have time to see a typical native, night-club dance!"

"Dance?"

He nodded. "Only in Egypt." He winked and contracted his stomach muscles under his uniform.

"Oh, you mean the belly dancers," Halla interjected.

At the hotel we arranged for an English baby-sitter for Davey and off we went to a club that featured such dancing.

The "club" was located in the former palace garden of the un-lamented ex-King Farouk. Innumerable ghostlike spectators sipped coffee while a native orchestra hammered out a strange syncopation with odd-looking musical instruments.

The dancer was a sensuous, well-proportioned, burning-eyed brunette, who wore a gossamer-thin veil, short, gem-encrusted jacket, and diaphanous, flowing skirt that descended from a low, hip-hugging girdle to her ankles, which were encircled by large, jingling golden rings. She was barefoot.

The "dance" consisted mainly of gliding about the floor undulating her abdomen and hips in tune to the music. Occasionally she would stop and quiver all over for a while to the shouted encouragement of the men spectators.

Our constable obviously considered the display "art" of the highest order. He watched us for our reaction.

As performed by this young lady, there was frankly no lewd aspect to the dancing, no overly suggestive movements such as are apparently featured in American burlesque houses.

"What a graceful, exotic dance," Halla whispered to me, as I filmed it.

The next day's train ride took us "over the burning sands of the desert." Air conditioning was unheard of in these trains. And if we wished to breathe it was necessary for us to keep our windows wide open in the *wagon-lit* sleeper compartment.

When we finally awoke at 6 A.M. after fitful periods of sleep during the clattering, lurching journey, we found everything—bedding, clothing, and baggage as well as ourselves—covered deep with Egyptian dust and sand.

The only hotel open in Luxor at that time of the year was the luxurious Winter Palace, and in the tremendous heat the name at least gave us a certain amount of psychological cooling but little else.

The hotel staff eyed us rather oddly when they learned that we were determined to visit the tremendous temples of Karnak and explore the famous tombs of bygone Pharaohs in the Valley of the Kings at this time of the year.

A genial, elderly guide or "dragoman" named Gasem Ahmed took us under his wing and told us that our routine would call for reveille no later than 6 A.M. with a departure from the hotel an hour later.

He took great pains to point out that the climate in August was absolutely unbearable out-of-doors between the hours of ten in the morning and three in the afternoon.

The over-all solicitude about our not being out in the midday heat reminded us of Noel Coward's famous song "Mad dogs and Englishmen go out in the noonday sun."

Halla amended it by saying: "Add the Linker family to that."

Our initial exploration of Karnak's temples found us stricken dumb by the eternal beauty of the centuries-old columns, granite statues, and fascinating hieroglyphics.

Like the Pyramids and Sphinx, which we had visited near Cairo, Karnak has been built on a mind-staggering, gigantic scale. Ahmed enjoyed our obviously awed reaction to the mighty ruins.

When he pointed out that the ancient Greeks and following Romans used to visit this identical place as "tourists" in the pre-Christian era we realized all the more the incredible antiquity of the Egyptian civilization on the Nile.

It was our son's first introduction to the meaning of "time without end." When he asked when the temples were built Halla answered that it had been many, many thousands of years before.

"Before I was born?"

She nodded.

"Before you and Daddy were born?"

"Long before our grandfathers and grandmothers and a hundred great grandfathers and grandmothers were born——"

Our son stared at the towering pillars. "Will they be here always?"

Halla stared up at them. "They'll be here, David, when your grandchildren a hundred generations from now come to visit Egypt!"

Ahmed, who was taking this all in, nodded his fezzed head. "We are," he said dramatically, "mere gnats on the flank of the great camel called time!"

Our guardian angel then cast a worried look at his watch. It was just past 9 A.M. "We must go back," he insisted.

"But we hardly got here," I protested.

He shook his head. "The sun. You must return to the hotel. Otherwise—" He shrugged.

At the time we thought that he and the others were overemphasizing the heat. After all, we had experienced the heat of India and Pakistan, Cuban sultriness, the impact of the sun in Equatorial Africa.

By the time our car, a rather ancient affair, got us to the Winter Palace we began to feel stifled. Every breath of air we took in was like breathing at the open door of a blast furnace. In this truly awful heat the thought of food was out of the question.

We partially solved the problem of survival during the noon hours by taking turns at sitting in a tub filled to the brim with tepid water.

The legendary Valley of the Kings was on the other side of the Nile from Luxor. When Ahmed called for us the following morning he explained that "our" side of the river—the eastern bank—had been set aside by the ancient Egyptians as the site for Karnak—the side for "living" since the sun rose in the east to start the day.

The Valley of the Kings, location of the royal tombs and the Necropolis of Thebes where ordinary people were buried, were both on the western or sun-setting side—"the dying side," as Ahmed put it.

Halla remarked on the similarity of this legend with that of River Styx of Greek mythology. When we arrived at the bank of the Nile to board a lateen-rigged felucca for the river crossing to the "dead" side I pointed to the waiting boatman. "If this is the Styx then here's Charon, come to ferry us to Hades."

In a manner of speaking I was not too far off. Within the matter of another two hours the sun would climb and the entire area would be baked by hellish heat. When we reached the other bank an ancient car whisked us from the landing, through several tiny native villages and past the fabled Colossi of Memnon.

Ahmed, an ambulating Baedeker of Egyptology if ever I saw one, told us that the two huge statues actually were named after the Pharaoh Amenhotep. The Greeks called him "Memnon." In the days of the Roman Empire the stones used to make strange, whistling sounds when the sun warmed them," he said.

The Romans, from the time of Marc Antony and Julius Caesar, used to come here as tourists just to hear the whistling of the Colossi of Memnon—" He sighed. "Alas—they no longer whistle. Wind and sand have worn the stones down and an earthquake centuries ago finished the job. Now they are silent."

The Valley of the Kings, a city of the dead, contains over one hundred tombs of Egyptian rulers. At the time of our visit approximately sixty-three of the burial crypts had been opened by archeologists. The most famous, of course, was that of King Tutankhamen the "boy" Pharaoh, better known as King Tut.

We had heard of the curse which had overtaken the discoverers of the tomb. It is true that since the first opening of Tutankhamen's treasure-laden crypt some thirty-five years prior to our visit a number of the scientists who had excavated the tomb had died under obscure, if not downright mysterious circumstances.

It is easy to scoff at this as mere superstition. And certainly one would suppose that in the blinding glare of Nile summer daylight the tomb-covered Valley would be anything but eerie. Yet Halla and I had a distinct feeling of being intruders. Not that Ahmed or the handful of retainers were unfriendly in any way. To the contrary, as mid-August tourists, we were more than welcome. It was just that the vast valley seemed haunted.

We entered and examined several of the tombs and we actually filmed inside the tomb of Ramses VI. There was wiring connected to an ancient generator which provided sufficient 220-volt current for a solitary light bulb in the famous burial place.

When I explained that I wanted to film in Tutankhamen's tomb as well, Ahmed was dubious. "Official permission—" he began.

I pointed out that the sun was climbing higher and that we couldn't waste time. Our dragoman's sunny disposition gloomed. He spoke to the caretakers, who were equally disturbed. After a muttered council Ahmed shrugged. "Very well—but be careful——"

"Of what, the famous curse?" I said banteringly. I began to set up my lights.

Ahmed did not answer. The expression on his face told me that he did not consider my remark the least bit humorous. Halla usually held floodlights for me when I had to use illumination. Ahmed stood toward the entrance while my wife directed the illumination toward the walls covered by hieroglyphics and paintings.

I recall obtaining several close-ups of the gold mask of the Sarcophagus of King Tut. "This should do it," I remarked to Halla. In the background Ahmed heaved a noticeable sigh of relief.

And then like a true photographer I decided that I needed one more shot, an extreme close-up of the mask of Tutankhamen. I reconnected the lights and commented: "Just one more shot, Elskan-mín."

Halla obediently flicked the switch. There was a blinding flash accompanied by a loud, sharp explosive sound. The tomb was plunged into darkness. Ahmed uttered a strangled sound. For a wild moment I stood still, my heart pounding. I called out "Halla, are you all right?" "I—I guess so," she managed to reply. And then, practically instantly, I realized what had happened: my lights had short-circuited.

"Guess I've blown a fuse in my lights." I tried to laugh.

"Hal—let's get out of here," Halla said.

"Of course. Got more than enough footage anyway."

We headed for the exit and emerged into daylight. Ahmed's fez bobbed as he excitedly told the caretakers what had happened. The light switch was a blackened melted mass of wiring. I tried to explain to him that the light switch must have worn out. "It wasn't King Tutankhamen's curse," I concluded with a chuckle.

He looked at the dark opening of the tomb. "Of course not," he said laconically.

Still there was a strange note in his voice. Halla and I looked at each other . . . Had King Tut decided that he had had enough of bright lights shining in his eyes?

Lolling on the verandah of our hotel suite on the French Riviera the discomforts of our Congo and Egyptian expedition faded and only the color and excitement remained.

We were resting for a fortnight as a self-awarded reward before returning to the U.S. via Iceland and the customary annual visit with Halla's family in Reykjavík. David was sound asleep.

I recall discussing with Halla the fact that we had in our possession over 16,000 feet of color motion-picture film covering the Belgian Congo and Egypt.

Much of our footage was unusual. We had gone to many places

far from the beaten tourist path. "When we get home I am going to see if I can't get my own television travel show launched," I told my wife.

She nodded. "It's time, Elskan, people are interested in the world. I think television audiences in America would like to share our trips——"

We already had roughed out a format. My television show would not differ too greatly from my lectures: the three of us, Halla, David, and myself, would personally be seen at certain times during a telecast. The balance of the program would consist of my footage with myself and Halla alternately narrating "behind the scenes" so to speak. It would be a "family show" in every way, aimed at appealing to the entire television-viewing family. I believe we were just on the verge of counting our future wealth when a sudden whimper from David brought us back to reality.

Our son had complained of feeling out of sorts before going to bed. Now when we investigated we were alarmed to find he had a high fever. Suddenly he awoke and began to regurgitate all he had eaten that day.

While I tried to find a doctor I wondered what could be wrong. And then I remembered with dismay: it had been exactly two weeks since he had been bitten by the mosquitoes in Stanleyville. The incubation period for malaria is approximately fourteen days!

Although he could speak little English, the doctor was like M.D.s the world over who deal with frantic parents. He listened as I tried to tell him that I was fearful my son had contracted malaria in the Belgian Congo.

"That insufferable name-of-a-name of a hotel manager there," I exclaimed. "It was he who caused this: by not giving us the air-conditioned, screened room we had reserved. If I could get my hands on him——"

"M'sieu, it could be malaria," the doctor agreed while he carefully scrutinized David, "but frankly I cannot tell yet what ails your son. We can only wait——"

Our rest on the Riviera became somewhat of a nightmare as Halla and I worried about our son. I found myself berating myself for having thought of bringing the boy to the Congo in the first place. His fever did not abate in spite of the various medicines suggested by the physician. And then, on his third visit, the doctor subjected Davey to an even more rigid scrutiny. Halla and I were both silent when he examined our son's body and inside his mouth. He finally removed his stethescope and turned to us.

"Is—is it malaria, Doctor?" I asked.

His eyes began to twinkle. "M'sieu, madame—your son has —the measles!"

Chapter Seventeen

"Wonders of the World"

MAKING GUEST APPEARANCES on established television shows with experienced masters of ceremonies at the helm was an easy matter, as was daydreaming about our own TV travel program. But completely producing our own program without help was another story. Since making contacts and getting contracts for such a venture would certainly be a full-time job and I had to concentrate my full attentions on the forthcoming travel-film lecture season where I had a sure source of income for my family, I decided to contact a nationally known advertising agency in Los Angeles and place in their hands my complete plans. When they had all details as to what films I had and how much I thought we should receive for such a program, I then promptly put the matter out of my mind for the more pressing needs of the immediate lecture season's requirements.

Only a few weeks later, while we were in San Francisco for an appearance for the Town Hall Forum series, the phone rang in our hotel. "Hal, is that you?" The voice of the account executive who handled our proposed series for the advertising agency came in over the imperfect connection. He rattled off some information. I weakly thanked him and hung up. "What was it, Hal?" Halla asked worriedly, noting that the color had drained out of my face.

"I'm not sure, Halla-mín, because the connection wasn't too good, but I *think* he just told me that they have signed us to a full thirteen weeks contract with television station KCOP in Los Angeles. We are to have our own show!"

It was true, we found when we returned to Los Angeles. In a conference with Al Flanagan, the program director of KCOP (now manager of the station), we learned that he had seen us

209

on our guest appearances on other travel programs and had been favorably impressed with our presentation. Thus, when he was contacted by the agency about us he agreed with them that our program *should* appeal to all members of the television-viewing family. The thirteen-week contract had resulted. But at that conference with Mr. Flanagan a chilling reality arose to haunt us.

Each week's program was to be one-half hour long and after carefully checking my film footage I had assured the agency that I was pretty sure I could come up with thirteen complete programs. Now as we sat in Mr. Flanagan's office, my unbelieving ears heard him say, "And if this series goes over, will you be able to give us another thirteen weeks?"

I found myself saying, "Well, I think so—in fact I'm pretty sure I can do it." I couldn't imagine that we would be on the air for twenty-six consecutive weeks and it seemed to me that I was taking little chance in making that statement so glibly. We really felt that thirteen weeks would be our fling on television, with the glory of knowing that it was all our own program.

We chose "Wonders of the World" as an appropriate title for the series and took an episode called "The Mysterious Congo Witch Dancers" for the opening program. We also chose a scene of those remarkable dancers, the Watusi warriors, to be used as the theme of every episode, with a sequence of the dancers of Bali to close each program. But as yet we had no inkling as to the exact date our series would start.

Finally, just before Christmas of 1956 we learned that we were scheduled to begin our programs on January 16. "Remember," said the voice from the agency, "rehearsal for the live portion of the program will be on January 15, the day before the show. It's at four o'clock and don't be late."

When we appeared for rehearsal in a bewildering chamber of cameras, cables, props, and aloof technicians it was to learn that we were on our own. Luther Newby, the capable director assigned to us by the station said, "And how do you plan to start the program, Hal?" and I could see him wince when I replied, "But I thought the station was going to tell me how they thought it should start!"

Unknown to us, the sales staff and Mr. Flanagan were watching this rehearsal on a monitor in another room, and I am sure they must have blanched to hear me say this, just the day before our show was to go on the air.

I was a thoroughly worried performer that day. The awful realization hit me that appearing as a guest on someone else's program was one thing, but having the full responsibility for completely producing our own program was quite another. Halla was simply petrified, but I managed to look confident to keep her from bolting. David was unconcerned. He seemed to regard the experience of being under the klieg-lights as just an elaborate "grownups' game."

The rehearsal seemed just awful. I felt that the agency and the station might reconsider and decide that it would be a mistake to allow us to go on. Before we left the station I waited, half-expecting someone to shake his head and say, "I'm afraid Mr. Linker that—" Instead Newby cheerfully called out, "Remember, tomorrow at five for make-up. See you then."

The actual telecast, up to the moment when the Watusi drums began to beat and our program went on the air seemed a hodgepodge of general confusion. I was positive in my own mind that the program had gone miserably. Although the studio staff congratulated us afterwards—even the hitherto blasé cameramen—I chose not to believe them.

"They're just being kind to us," I told Halla as we drove home from KCOP. Davey fell right asleep in the back of the car, completely unconcerned.

Our phone rang almost at the crack of dawn on Friday. It was the advertising agency executive. "Have you seen what *Daily Variety* said about your show?"

My heart sank. "What did they say?"

"It's great, terrific. You've got a good one, Linker!"

I hung up feeling limp. "He must be kidding, Halla," I said.

The phone rang again. This time it was a personal friend. Her enthusiasm was unmistakable. She had also caught the review in the daily entertainment newspaper, which is considered a Bible by motion picture, TV, and radio people.

Halla and I stared at each other. "It—it can't be!" I finally gasped.

"And why not, Hal-minn? It's like you said—lecturing on a large scale. Audiences like it—why not the TV audiences!" Halla's eyes sparkled.

I grabbed a pair of trousers and shoved them on over my

pajamas, jumped into the car, and tore off in search of a news-stand. I must have been quite a sight, still unshaven, wearing my pajama top for a shirt, standing on a street corner devouring the copy of the *Daily Variety*. And here's what it said:

WONDERS OF THE WORLD

(*The Mysterious Congo Witch Dancers*)

Filmed by Hal Linker. Producer-Writer, Linker. Director, Luther Newby, Cast: Hal, Halla and David Linker. KCOP, Wednesday 8 p.m. Running time 30 min.

"Producer-cameraman Hal Linker tees off his true-life adventure series on KCOP with conspicuous success, in an interesting expedition into the Belgian Congo. Quality of the films is far better than the usual seen in series dealing with faraway places and strange-sounding names, as the song goes.

Preem show saw Linker, his wife Halla and their son David trek to the Belgian Congo for interesting shots of the Mai Munene tribe and the diamond mines. Outstanding was the sequence of an actual witch dance, wherein the Africans make Elvis Presley look rather sedate as they gyrate madly "to drive the demons out of the village," explains Linker. He also lensed a brush fire at close range and altogether brought back above-average footage of the Congo and its inhabitants.

The Linkers are on live, to explain the various scenes, and do a good job of this, adding to the entertainment and never intruding."

The issue cost ten cents. The vendor had nine copies left on the stand. I fished into my pockets and found exactly ninety cents left in change. I poured the collection of nickles, dimes and pennies into his surprised palm, grabbed the papers and rushed home.

I remember bursting in and waving the paper. "It's true, it's true," I yelled.

On that glorious day, January 18, 1957, all we could think of was that now, probably, we wouldn't be taken off the air before our thirteen weeks were up. Not in our wildest imagination could we dream that after those thirteen weeks we would be renewed for another thirteen weeks, then for an additional twenty-six weeks, then for fifty-two weeks more, than seventy-eight weeks still more, and that after *two hundred weeks on the air* our program would still be continuing week after week! Nor did we dream that some-day our programs would be seen in Germany, in England, in East Africa, and even in Siam (just mention our name in Krung Thep!) and Hong Kong among other countries. Not to speak of being shown in cities of the United States from coast to coast, New York, Washington D.C., San Francisco, New Orleans, Miami, Dallas, and many others. And most of all, I did not realize that television would become my prime business, with lecturing reduced to a sideline in which we gave personal appearances whenever we wanted to once more have personal contact with our viewers. The day of the *Variety* review, when the first excitement had worn off, the thought hit me with the force of a sledgehammer that for the next thirteen weeks I would not only have to edit, write, and produce a different show each week, but also, since lecturing was then my primary livelihood, I would have to continue to make personal appearances all over the United States with my films during that same period. I could not cancel the contracted-for lectures without risking my future in that field, so I decided that contrary to all known laws of physics I would have to be in two places at one time. My magic carpet, enabling me to accomplish this impossible feat, was to be the many airlines of the United States.

We carefully went over my lecture schedule. I had only two lectures on Wednesday, our television show day, during the thirteen weeks. For these, when I couldn't possibly be back in time, we decided we would pre-record my voice on tape to be played with the film and Halla would be there in person to make the introductory remarks. For the other programs I planned to simply use the airlines to rush back to Los Angeles from wherever I was, in time to do the program, then dash just as madly back again by air to do the next day's lecture. I couldn't risk damaging my lecture season for the ethereal possibilities of a television career.

My weird aerial zigzag across the United States and into Canada began after our third telecast. I was giving a series of travel film lectures at the Eaton Auditorium in Toronto at that time. Performances were on Monday, Tuesday, and Thursday only, fortunately. Tuesday night I finished the show at 11 P.M. The first plane out of Toronto westward was at 7 A.M. the next morning. I was on that plane, bound for Chicago bright and early, although frankly since it was so early I was *not* feeling so bright. At Chicago I had a wait for my connection, and finally arrived at Los Angeles at 4 P.M. Here I had just time enough to say "Hello, family," grab a quick snack, and then dash off with them to the studio, where after make-up and rehearsal we put on our program from 8 to 8:30. Eleven o'clock found me back on a night plane for Chicago, where after a long wait I boarded my flight back to Toronto to arrive in the early afternoon. That night I gave the Thursday show to an audience unaware of my mad transcontinental dash.

Several times I had narrow escapes in my hectic travels. Once I was giving a lecture in Boston. I had everything worked out. I would catch the non-stop flight from Boston to Los Angeles at 11 P.M. and be in Los Angeles early the next morning, in time to check over the film and perfect the narration to go along with it. Then I would board a midnight return flight to New York, where I was scheduled to give a performance at five o'clock the next afternoon! That night in Boston, though, as my taxi neared the airport, to my horror we entered a heavy bank of fog. At the ticket counter I was told that all flights were canceled. There was just nothing to do—no flights were going out and the Los Angeles flight had definitely been canceled. Ordinarily I should have given it up as a bad job and gone to a hotel to call Halla and tell her the bad news and to lick my wounds. But sometimes I can be terribly persistent when much is at stake and I determinedly sat down on my baggage in the terminal, after all the other passengers had left, vowing that I would wait there until I could get some sort of transportation out of Boston. At 2 A.M. the airlines clerk to whom I had told my tale of woe shook me out of my dozing to excitedly inform me that there was a slight break in the fog and a plane would be leaving for New York and Miami in five minutes. I was sure I could get a plane from New York to Los Angeles, so I managed to dash aboard the flight barely in time. In only a little over an hour I would be in Gotham, so I relaxed with a sigh, only to be startled almost out of my seat when the stewardess anounced that fog had closed down all the New York City airports and we would have to continue on to Washington D.C.! At the Washington National Airport our plane landed just before that airport was closed down by the same fog, which was sweeping down the coast, and there I was, marooned in the Nation's capital, still almost three thousand miles from my destination, at three o'clock in the morning on the day of our program. I was told that at 9:45 A.M. a flight to Los Angeles was scheduled. It probably would not go out because of the fog, but I booked a seat on it anyway and went to a nearby motel to rest for the few hours remaining. I had little rest though, since I called Halla and spent half an hour talking to her about my predicament and making suggestions as to how she should handle the show if I couldn't get there.

Here again Halla's mettle showed itself. Not a peep of complaint came from her about this tremendous new unexpected burden that was thrown in her lap. She had never given a program by herself. I always had prepared a continuity for her which she followed on the air, although I used no script myself for my comments during the film shows. And since there was no script which she could read with the film, she would have to ad lib as she went along. But perhaps she was more than sustained by my own attitude. I kept telling her, "But don't worry, Halla-mín, I'll do everything possible to get back there, and if I don't, whatever you do on the show will be fine."

After a fitful cat nap of three hours or so, I awoke to find the mists still hugging the ground, but to my anxious eyes it seemed to be thinning out. At 9:15 the plane was called, and 9:45 saw us on our way with just barely minimum visibility to permit our take-off. The plane arrived at Los Angeles at almost 6 P.M. with the program scheduled at 8. But we did the show successfully, with none of our viewers aware of the tensions of the day, and midnight found me back on a plane for New York where I arrived safely and in time to give my Town Hall presentation! With cross-country trips like this every week I soon became an airline "regular" to flight crews and ticket agents.

Once an American Airlines stewardess paused by my seat while in flight and asked me if there were any opening for girls in Pan Am. I explained that I had nothing to do with Pan American except that I had once ridden in one of their planes overseas. She frowned perplexedly, "Isn't that odd. I've seen you before. I could swear—" For the rest of the flight she eyed me with a certain amount of suspicion. I'm sure she had seen me on one of our programs during a layover in Los Angeles, since I soon heard that our series was a favorite with airlines personnel because we only showed films we had actually taken ourselves in places which we had visited, and they felt that our comments were soundly based.

It was a thrilling moment when I was finally recognized in a plane to Los Angeles by a fellow traveler. He peered rather closely at me and then said: "Haven't I seen you on television, Mister—Mister——"

"Linker," I filled in. "Yes, you have." Tired as I was from an unusually difficult trip I was thrilled by this encounter with "my public."

"Thought so," he nodded. "Now I remember where it was. You were guests on the Groucho Marx show about four years ago. That sure is a pretty wife you have!"

Ah, well, such is fame, I thought. Here we have been on the air for two months with our own program and our guest stint on a famous comedian's show is the way we are known. But then I consoled myself with the remembrance that we had won 265 seriously needed dollars on that "You Bet Your Life" appearance. Besides, what man worth his salt wouldn't swell with pride if he is remembered as the man with the beautiful wife? And then our television rating was climbing healthily, even though we were pitted against the most formidable opposition on the air at that time, the popular "Disneyland" show.

The advertising agency now came to us with a proposition. If I would put up half of the financing for production costs they would match the amount and distribute "Wonders of the World" on a national scale. This would take all the money we had earned to date on television—but with Halla's enthusiastic approval and growing confidence in ourselves we agreed.

Pressed and harried as we were by deadlines piling on top of deadlines we would produce a filmed series of twenty-six episodes. But since I had scheduled a summer trip to the South Seas for additional TV and lecture footage it meant that I would have to not only meet existing lecture and television commitments but also put together eight shows for the new series. These would be filmed in their entirety and televised during the eight weeks we would be gone! The remaining eighteen would be made upon our return from the Pacific.

The spring and summer of 1957 were distinguished by a prolonged and record-breaking heat wave in southern California.

Every spare moment between planes was spent cutting and editing film or in the studio where we were to film the studio sequences and record the sound tracks.

When it was over 90 degrees "in the shade" outside it was over 120 in the studio. And when the electricians turned on the juice for spotlighting, the mercury zoomed up out of sight and we slowly but steadily wilted beneath our make-up!

By the time we were able to board a plane for the beginning of our South Seas swing we had almost had it. As we sat in the blessedly cool cabin of a DC7C airliner winging westward across the Pacific toward Hawaii I stared at the distant smudge behind us on the eastern horizon which marked southern California and told Halla that I finally had a notion of how it felt to be an escapee from Devil's Island!

Chapter Eighteen

New Zealand and American Samoa

NEW ZEALAND, member of the Commonwealth, has the unanimous Linker vote at any time as a land of pleasant people, a wonderland of scenery, a "promised land" for sportsmen and a delightful place not only for vacations but for hard-working movie cameramen as well!

We could have spent much more time there. But our schedule included Fiji and Tahiti, so we confined our activities primarily to the North Island, where we encountered the fabled and almost extinct kiwi bird, a weird creature which sees only in the dark and can only walk—since its wings disappeared eons ago.

There were only two kiwis alive in the Auckland Zoo at the time. It was broad daylight and since the birds cannot see in the daytime I was not too hopeful when I asked if the birds could be brought out of their cages for a close-up shot. To my happy surprise the zoo keeper agreed to show them to us.

Halla and David, not without a certain amount of trepidation, each held a bird while I moved in with my camera. Their feathers are no longer suitable for flight, being too skimpy. A little bump on each side of the birds' bodies was all that remained of what had been wings, and their beaks contain breathing nostrils almost at the tip.

They were indeed a unique species, once almost extinct, but now making a comeback protected by the government.

Rotorua was, by far, the highlight of our visit. The area proved to be a fascinating potpourri of lakes teeming with husky, game trout, snow-capped mountains, boiling mud baths, and spouting geysers (Halla felt right at home).

The Maoris, native New Zealanders, were more than gracious hosts and willingly demonstrated their dances and songs near Waharewarewa, an authentic Maori village.

It was here that we met guide Rangi, a medium-sized, vivacious, good-humored Maori woman who had won world renown when she "pressed noses" with Eleanor Roosevelt—the traditional form of affectionate Maori greeting. Rangi was so taken with David that she vigorously pressed noses with *him!*

Our son was mightily impressed by this bronze-skinned, affable, and highly cultured representative of a great Polynesian race.

"I bet you're strong." She smiled. "Tell you what: we'll go to Lake Taupo where you will be able to throw stones larger than your head!"

Our son wore a skeptical look as we drove along the banks of the tremendous lake from our headquarters at the Wairaki Hotel. Rangi bade us stop and park by an embankment which was studded with huge boulders.

She took David by the hand and led him to a rock approximately the size of an overgrown pumpkin. "Here," she said, pointing, "pick it up and throw it into the lake!"

David's eyes bulged. "It's too big," he murmured. "I can't——"

"Of course you can," she said. "Here—I'll utter magic Maori words that will give you the strength." She winked at me. "And if I were your daddy I'd get set with that camera for a picture of you throwing this rock!"

I unlimbered my camera and watched while she waved her arms and uttered a few sentences in her language. Then she tapped our son on his chest. "There—feel that strength flowing through your arms?"

Spellbound, he nodded.

"Pick up the rock and throw it," she commanded.

Now it was our turn to stare as David picked up the comparatively huge rock and easily tossed it into the water!

Halla gasped and pointed: "Look, Hal—it floats!"

Rangi laughed. Her "spell" was no longer secret. The rocks and boulders were pumice stone—almost feather-light. For a happy fifteen minutes all of us had fun playing Atlas. I have often thought of making a deal with the New Zealand government—to import the light weight pumice-stone "boulders" as props for motion picture and television studios.

Ever since the days of Gauguin, and since George Nordhoff and James Norman Hall, penned *Mutiny on the Bounty* and *Men Against the Sea*, people have regarded Tahiti as the mystic island of tropical South Sea splendor and romance.

During my World War II wanderings through the South Pacific I had often thought of Tahiti. Like many other shipmates I had been both disappointed and thankful that the campaigns had bypassed the lovely French possession. Disappointed because there was no reason to touch upon its shores; thankful that it had been spared the destructive visitation of the gods of war. Even though Tahiti was high on my "must see" list in the South Seas, when we left New Zealand I was by no means assured of transportation to that island paradise. Although the capital Papeete (pronounced Pahpay-ehtay) with its population of 17,000 was a mid-Pacific dot far removed from the beaten tourist paths, there was already a rather heavy movement in its direction.

An airline provided service every two weeks from the Fijis, via a World War II Solent flying boat which could airlift some forty passengers at a time. There was sea transportation available, but only from Los Angeles. We had hurried first to New Zealand to get there before the worst part of their winter set in and now we were ready to go to Tahiti directly from New Zealand and the Fiji Islands.

We tried in advance through both the airline people and the French government to obtain reservations on the flying boat. The word was: "Sorry—all sold out." We flew to Fiji anyway on the off chance that we might be able to "luck in" on a flight to Tahiti. My stateside airline experience had taught me that a "sold out" flight often had a few empty seats just before departure, due to last-minute cancellations. Our problem was that we needed *three* seats and this was almost too much to hope for. But I felt we would be better off waiting in Fiji. Should it be impossible to reach Tahiti, we could still fly from Fiji to American Samoa. And Samoa *could* be construed as an "island paradise" next to Tahiti in interest—sort of.

When we reached the Fijis I learned that while there are many last-minute openings on airliners elsewhere in the world the sign above the TEAL Airways flying boat service for Tahiti was SOLD OUT. And they meant it.

It was a bitter pill to swallow. A segment on Tahiti would have embellished our "Wonders of the World" TV show. Well, there was always tomorrow. It would be "Tahiti, lads" a year later perhaps. Meanwhile we boarded Pan Am's DC4 and arrowed toward American Samoa, Pacific Island Paradise Number 2. We landed there—smack in the middle of an epidemic of the Asian flu!

A contemporary best-seller novel, *The Ugly American*, purportedly points out why many of our State Department representatives in various countries do not win friends and influence people for us.

Samoa, we discovered upon our arrival, is divided into American Samoa and Western Samoa which is under New Zealand jurisdiction. Compared with the area supervised by Her Majesty's Government our sector was "ugly," if I can use that word for neglected.

The history of American Samoa dates back to the turn of the century when a chief granted the entire island of Tutuila to the United States. At the same time the then German imperial government gained control of the adjacent island of Western Samoa. We established a naval base at Pago Pago (pronounced Pango Pango) while the Germans put military installations into the settlement of Apia.

New Zealand took over Western Samoa after World War I. The United States retained Tutuila as a "non-self-governing" territory ever since. Until approximately five years prior to our visit in 1957, the Navy had "governed" Tutuila. In 1951 the Department of the Interior superseded the Navy and I am sorry to relate that the plight of the "American" Samoans had not improved since.

When we landed at the Tafuna airport we were surprised to find ourselves greeted by a tall, rather worried-looking individual who turned out to be none other than the "Attorney General of American Samoa."

He told us that we had arrived at an "unfortunate time"—during the Asian flu epidemic—but that he would help us in any way he could.

We could tell that the sickness had blighted the area. Never a bustling community (Pago Pago has long since lost its strategic importance as a naval and shipping base) the community had only about 2000 population.

Our headquarters was a collection of boards called the Rainmaker Hotel—deriving its name from a 1500-foot "mountain" of that name which dominates the harbor from the opposite side.

Our proprietress was an amply girthed, good-natured Polynesian named Mary. Over dinner she told us that more than 75 per cent of the population was "down" with the flu. It worried me enough to take Halla and David to the hospital, one of the few substantial installations in Pago Pago, for preventive flu innoculations.

The physician in charge, Dr. Kramer originally from Europe but now a naturalized citizen, was apologetic. There was no vaccine available.

"But—with this epidemic," I protested.

He shrugged. "We've sent request after request to Washington. They've been ignored."

"You mean—they simply have not answered?"

He nodded.

It literally took the wind out of my sails. Here was American Samoa—a U.S. possession. Surely, I had reasoned, here I would find a "model" possession—something which undoubtedly we could hold up as a shining example to support our criticism of the way the British, French, and Belgian governments manage their possessions elsewhere.

Instead, I found "absentee" government of the worst possible type from the standpoint of indifference and ineffectiveness. The doctor sadly explained that although the Department of the Interior was responsible for American Samoa the actual "Governing" was done by private individuals under contract to the department.

"These people are hired to come here and run things," the doctor related. "That goes for the 'Attorney General,' myself, and others. We are private citizens 'governing' by virtue of a signed document. We are not members of the Department of the Interior!"

The rest of his story was depressing. Uncle Sam annually granted this "contract" Samoan government one million dollars. From this meager sum had to come sufficient funds to maintain and operate every one of the island utilities including the police department, public health service, and school system.

"The natives—actually more pure-blooded Polynesians than the type you'll find in Hawaii or Tahiti—are not much better off than they used to be during the pre-European era," the doctor added. "Even though they're not starving, nor are they being abused."

"But what have we done to help them to elevate their own living standards?" I asked.

His lips parted in a wry smile. "Well—we tried an experiment about five years ago. We decided that in order to put American Samoa on its feet we'd build a big fish cannery here in Pago Pago.

"The theory was that the Samoans would go out, maybe two or three hundred miles offshore, and develop a fishing industry. We overlooked one thing."

"What was that?"

"Unlike other Polynesians the Samoans are terrible sailors. They get seasick! We had to contract with Japanese deep sea fishermen to catch the fish. It's true that Samoan women, several hundred of them, work in the cannery itself. But the Samoan men still have nothing to do. And that's bad for family life."

"Then how do the men and boys occupy themselves?"

The doctor sighed. "They don't. Many of them, in desperation, enlist in the armed forces, the merchant marine, anything to get away from here!"

It was an unhappy picture. "You say the cannery is still in operation?"

He nodded. "An American firm leased it and has been exporting over $4,000,000 worth of fish to the States and elsewhere each year. For this company and the merchants in Pago Pago things are perfect. Here—" he eyed us—"you see, there are no corporation or income taxes here. American citizens on the mainland, with *their* taxes, are paying money the local businesses should be paying!"

We visited a house in the center of Pago Pago where Sadie Thompson, the legendary heroine of Somerset Maugham's story was supposed to have lived during the olden days. At the time of our visit it was a white-painted warehouse.

The adjacent land was dotted with small communities which were clusters of oval-shaped, thatch-roofed houses, and occasional copra plantations.

What absolutely amazed us was the tremendous number of

223

churches. Our friend, the doctor, told us that American Samoa had more churches per capita than any other country in the world. "And that even includes Cholula, Mexico, where there are 365 churches, one for each day of the year," he added.

Evidently the Navy, tolerant of religious matters, permitted every and any religious group mission to invade Tutuila and collect donations from the rather devout Samoans for the purpose of erecting these houses of worship. When the Department of the Interior took over control it fortunately put a halt to this practice.

We saw—and filmed—a dramatic reminder of this. About five miles from the heart of Pago Pago we discovered a small village with a population of 200. Dominating the village was a tremendous, partly completed structure consisting of huge walls minus roof. This was to have been a church. The size was that of a cathedral. One could have put all 200 villagers into the structure with sufficient room to spare for the rest of Pago Pago's population.

We could not swim in most of the Belgian Congo waters because of the parasitic flukes. We learned that it was equally as dangerous to swim anywhere near Pago Pago's spectacular harbor for a different reason—raw sewage!

Despite American sanitation know-how, Pago Pago, at the time of our explorations, had no decent sewage system. The harbor was dotted by outdoor privies which were mounted on stilts sunk into the bottom of the shallow edge of the bay. To say that the water was contaminated would be putting it mildly. And what irritated us most about Samoa was the fact that the natives there were a fine looking, pleasant people who obviously want to be our friends and who obviously are being disregarded because they do not threaten each day to go communist!

We liked the people there and their beautiful island but we certainly were disappointed, as Americans, in our administration of those islands.

When we returned to the States I immediately started a "one-family" campaign to tell the Americans the truth about American Samoa. I pulled no punches with my narration on the TV show.

Letters began to come into the studio. People were shocked at my report. I sent batch after batch of the increasing mail to Washington. I especially stressed that after ninety years of U.S. control there wasn't even a high school in American Samoa.

The chief counsel of the Senate Committee on Interior and

Insular Affairs at first denied that anything was wrong. However in the face of my insistence, and the entry into the picture of U.S. senators, Washington decided to send an investigating committee.

Some good is coming of this solitary attempt by the Linker family to tilt with "bureaucratic dragons." New laws are being written for American Samoa. The wonderful Polynesian people there may someday have reason for pride in living under U.S. rule.

Chapter Nineteen

Ticketless to Tahiti

THE "DAY OF OUR TRANSPORTATION MIRACLE" began inauspiciously.

Halla and I sat with our son in the dining room of the Rainmaker Hotel and tried to summon up some enthusiasm for our breakfast. We'd had our share of American Samoa. All we wanted was to leave. Alas, the next plane was not due for another week.

The swinging doors leading to the kitchen were flung open. "Gooood morning!"

It was the cheerful voice of Mary, our Samoan hostess. We acknowledged her greeting and barely glanced in her direction. And then I sat bolt upright and stared. She was radiant in a colorful Samoan costume, which consisted of a long tunic draped over an almost ankle-length skirt. A garland of flowers was worn like a crown around her carefully combed black hair while heavy, fragrant leis caressed her neck.

She sparkled with infectious good humor as she poured our coffee. Halla's eyes widened. "You look simply wonderful, Mary," she exclaimed. "Is today a holiday?"

The Samoan beamed. "Mebbe yes, I think. Big ship, she come today!"

"Big ship?" I squinted toward the bay. "I didn't know a cruise ship was due in Pago Pago at this time of the year."

"Oh, no cruise ship." Her smile widened. "She big U. S. Navy ship."

I was somewhat startled. Since American Samoa was no longer a naval station the impending appearance of the vessel was quite intriguing. Noting the expressions of curiosity on our faces Mary volunteered an explanation.

To escape the boredom of life here many young Samoans en-

226

listed in the U. S. Armed Forces for duty in outposts throughout the world.

But because commercial air and sea transportation to Pago Pago was not only expensive but uncertain, it meant that the uniformed islanders had to spend their furloughs away from home. This created a morale problem.

The Navy solved it with ingenuity. At certain intervals it collected at Honolulu all Samoan servicemen whose furloughs happened to coincide. The happy group was then placed aboard a vessel and dispatched on what amounted to a leisurely cruise to Pago Pago "on Uncle Sam."

The arriving ship this day was an AK 213 named the U.S.S. *Sussex* carrying 113 Samoan servicemen. The ship was scheduled to dock just before noon.

"Very nice day," Mary concluded, vigorously nodding. "Everybody go dockside, meet ship. Chiefs, Governor, everybody!"

When we reached the scene of the homecoming it seemed as though half the island's entire population had turned out. The women, for the most part, were elaborately costumed and flower-bedecked like Mary. A goodly number of the men had forsaken Western clothing for traditional brilliantly hued, skirtlike *lava-lavas* wrapped around their legs. One of the stalwart chiefs present was particularly impressive in an outfit consisting of a smartly tailored, modern sharkskin jacket over a brilliant blue lava-lava.

Of particular interest was the appearance of the newly appointed governor of American Samoa, Peter Coleman. A stocky man in his early thirties, Coleman bore the distinction of being the first native-born Samoan ever to hold that high office. Mary told us that he was "determined" to bring about improvements for his people. In almost the same breath she noted that he was working under a handicap. The son of a U. S. Navy petty officer and Samoan wife, Coleman had been sent to the mainland for his education. Now that he had returned and assumed the mantle of high office, the old-line Samoan chiefs felt that because he had been brought up and schooled away from the island he would not understand Samoan problems.

Many of the women present, particularly some of the wives of the assembled chiefs, were massive. One of them must have easily weighed 275 pounds. A towering person, she appeared as wide as she was tall.

The Attorney General, noting my interest in her, remarked that in Polynesian circles a man's prestige increases in proportion to his wife's poundage. "The stouter she becomes the more evident it is to all and sundry that her husband is a good provider, therefore worthy of being a chief."

I turned to Halla who had been taking all of this in. "Halla-mín," I said in mock seriousness, "starting tomorrow you'll have to eat at least four meals a day. With your weight at 118 pounds I'm sure everyone here must be gossiping about what a poor provider I am. You don't want me to be disgraced, do you?" Halla just wrinkled her nose at me.

As I stood on the dock filming the excited populace, people began to shout and wave. I turned, and there in the harbor was the *Sussex* making a tight 360 turn and heading for the dock.

When the ship approached us (it was just a shade larger than the S.S. *Tröllafoss* on which I had sailed to Iceland) I could see the decks a-swarm with uniformed men—sailors, soldiers, and marines—all waving to us and singing Polynesian songs.

While the officers and crew maneuvered the *Sussex* to a feathery contact with the dock people ashore joined in the singing. Parents recognized sons and tears of joy began to roll down their cheeks. It was an emotional experience for Halla and me. Her eyes were moist, and as I filmed there was a lump in my throat.

No sooner was the gangway in place than the arriving men and waiting people made a concerted rush toward each other. Many of the servicemen had been away from home as long as four or five years. Some had been gone almost twice that long.

The happy confusion was heart-warming. And then non-coms began to shrill on whistles. There was an official ceremony to be staged. The servicemen lined up in units—marines, sailors, and soldiers. They stood at attention while the Governor, Attorney General, and chiefs walked up and down the ranks, shaking hands with each and every furloughing "returnee."

I finished taking the sequence of this part of the official welcome and had started to dismantle my equipment when a pleasant voice remarked at my elbow: "That's quite a camera rig you have, mister—mister—?"

It was a young naval officer, a lieutenant.

"Linker," I volunteered, extending my hand.

"Riley," he replied with a sunny grin. "Stuart Riley."

I nodded toward the *Sussex*. "Your ship?"

"I'm the 'exec'—" He pointed his chin toward the bridge. "The skipper's Lieutenant Commander Tilley."

"How long will you be here?" I asked.

"We're pulling out tomorrow!"

"Where are you heading for?"

He lit a cigarette. "Well we're just going to cruise a spell. Y'see, the men we brought have a fourteen-day furlough. So while they enjoy themselves here we'll go somewhere else and then come back in time to pick 'em up and return 'em to Honolulu!"

This didn't sound like the Navy I knew during World War II. "Where are you planning to go, Lieutenant? Fiji or someplace like that?"

He shook his head. "We all took a vote on where we wanted to kill time——"

My jaw dropped. "You—voted?"

"Yeh. The skipper didn't want to decide on his own and since the Navy Department said we could write our own ticket the captain put it up to the officers and men."

I swallowed. The Navy quite definitely had changed.

Riley took a last drag on his cigarette and flipped it into the bay. "We put up half a dozen places within easy sailing. Tahiti won by a landslide!"

Tahiti! I tried to suppress my sudden excitement. "You mean that you'll sail for Papeete tomorrow, anchor there, and return to Pago Pago in time to take your passengers back to Honolulu?"

He nodded. "We're all looking forward to it."

I could well imagine. "Lieutenant, let me tell you about my problem," I said. I explained my predicament, how I'd hoped to film in Tahiti only to find that there was no available space on the sole airline which linked the fabled island paradise with the outside world. I took a deep breath. "D'you think there's the slightest chance I might be able to hitch a ride with you to Tahiti and back?"

Riley shoved his cap onto the back of his close-cropped head and frowningly rubbed his chin. "Well, golly, Linker, I don't quite see how—we're not supposed to carry civilians and——"

"Well I'm not actually without a naval connection," I pulled out

229

my old World War II ID card. "I used to be a 'Jaygee' myself. The Department knows of me. Maybe I could be included in the ship's roster—just for the round trip."

Riley pursed his lips and scuffed the toe of a shoe along the planking of the dock. "Well, it's something I can't answer. Anyway you'd have to talk to the captain. It'd be up to him."

He turned and beckoned for me to follow him up the gangway. Stepping aboard a naval vessel for the first time since I had been given my honorable discharge was a strange sensation which brought back crowding memories. Seamen engaged in their varying duties curiously eyed me as I followed the young executive officer to the "Old Man's" quarters.

Lieutenant Commander George Tilley, Captain of the U.S.S. *Sussex* proved to be sympathetic to my tale of woe. When I had finished he leaned back. "I can't make a decision on something like this, even though you are—or were—a naval officer, as Mr. Riley indicates. The fact is you are now a civilian."

I felt my sudden hopes begin to fade.

"However—" He paused, his weatherbeaten features furrowed with concentration. "If the Navy Department will approve it I certainly have no objections to taking you with us to Tahiti——"

My hopes bounced up once more.

"Tell you what, Mr. Linker. You go ashore and get the Governor's permission to send a wire to the Navy Department. You'll have to get his okay to use the cable facilities here for a matter such as this. I'll give you a note, telling him I'm all for it provided Washington goes along with it!"

I was overjoyed. I could not ask for better co-operation. And then it dawned on me that I had not been entirely candid with either officer. "There's something I'd better tell you, Captain!"

He eyed me.

"I am not traveling alone."

Both officers leaned forward. "Y'mean someone's with you?" the skipper asked.

I nodded. "My family."

Riley's jaw dropped. Tilley's eyes widened. "What d'ya mean by 'family'? What does it consist of?"

I took a deep breath. "My wife and a six-year-old son!"

Tilley sank back in his chair, bafflement on his face. He kept studying me for a long moment. "A civilian, and now he wants us to not only carry him against all regs but pack along a wife and kid as well!" Riley merely shrugged.

The skipper's expression was somewhat stern. "You've been in the Navy, Mr. Linker," he said. "You know that we do not have facilities for women on naval vessels."

I could only nod unhappily. Tahiti seemed to be fast receding.

"As for the *Sussex*, we probably have only one very small cabin which might be available. It'd be confining." He shook his head. "I don't think it'd be possible for you three to squeeze into those quarters——"

"They're part of my team, sir," I said. "We never go anywhere without each other." Although I had virtually given up hope by this time I briefly sketched in the details of Halla and myself and how we traveled around the world together.

The facts intrigued them. Tilley stood up. "Never heard of a husband-and-wife team like that." He put on his cap. "I'll show you this storage-locker-sized cubbyhole," he said. "If you think your wife and kid won't mind the tight squeeze it'll be okay with me— provided Washington approves!"

Tilley had not exaggerated in his description of the available cabin space. The compartment, roughly the size of a tract-home bathroom, had two bunks. I turned to the two officers who stood by with quizzical expressions. "Hope the Navy says okay!"

When I explained my purpose and showed Tilley's note Governor Coleman gave me permission to send my cable to Washington. The "contract" Attorney General accompanied me to the cable office. Before I wrote out my request he looked pityingly at me. "You don't really think the Navy Department is going to answer your cable by tomorrow, do you?"

"Why not?"

"Well it's Sunday here, Linker——"

"So much the better. It means they'll have my wire first thing tomorrow morning—Monday, a working day—and they'll be able to flash back a 'yay' or 'nay.'"

He shook his head. "You forget, my friend," his voice was soft. "We're on the other side of the international date line. It's Sunday here, today, but in Washington it's only Saturday. Your cable will get there on their Sunday. Do you really expect to get an answer out of Washington on Sunday morning?"

His logic was like a bucket of ice water. "I've nothing to lose," I finally said. "It's sort of like a miracle: here I've been hoping all this while to somehow get to Tahiti. And just when we'd given up all hope along came the *Sussex*. It's not just a coincidence, it's almost miraculous. I'm going to send the cable. Maybe someone'll be working in the Navy Department during Sunday. Who knows!"

He stood by with skepticism while I tried to cram all the pertinent facts including the tentative approval by Commander Tilley into as short a message as possible.

Later that night I told Halla that on the face of it the true miracle would be to receive any sort of acknowledgment of my message, let alone an approval. The *Sussex* was due to weigh anchor just before noon the next day. As a "just in case" precaution we partially packed before retiring. I did not get too much in the way of sleep that night. Tossing and turning I began to feel more convinced than ever that we'd wind up standing on shore and forlornly waving farewell to the *Sussex*.

A rapping on our door, almost at the crack of dawn, brought me to my feet. I opened it. Mary stood there, her eyes wide with excitement. "Rush cable for you—from Washington," she exclaimed.

My hands almost shook as I ripped open the envelope. And then I whirled and shouted to Halla. "It's come—it's okay—we can go on the *Sussex* to Tahiti!"

The *Sussex* was a beehive of activity as officers and crewmen prepared for the start of the five-day voyage to Tahiti. That is, until our taxi stopped and disgorged Halla, David, and myself.

At first the seamen, clad in dungarees, merely glanced at us, eyeing my wife with quiet but obvious appreciation, while continuing to work. However when we determinedly picked up our luggage and advanced up the gangway the effect was electrifying.

Sailors literally froze in their tracks. Petty officers shook their heads in silent disbelief. As we stepped aboard a series of long, low, drawn-out whistles emanated from the crew.

Lieutenant Riley met us. His narrow-eyed look choked off the whistles and then, after being introduced to Halla and David, he smilingly touched the peak of his cap. "Welcome aboard, ma'am," he said and led us to our cabin.

By the time we had steamed along the coast of Tutuila, passing Swains Island and then heading into open sea the shock of having a family of civilians aboard had worn off and we were gradually admitted into the ship's family, which consisted of thirty crewmen and six officers.

For Halla the experience was intriguing. David was thrilled beyond description and found himself popular with both the engine-room gang and deck division. As for myself, being on a naval vessel, after an absence of twelve years, was pleasantly nostalgic.

It was an almost idyllic journey. We ate with the officers and were frequently invited to the bridge, exclusive domain of the skipper and navigating watch officers.

Commander Tilley, it turned out, had been a non-commissioned officer during World War II. Since then he had been commissioned. He was looking forward to retiring to his home in Hawaii after twenty-five years in the service.

We were surprised to learn that he was then in his late forties. He looked younger. Lieutenant Riley, we found out, was nearing thirty. The rest of the officers, mostly ensigns, were in their early twenties. During a bull session with them my encroaching old age was pointed up.

I had been remarking about the service I had seen on naval vessels. One of the ensigns questioned me rather closely, asking what type of vessel I had been aboard. I explained that I had been assigned to an APA, the *Carteret*, which had transported assault troops into the Iwo Jima and Okinawa invasions.

At that point comprehension dawned on his face. "Oh," he explained, "you had me confused. I was trying to figure out what kind of a ship it was from your description of it having two stacks with a raked bow. Now I can understand when you tell me what invasions you were in. You were in the Old War!" The Korean War was the "new" war to him!

The routine of navy life at sea was a revelation for Halla and David. Before sighting Tahiti we watched a gun drill wherein the *Sussex*'s three-inch gun received a workout with live ammunition.

Although Halla and I took turns having David share our bunks the cabin was not too uncomfortable. However there was only one bathroom ("head" in the vernacular of the Navy) with a shower assigned to the officers. And since there were no locks on the door

I had to post myself as a sentry whenever Halla had occasion to use those facilities, just in case an officer happened to come along, forgetful of the fact that there was a woman passenger aboard.

Each evening a motion-picture projector and screen would be set up on the aft hatch and the entire ship's company, with the exception of the men on watch, would assemble for their nightly movies. Commander Tilley, having spent most of his time at sea, had the sailor's classic love of the land, especially the Wild West. The library he selected consisted mostly of what Hollywood people refer to as "horse operas." Whenever Halla and I joined the group we had the feeling of watching the "late, late movie" on television.

Before landing at Papeete, Tahiti's picturesque seaport, we learned that Lieutenant Riley had his own "sweetheart" stowed away aboard the *Sussex*. We noticed that whenever he was off duty he would disappear. Several of the junior officers had made oblique references to "Riley being 'below' with his 'love.'"

The lieutenant himself grinningly cleared the mystery for us before we docked. He took Halla, David, and me into the hold and showed us his "love." It was his gleaming, brand-new Corvette sports coupe. "I took delivery just before we shoved off from Hawaii," he explained while delicately flicking imaginary dust from its glittering flanks. "Can't wait to get her on a road and let 'er rip!"

On the morning of the fifth day we were up in time to see the island of Moorea which is situated some ten miles from Tahiti. It was a scene of spectacular beauty. The sun was just coming up and highlighting the mountains which still wore the dark purple mantle of night.

A short while later we saw the entire main island of Tahiti dead ahead. It seemed to be one tremendous fold of mountains, the highest of which was the 7000-foot peak of Orohena.

Although it was after seven by then the air was still cool and the sky cloudless. There was an indescribable excitement for me, watching Tahiti draw closer. Fragments of the stories I had read, memories of Captain Bligh, the *Bounty*, "MIST-er CHRISTIAN!" came crowding to mind.

Frequently a place so fabled turns out to be a letdown in reality. Such was not the case with Tahiti. From the moment we came to a stop just outside the harbor area of the capital, Papeete, to wait for our pilot to guide us to safe anchorage through the reef barrier, I knew that actuality would exceed documented fact and fiction.

When the small pilot boat came alongside and the pilot himself, a short, slender, voluble Gaul, clad in white shirt, dark trousers, and wearing a flopping-brimmed Panama hat stepped aboard, I knew that we were in for a delightful, storybook experience. Nor did subsequent events of our visit prove otherwise.

Papeete sprawled along the water's edge. Boats of every imaginable type and description were tied up to the docks.

Traffic in the streets consisted of a few contemporary and many vintage cars, somewhat ancient jitney-buses, numerous bicycles, and an amazing number of Italian motor scooters. To this varied selection was now added Lieutenant Riley's zooming new Corvette and for the duration of the *Sussex*'s sojourn in Tahiti we were constantly catching glimpses of Riley's car as it roared by carrying the other ship's officers, or Captain Tilley, or more interesting yet, a giggling squealing group of long-haired Tahitian girls.

Tahiti was discovered about 1767 by an English explorer, Wallis, but it was the French who took over the island in 1880 after a period of "control." In the two hundred years since the discovery of this island paradise there has been great intermarriage with Europeans by the natives and hardly a full-blooded Tahitian can now be found. The intermarriage has, however, developed an extremely attractive race, especially in the women, who still favor long hair reaching to the waist if possible.

Papeete itself is quite tropical-looking, with no extensive areas of new and modern buildings. It looks just as most of us think a tropical town in the South Seas should look.

We stayed at a fanciful collection of thatched roof bungalows called the Hotel Les Tropiques on the outskirts of the city. Although from the outside it looked like the "little grass shack" of tropical fame we happily learned that our bungalow had completely insect-proof netting, a tile bathroom with modern plumbing, and an excellent shower.

The hotel's lagoon provided wonderful swimming. Using borrowed diving masks we were able to see and pursue schools of beautiful, tropical fish while gliding over brilliant formations of coral—an experience that had David simply agog.

Food at Les Tropiques was excellent. And although, to Tahitians, the price was considered high we decided that according to

U.S. standards they were not excessive. At the rate of exchange during the time of our visit in 1957 we were paying 1000 Pacific francs a day—about $14 U.S. for our bungalow, while the à la carte meals cost about $3 each.

We were easily able to obtain modern conveniences such as an experienced baby-sitter who took care of our son while Halla and I went to explore Papeete's night life.

It was a Saturday evening and, as the vernacular has it, the "town was jumping." Especially at a place called Quinn's—an establishment whose atmosphere and dècor could be construed as "early piratical." However the "tough atmosphere" was merely that. The occupants were good-natured, happy-go-lucky citizens with a small sprinkling of foreigners like ourselves out to enjoy themselves.

The band was not only good but enthusiastic. The tempo of Tahitian music has a rapid-fire, almost machine-gun cadence—strange, considering the fact that those people rarely if ever move at a pace faster than a graceful, indolent walk. But their rhythm and dancing: that was something else again.

Halla and I had seen Hawaiian hula dancing, Egypt's "belly" convolutions, the weird gyrations of Pakistani North-West Frontier tribesmen and Congolese witch dancers. They all seemed tame in comparison with the "pape-o" demonstrated by inspired Tahitian couples.

An English couple sitting nearby noticed our startled expressions. The man recommended that we should visit the nearby Club Lea. "There they *really* let themselves go!"

He was correct. The effort extended by the dancers made us feel tired merely from watching them. These were not professional entertainers: just ordinary residents letting off steam on a Saturday night. Before we were to leave the island for our return to Pago Pago on the *Sussex* I got the opportunity to film, in its entirety, a succession of the wildest of the authentic Tahitian dances performed, believe it or not, by devout members of the island's Mormon Church!

Although the night clubs remained open until almost dawn, Halla and I called it quits shortly after midnight. We had arranged for a Citröen which would take us almost completely around the island. And the start of our filming trip would be rather early.

The roads were good. Our first stop was at Point Venus, a

peninsula which offers a beach of fine, black, volcanic sand. A nearby monument attested that here, in 1769, England's intrepid naval explorer, Captain Cook, had landed a group of royal astronomers to observe a transit of the planet Venus across the sun.

Our visit to the nearby home of M. Jacquier, head of the Tahitian Tourist Office, rewarded us with pleasant company, an excellent luncheon—and then delightful swimming in velvety water. Surfing in Tahiti is wonderful experience. There is, however, one drawback: spiny sea urchins which can inflict nasty wounds on unwary feet.

When we reached the village of Tautira it was like finding ourselves living out a chapter of the Tahitian segment of the celebrated novel based on fact, *Mutiny on the Bounty*.

The cheerful, friendly nature of the people and their genuine fondness for playing lavish host were excelled only by the beauty of the women and girls.

Tahitians would rather feast, sing, dance, and play than do anything else. They are known to seize upon any occasion as an excuse for their version of a fiesta. Our advent triggered an impressive celebration.

Our "host" was a smiling half-Polynesian, half-Chinese named Pepe. Almost *au naturel* in dress (and who needed too much in the way of clothing in that delightful climate?) Pepe wore a costume consisting of a floppy straw hat and colorful loincloth.

People came from all directions and helped prepare the feast under his supervision. The conversation on all sides was a melange of Polynesian and French with smatterings of Chinese thrown in for good measure.

Our food consisted of fruits, a bewildering variety of sea food prepared in various ways, roast pig, fowl, and, of course, the staple of native Tahitian life, breadfruit. The latter is actually the staff of life, not only in Tahiti but in islands throughout Oceania. About the size of a cantaloupe the breadfruit is picked from trees. I filmed sequences of laughing men and women preparing the fruit by scraping the rough exteriors with cowrie shells and then cutting up the meat, which resembles a raw potato.

The breadfruit meat itself is baked along with the rest of the food in ovens consisting of hot stones sunk into a pit and covered by bundles of banana leaves. During the course of the feast Halla, David and I sampled the breadfruit which, according to legend was handed down to the Polynesian ancestors by their gods in order to prevent starvation. This legend as well as others made me ponder upon the curious similarity of racial beliefs throughout the world. As I pointed out to Halla the breadfruit legend was amazingly parallel to the biblical account of Jehovah showering life-giving manna upon the Israelites during their wandering in the wilderness.

The other side of Tahiti's social coin was demonstrated on our return to Papeete at a dinner party at Les Tropiques. Our hosts were a charming New Zealand couple, Mr. and Mrs. Donald Donald. The dinner party included the British consul as well as Jules Verne, grandson of the famous French author, and his wife, with Mrs. James Norman Hall, widow of the American novelist.

Whereas at Tautira we had feasted straddle-legged on grass mats, eating everything in sight and using our fingers instead of utensils, as was the custom, now we attended an exquisite French dinner served with magnificent cutlery on a background of spotless linen.

Mrs. Hall suggested that we would be doing ourselves and our television and lecture-hall audiences a disservice if we neglected to take the two-and-one-half hour crossing, by motor launch, from Papeete to Captain Cook's Bay on the island of Moorea. "Although you may not think so, Tahiti is now 'built up' in comparison with Moorea. There you will find the pure Tahiti that my husband and I first discovered, and fell in love with, here shortly after World War I."

The trip to Moorea would be possible if we squeezed it into the frame of a single day. In that way we would be able to be on hand for the departure of the *Sussex*. We accordingly took only the barest essentials, primarily the cameras (motion-picture and still) and sufficient film. The launch, or ferry, was barely thirty-five feet long and jam-packed with passengers and cargo for the eighteen-mile crossing of the intervening strait.

The island itself, protruding from the surface of the water, is spectacular at a distance. As we came closer to Captain Cook's Bay it became simply magnificent.

Accommodations on Moorea consisted of a tiny, truly primitive hotel. The principal activity there consists of vanilla plantations primarily owned by Chinese. Actually vanilla is a vine that seems to be as stubborn and unpredictable as a Missouri mule.

One overseer explained that the vanilla vine will not grow just anywhere. It seems to have a mind of its own as to on which side of a hill, for instance, it will thrive. Trying to raise a successful crop is a gamble. And since Chinese seem to be inveterate gamblers perhaps that is why they cornered the vanilla-growing industry in Tahiti.

The process of raising a crop is extremely tedious. If the vines "like" the tree around which they wrap themselves, they produce tiny, orchid-like flowers which are carefully opened by hand and pollinated. The process is called "marrying the flowers."

Our return to Papeete took place at two the following morning. The night was stormy on the beach at Moorea. The moment we sailed into the straits gigantic waves hit us. Before long a small-sized gale was in the making and our passage became something of a nightmare.

There was absolutely nothing in the way of cabins on the lurching, rolling, tossing launch. The three of us, together with four Tahitians, huddled on the deck under blankets that quickly became drenched. Sharing deck space were a dozen huge pigs, destined for the markets in Papeete. These porkers seemed to us in the wind-swept dark, as large as St. Bernards.

As the jolting, swaying motion of the launch grew progressively worse all the passengers, four-legged as well as two-legged, became seasick. We humans were miserable enough. What the pigs must have gone through can well be imagined. We have never heard such grunting and wailing as we did that night from the seasick pigs. The eighteen-mile trip took us six awful hours.

As it must to all transients in Tahiti the time for our departure finally came. Like almost everyone else who has visited that island paradise the Linker family had truly fallen in love with its people, climate and way of living.

A small entourage of well-wishers including Mrs. James Norman Hall and Mme. Jacquemain, assistant to Monsieur Jacquier of the Tourist Bureau, a handsome woman and an acknowledged authority on Tahitian dancing, music, and art, came down to the dock to wish us *bon voyage*.

While our commissioned and enlisted friends of the U.S.S. *Sussex* watched, the two women placed leis around our necks and then stood there waving to us after we had boarded the ship.

The sight of lovely Papeete slowly receding made the three of

239

us somewhat melancholy. Lieutenant Riley joined us on the stern where I was getting some last-minute footage of the city.

For a moment he silently watched the water widen between the ship and Papeete and then he gently dropped a lei which he had been holding into the bay.

"Why did you do that, Lieutenant?" Halla asked.

"There's a saying here that if a friend gives you a lei when you depart and you cast it into the water it means you will someday return to Tahiti!" The lieutenant kept staring at the island.

Halla and I looked at one another. Without another word we took off our leis and dropped them into the bay.

Chapter Twenty

Corrida and Casbah!
Portugal, Spain and Tangier

MR. VLADIMIR SPIRIDINOV was a tall, lean gentleman with distinguishing touches of gray at his temples.

Attired in fastidiously tailored gray flannel embellished by properly matching accessories, he looked more like a Madison Avenue advertising executive than what he actually was—head of the New York office of Intourist, the official government-controlled Soviet Russian tourist agency.

We were seated in a restaurant in lower Manhattan and as I stated my case he listened with detached politeness. My request was quite simple: permission to visit and film Russia. I launched into a brief resumé of our activities, the family, lecture engagements, and the growing success of our TV show, "Wonders of the World" which, since our return from the South Seas, was being shown in twenty-four cities across the United States.

Comrade Spiridinov quashed his cigarette in the tray between us. "I am familiar with your background, Mr. Linker." His English contained a mere trace of Muscovite accent.

"Then can I count on Intourist's co-operation?"

He shrugged. "Of course. However, obtaining the necessary permits for a full-scale, professional filming expedition will require time." His eyes momentarily flicked in my direction.

"How much time?"

"Six months, perhaps!"

His remark jarred me. It was early April and I planned our departure for Europe to take place no later than the beginning of June. The happily surprising popularity of our program had one drawback: the insatiable appetite of television.

To obtain sufficient material for the forthcoming winter season of 1958–59 we would have to cover Russia and other European countries during the summer months, when the weather and light were most favorable for color motion-picture filming. I hinted at our problem.

Mr. Spiridinov merely lifted his eyebrows. "I have a suggestion. Rather than make a 'production' of your trip to Russia why not go merely as regular American tourists under the 'deluxe' arrangement!"

I was surprised. He seemed to be thinking more like an American than a representative of the inscrutable Kremlin. "What about my camera, taking pictures?"

He faintly smiled. "We Russians expect tourists to take pictures. Whether with kodaks or movie cameras makes no difference."

At that time "deluxe" Intourist tours cost $35 per day per person. Since David was under twelve years of age his rate was reduced by half. The fee entitled us to rooms, meals, cars, chauffeurs, and guides. I spread my contemplated itinerary before him. Before we would reach Russia we were scheduled to visit Portugal and Spain, detour to Tangier and then return to the European continent, to Istanbul via Italy and Greece.

"You'll be covering a lot of territory," was his comment.

"We then want to go from Russia to Finland, so that we can wind up our trip in Iceland, my wife's birthplace. I'd like to be able to travel to your country by ship from Istanbul, through the Black Sea, to Odessa."

For the first time in our interview Mr. Spiridinov showed genuine interest. "An unusual routing, Mr. Linker." He pursed his lips. "We do have steamer connections from Turkey to Odessa. So far as I know if you use that route you'll be the first American tourists to do so."

"If?" I leaned forward. "Is there a problem?"

He shook his head. "Not so far as Russia is concerned. Your problem might be with your own State Department."

"But there's no restriction on travel to Russia right now from the U.S. government."

He smiled. "No, not to *our* country. Unfortunately your government severed diplomatic relations with Bulgaria. If you'll examine your passport you will see, in rather bold print, that American citizens are not permitted to travel to that country. And since our steamer service to Odessa makes a stop at Varna, Bulgaria, I'm afraid you'd have to obtain a special approval from your State Department."

His smile broadened. "And as far as I know such an okay has never been issued by Washington to one of its citizens!"

When I returned to Los Angeles I visited the U. S. Passport Office and, not without misgivings, explained our situation. The agent in charge handed me a pleasant surprise. The week prior to my call had seen the beginning of a "thaw" between the United States and Bulgaria. Recognizing that many European routings, whether by surface or air, had to cross the fringe of Bulgaria, the State Department had at long last decided to make the lot of traveling Americans easier.

Consequently they now stamped into our passports a special permit which allowed us to "transit the territorial waters of Bulgaria."

Despite Mr. Spiridinov's assurances that there would be no delay on our Intourist deluxe tour arrangements, I still kept my fingers crossed. However the details were quickly and smoothly accomplished and we found ourselves on our way by transatlantic airline to Lisbon, Portugal, initial stop on our venture.

A small nation of 9,000,000 people—geographically as large as Indiana—Portugal was, for us, bright, gay, and crammed with a bewildering profusion of color, places to go and things to see, and film that could easily occupy a dozen episodes of "Wonders of the World."

Lisbon and the Linker family took to one another with wide-open arms. Like ancient Rome the Portuguese capital has been built on seven hills. The buildings, ranging from modern downtown edifices and spectacular hotels to pastel-hued homes wandering over hill-and-dale, contrast with the brilliant blue and green background of sea and mountains.

A short distance out of the city is the famous Belém Tower, a breathtaking example of the Manueline style of architecture with suggestions of Moorish influence. Nearby we visited and filmed the Jeronymos monastery and church, with its cloisters.

One of the interesting subjects filmed was the Morrish castle called St. George's which dominates the city. In contrast was the native fish market where we enjoyed watching and filming the "varinas" bargaining over their wares.

Black Horse Square in the lower part of Lisbon, which was rebuilt after the terrible earthquake of 1755 gave us an opportunity to film handsome, classic structures. Getting about the hilly portion of the city became a lark. *Ascensores,* outdoor elevators, carried the three of us including camera gear up steep inclines for less than half a cent per trip.

The scene from these lifts as the city and bay came into view reminded Halla and me of our ride on the cog railway to the top of the mountain overlooking Victoria Peak in Hong Kong during our first round-the-world trip.

A drive along a wide boulevard brought us to Estoril, a fabulous seaside resort some fifteen miles from Lisbon. There were accommodations to suit anyone's purse. Halla and I could not understand why more American tourists had not flocked to this intriguing vacationland.

An experience worth mentioning was our visit to a café frequented by Portuguese where eerie, spine-tingling songs called *"fados"* (meaning fates) are sung in a smoke-filled atmosphere before an audience of intense listeners. The songs, all of which deal with tales of violence and tragedy, are performed with a shuddery realism as though the singers themselves had been personally involved. The men spectators kissed the backs of their hands with loud smacks and sighs of rapture whenever the singer hit an especially fine note.

Our Portuguese visit turned out to be a delightful vacation despite the fact that we were on the go from morning until night shooting hundreds and hundreds of feet of color film and still pictures. Before we left I decided to obtain footage of a Portuguese bullfight. Halla was not sure she would care to watch the sport until I explained that unlike the *corridas* of Spain and Mexico, Portuguese bullfighting was comparatively bloodless.

"The animals are not killed," I told her. "Compared to the fights elsewhere the contests here are rather tame!"

So I thought! We went to a little town near Salvaterra de Magos where an "amateur" meet was scheduled to take place. The arena resembled those of Latin America and Spain. I was allowed to go down to the *barrera* of the arena. David and Halla sat up in the stands on the *sombra,* or shady side, while I got my camera set up in the space behind the five-foot protective barrier where the matadors and his assistants can take refuge if necessary.

While I began to film the activity in the arena itself Halla, using another camera, was obtaining footage of the spectators packing the stadium.

When the first bull came trotting into the arena the crowd went wild. I got close-up shots of the animal as it stood still, taking stock of its situation and we could see that its horns were deliberately blunted. The tips had been cut off. And then it sighted its first opponent, a beautiful, spirited stallion ridden by a horseman picturesquely clad in a costume reminiscent of those worn by South American Gauchos. The bull snorted and charged. The horseman with consummate skill managed to sidestep the attack with less than an inch to spare.

As I filmed the intricate maneuvering of the rider and his animal, performing hair-raising escape after escape from the charges of the infuriated bull, I began to appreciate the skill, daring, and high drama of the Portuguese brand of corrida. Here the odds, definitely, were against the man, not the bull. No matter what happened the bull would not perish. At the end of the contest he would merely be corraled and turned out to pasture. But should the horseman or the following fighters who battled on foot make the slightest mistake, they could expect either instant death or else crippling injuries.

After the rider had demonstrated his equestrian skill he began to place *banderillas* in the fatty hump on the bull's neck. This, while painful to the animal, does not cause lasting injury. The rider placed perhaps six of the bars into the now frustrated bull and then took the crowd's applause and cantered from the arena.

And then into the scene of battle stepped a huge man clad in tight-fitting breeches, white shirt, sash wound around his waist, a small vest-sized jacket, and a woolen Portuguese fisherman's cap with a long tassel. Behind him strode a squad of eight other men similarly attired. They came to a halt, and the giant slowly approached the bull who was standing stock still, eyeing this new development with obvious perplexity.

The man paused and then began to jeer at the bull. Whether or not he used "bull" language I couldn't say. Regardless of what it was, the animal's reaction was immediate and violent. It charged with head lowered and the horns menacing.

I expected to see the man step to one side. Instead he dove over the bull's horns, grabbed the thousand-pound animal around

245

its neck and proceeded to wrestle! For a moment I almost stopped filming this Portuguese version of American rodeo "bull-dogging" and then I continued to furiously grind out footage of this utterly bizarre contest. The bull twisted and turned his neck, flinging the huge man up and down and from side to side like a grotesque stuffed doll. I could not for the life of me see how the man could survive a shaking like that, but survive it he did. After he had demonstrated to the crowd that the bull could not loosen his grip his assistants immediately closed in and subdued the animal by holding it so it couldn't move.

By this time I thought that surely the fight was over. Instead the men suddenly scattered leaving one of them gripping the bull's tail with both hands. The exasperated animal snorted and began to lope around the arena. A door opened and out came a small herd of cows and tame bulls urged by pole-carrying herders. The fighting bull spotted the approaching herd and made a beeline for what he rightly assumed to be refuge. The man who had been dangling from the animal's tail now relinquished his grip and joined the horseman who had previously performed. Both bowed and the crowd cheered.

So this was how bullfighting is accomplished in Portugal. I put a fresh roll of film in my camera and turned to wave at Halla as though to say: "See—I told you a Portuguese bullfight is more comedy than tragedy!"

The next bull was a huge black devil. He took one look at the horseman and decided that he wanted out by simply leaping over the barrier at the opposite side of the arena. I chuckled and relaxed, assuming that he would be chased back into the arena.

A sudden, alarming note from the crowd made me whirl. People were standing up, waving and pointing. Halla and David were both screaming at me. And then I realized what had happened. The bull was evidently circling the arena *behind* the barrier. I didn't wait for him.

I grabbed my camera, heavy tripod and all, and vaulted to the top of the five-foot barrier. Perched on the narrow top rail in a state of precarious balance I suddenly heard the thunder of approaching hoofs and then the bull came into sight.

Instinctively I aimed the camera his way and started to take footage. My right leg happened to be dangling. The bull spotted it. To him I was a target of opportunity and he came charging!

246

Instinctively I pulled up my leg to get it out of harm's way. As the animal roared past, just beneath where I was perched, the camera and heavy tripod completely unbalanced me and I tumbled five feet to the floor of the arena itself, landing with all my weight on my left hip.

For a moment I lost consciousness. When I came to it was to find concerned Portuguese bullfighters helping me to my feet. The bull was now back *inside* the arena and that's where I had fallen. Halla of course had seen all this happen.

My first concern was for my camera. That seemed intact. In response to questions about my condition I shook my head and told them, to the best of my ability, that I was "okay." At the time I merely felt a little soreness where I had landed.

After the last bull-versus-man contest I packed up my gear and rejoined Halla and David. We left the ring and picked up a chauffeur-driven car which was to take us twenty-five miles to the picturesque, walled medieval city of Obidos. There a formidable castle had been converted into a unique hotel with accommodations for only six guests.

As I walked to the waiting car I found myself hobbling. My hip felt as though the socket had run dry. There was no serious pain. I was merely uncomfortable and as we got into the car I told Halla that it would be nice if people had places for lubrication like automobiles. "The way I feel," I commented, "I'd like to stop at a service station and have 'em squirt some grease into my hip!"

It would have been pleasant just to lie down for a rest. Unfortunately the Obidos castle hotel's rooms were in heavy demand. We had been lucky to obtain our accommodations for the night at the last moment. And since Obidos would be an important sequence of our film of Portugal we could not afford to pass up the visit because of a sore hip.

During the drive I joked about my fall. Actually it had its humorous aspect. After all the "American cameraman" was the only casualty to spice the entire program!

But when we finally pulled up to the magnificent entrance of the castle my injury was no longer funny. When I tried to climb out of the car I almost could not move my hip. I finally did manage, at the expense of excruciating pain, to get out of the car.

The entrance to the castle was at the top of a very long and steep flight of stone steps. While Halla and David assumed part of the burden of my gear I took the tripod apart and used one leg as a makeshift cane. By the time we reached our room I was bathed with cold perspiration.

After a sleepless night I continued to hobble laboriously around the castle, using the tripod-leg "cane" as an assist while I filmed it for our program. It was a miserable experience and we were thankful when it was finished and we left the castle with its innumerable steps.

The sight of my left side was enough to give Halla the jitters. From the waist down to the knee it was a massive blue-black in color. I was convinced that nothing had been broken but even so there could have been serious complications. The thought of an enforced hospital stay was as worrisome as the stiffness and pain. If I had to undergo extensive treatment it meant we would have to change the balance of our itinerary. And with the Russians one just does not make itinerary changes, not if one wishes to travel through the U.S.S.R., even as a "deluxe Intourist guest." I had the unhappy feeling that if we did not make our appearance at the properly prescribed time and place the Soviet attitude would be "Sorry—you didn't come as scheduled."

Moving about seemed better than being still. Our next stop, prior to returning to Lisbon, was the quaint fishing village of Nazaré. Halla wanted me to pass up the visit but I felt we should go there and obtain the footage while returning to the Portuguese capital. We spent two days filming at Nazaré.

When we finally got to our Lisbon hotel I obtained the name of an orthopedic specialist and phoned for an appointment for X rays and some sort of alleviating treatment. At the last minute the doctor called to explain that he would have to postpone my examination. He had to leave on an emergency case.

When I hung up I looked at Halla. We were due to leave for Madrid that night on the crack overnight Lusitania Express.

"Let's be on our way to catch the train," I exclaimed.

"But what about your hip, Hal-minn?"

"I'll find a doctor in Madrid."

Although we are firm believers that tourists should try, as often as possible, to stay in "native" hotels so as to fully savor the atmosphere of the country they happen to be visiting I must confess that

I appreciated the modern, air-conditioned luxury of the Castellana Hilton when we finally reached Madrid.

The vast establishment, first of Conrad Hilton's hostelries to be opened in Europe, was mid-twentieth century Americana in the fullest sense. Our accommodations were super-luxurious and the almost instantaneous room service was appreciated, what with that vexatious hip of mine.

The hotel people put me in touch with an excellent doctor. We made an appointment. And then the phone rang again and it was a gentleman named Señor García Loygorri, head of the Spanish National Tourist Office, on the other end of the line.

He was exceedingly friendly and quite enthusiastic about our being in his country. He had a "special agenda" of unusual places for us to see. While I listened I mentally calculated time and distance and tried to fit them into the framework of the two short weeks our over-all itinerary allowed for Spain.

Within the hour we could expect a chauffeur-driven limousine which would take us on a highlighted tour of Madrid itself. The next day we would drive to Pamplona with a "unique" and fascinating detour especially arranged for the Linker family. I thanked Señor García Loygorri and hung up. To Halla I said: "Looks as though I'll have to postpone my appointment with the doctor!"

Still using the tripod as a cane and hobbling with my creaking hip I embarked on our inspection of the Spanish capital. A metropolis of over 1,800,000 population, Madrid combines the spectacular past of the Spanish people with the present electronic and atomic age. Skyscraping buildings were beginning to change the skyline of the city, and to present quite a contrast with the Prado Museum, home of priceless paintings by Goya, Velasquez, Murillo, and El Greco, and the sprawling University City, rebuilt in 1939 after it had been almost completely destroyed during the siege of Madrid in the Spanish Civil War.

The innumerable scenes I had to capture on film made me forget the discomfort of getting in and out of the limousine and moving with my camera from one filming point to another.

At the royal palace, built by Philip V about 1734, I was able to obtain film not only of the celebrated *Guardia Civil* police with their strange, leather helmets but of a passing parade of Spanish marines as well.

Later we visited the celebrated Puerta del Sol, "Gate of the

Sun," which used to be located at the center of Old Madrid, and then drove through the incredibly beautiful Retiro Park, where I took footage of Halla and David strolling through gardens, gazing at the amazing profusion of statues and fountains and tarrying by the banks of postcard picture artificial lakes.

When we returned to the hotel my hip was giving me great torment. I tried to get the doctor but he had already left his office.

The next day we had to be en route to Pamplona via Burgos and El Escorial. En route Señor García Loygorri's "surprise" proved to be a stop in the Valley of the Fallen, a stupendous monument to the dead of the Spanish Civil War erected in the rugged and foreboding Guadarrama mountains.

This incredible and somber edifice, situated some fifty miles from Madrid, had not been entirely completed when we got there. Señor García Loygorri explained that the public had not yet been admitted to the area.

Shaped like a cross the monument towers 492 feet high. The arms of the concrete-and-steel construction are 410 feet above the ground. We were privileged to ride an elevator within the main framework to the summit and then walk inside the hollowed arms for a spectacular view of the valley and mountains, one of the most bloody battlefields of the Spanish Civil War.

Underground, beneath the base of the huge cross is a crypt some 853 feet in length, hewn out of solid rock. Thousands of Spanish war dead are buried here. We were surprised to learn that Generalissimo Francisco Franco, Spanish chief of state, victor of the Civil War, was engaged in a dispute with many of his followers over his desire to include the bodies of the opposing Loyalists in the vast tomb. His contention was that in the final analysis both sides were, after all, comprised of Spaniards. He felt that with the Civil War a generation in the past it was time to forget old wounds and for the nation to spiritually unite.

El Escorial, on the way, also proved to be a photogenic place of over twelve acres of magnificent architecture dominated by the huge monastery-palace built by Philip II which houses the tombs of Spain's kings.

Segovia was next, with its Alcázar, a tremendous castle-fortress which sits on a hill and looks like a scene from one of Hans Christian Andersen's fairy tales. Halla and David both instantly noted its resemblance to the type of castle favored by Walt Disney.

In the narrow, old-fashioned streets of the village lying at the foot of the Alcázar we filmed colorfully costumed people—girls in swirling skirts, men wearing soft slippers secured by ribbons wound around their ankles—dancing the *jota*, a gay Spanish folk dance.

Our arrival at Pamplona was timed to coincide with the annual fiesta of San Fermín. Originally a walled city, Pamplona has mushroomed to a city whose population is normally 85,000 but during the time of the fiesta, is increased to almost twice as much by visitors from all over the world.

An incredible celebration was the Pamplona show. People sing, feast, and dance, morning, noon, and all night long, to the playing of special turbulent music which seems to contain touches of Moorish melody, gypsy airs and Castilian folk songs, as well as Basque airs.

During the opening phases of the incredible fiesta we were thrilled by the unique parade of effigies, almost two stories high, made of wicker. Called *gigantones*, the figures purportedly represent King Ferdinand and Queen Isabella who originally made it possible for Christopher Columbus to "discover" America, plus courtiers, Moors, and medieval Spanish knights.

Each of the figures is "powered" by a perspiring man who bears the load of the towering structure by means of a special harness arrangement. The procession is paced by shrilling flute music and the syncopated beating of drums from northern Spain. The overall effect of the music, the nodding, swaying motions of these grotesque figures is rather overpowering. Every now and then they paused and performed the steps of a minuet to the gleeful pleasure of the celebrating populace!

However the high spot of Pamplona's fiesta is the "running of the bulls," called "the Encierro."

This formidable event takes place every morning of the six-day long fiesta. Bulls scheduled to fight in the afternoon corridas at the bull ring are permitted to run through specially barricaded streets which lead them to the arena.

Centuries ago the custom began when the people of Pamplona celebrated the anniversary of the transferring of relics of San Fermín from an old to a new chapel. A procession of bulls was included and the animals used to follow a mounted standard bearer. All Spaniards (as, incidentally, most Mexicans) consider themselves matadors. In the old days young villagers used to follow behind the processional bulls to demonstrate their bravery. In their enthusiasm they would sometimes prod the fierce animals with sharp sticks.

Occasionally the goaded bulls would charge into the horse carrying the standard-bearer, or the boys in their enthusiasm would "accidentally" prod the horseman. In the year 1717 the Pamplona authorities called a halt to this custom, simply by eliminating the mounted standard-bearer.

Since then the procession has changed from a religious pageant to a wild mob scene where, at the crack of dawn, crowds of young men throng the barricaded streets and wait to run with the bulls.

David, Halla and I were up at 5:30 the first morning. Our vantage point was the second-story balcony of a private home near our hotel, La Perla. I barely had time to get my camera set when we heard a loud explosion and a mighty shout, immediately followed by the growing thunder of approaching, galloping hoofs.

The next instant the red-eyed animals poured like an avalanche down the street just below the balcony. Boys and men ran ahead of them, but the animals often overtook them and many of the runners simply tumbled beneath the plunging sea of bulls. David and Halla blanched. I ground away with my camera but the sight and sound reminded me of my experience in the Portuguese arena and my hip seemed to get worse all of a sudden.

After the flood of animals and humans had passed, careening through the streets toward the arena, we almost dreaded to look down below, fearing that we would find nothing but trampled, mutilated corpses. There were a few casualties, but all were ambulatory. Clothing was dusty and torn and several bled from various bruises. But their expressions were those of pleasurable excitement and as I watched they variously hobbled, limped, or ran after the insane cavalcade.

The next day we visited the arena in order to obtain footage of what happened when the arriving swarm of bulls and people erupted from the street, through a special opening, into the bullfight arena. To say that the scene was spectacular is to put it mildly.

The precipitate arrival of the flood of men and boys is not the end of it. After the bulls have been driven by experienced handlers into special pens the same young men who had engaged in the marathon race now enter in a "corrida" with certain small cows.

Since the horns of these animals are blunted the action is slap-stick comedy from start to finish.

The crowds of boys and men use jackets and coats as matador capes or else whistle, wave their arms, wave handkerchiefs, and in many cases, grab the animal's tail. One after another the boys play matador only to find themselves taken for a ride on the head and blunted horns of the charging bull. The culmination of these "fights," so much like the Portuguese version, generally consisted of a swarm of humans grabbing the creature by the horns, tail and body and ushering it out of the arena.

The "free city" of Tangier (now part of Morocco) is a mere three hours by air from Madrid. We arrived there to find that it is an entirely different world.

Sprawled along the shores of the Bay of Tangier the metropolis fronts on both the Atlantic and Mediterranean owing to a spur of the bulging North African coastline.

From our spacious and luxurious accommodations in the Moor-ish Hotel El Minzah we could view the ocean on our left, the Strait of Gibraltar to our right and, dead ahead, a vague smudge on the horizon which denoted the presence of Europe.

A community noted for smuggling pursuits since the days of the Roman Empire, Tangier was in the process of becoming modern-ized. Broad thoroughfares jammed with glittering new American and European cars plus towering office buildings and apartment houses indicated that the mysterious and glamorous North Africa was in the process of conforming to the inexorable laws of change.

Three languages, Spanish, French, and Arabic, shared equal im-portance. All street signs were trilingual. The population was as polyglot as the languages would indicate in both nationality and dress.

While most of the people we observed in the new section wore European clothing we found many men wearing the ubiquitous fez while most of the Moslem women wore *djellabas*, robes which covered them from head to toe save for the eyes.

Unlike the *burkahs* of Pakistan, the *djellaba* does not cover the face itself. Instead the women wear a black or white veil which be-gins at a point starting at the bridge of the nose and extending down over the chin. This means that their long-lashed dark eyes peer directly at passers-by.

Since Moslem women never expose their faces to strangers, especially non-believers, I could only assume that each pair of glittering, mascaraed orbs which were curiously cast in our direction undoubtedly belonged to a beauty such as Omar Khayyám might have had in his mind when he discoursed in the *Rubaiyat*.

The visit to the Sultan's palace took us from today directly back through the centuries to the days when Tangier groaned under the absolute despotism of those free-booting potentates.

Although the furniture, jewels, and armor on display do not represent a tenth of the original wealth and treasure there was still enough there to show the glories of those olden days.

In the courtyard of the palace we encountered an elderly snake charmer wearing a white turban and dark blue robe. Assisted by an emaciated flute player the charmer produced a non-poisonous but quite large serpent to which he promptly offered his nose and tongue to bite!

While we took pictures the snake bit away, and droplets of blood could be seen after each bite.

Then, muttering singsong incantations in Arabic the charmer produced some straw and pretended to wipe the droplets away with the straw. As I moved in for a close-up shot, he held the straw before his lips and began to blow. Suddenly a slight wisp of smoke appeared. The next instant the smoke thickened and the straw burst into flame. With a triumphant expression as though to say "Eureka!" he dropped the burning straw at our feet!

He implied that it was the snake's venom which had ignited under the spell of his magic and that the blood drawn by the snake's fangs had supplied the fuel. Halla daintily expressed distaste for the entire display, magical or otherwise.

Our stay here which extended for three days had to include a visit to the famous Casbah. Actually there are casbahs—originally the old fortified sections—in all large North African cities. However Charles Boyer and Hedy Lamarr had endowed all casbahs with an overwhelmingly romantic atmosphere in the motion picture titled *Algiers*. While playing the role of Pepe Le Moko, he had hoarsely, passionately whispered to beautiful Hedy, "Co-o-ooome weeeth meee, to thuh Kahs-bah!"

Oddly enough I have heard that Mr. Boyer swears up and down that he had never uttered any such line in the picture, which had

254

been filmed in 1938. Whether he did or not, the casbah remark has ever since been attributed to him.

We had for a guide a young member of the Tangier Tourist Department named Ahmed Mechnin. He had a lively interest in everything we did, including how I went about filming our sequences.

When I explained that it would be necessary to obtain co-operation of native, veiled women to pose while we were in the Casbah, Ahmed shrugged. The Moslem religion frowned upon women posing for photographs, particularly those taken by non-believers!

This was the first time I had actually encountered the taboo. And then I had a brainstorm. Why not dress Halla in one of the djellabas! The hood would hide her golden hair and the veil would disguise her fair complexion. It would be a good sequence, since the audience wouldn't know at first who she was, then she could unveil.

While Ahmed followed us, shaking his head and obviously brooding, I obtained the proper costume for my wife at a small shop and also procured a typical Arab boy's dress, complete with fez, for David.

When we reached a spot in the teeming, narrow Casbah which I felt had "typical" color I set up my camera and we were "on location." It was getting quite dark, so I used a special fast color film.

Ghostlike native women and turbaned and fezzed men passed us, eyeing us with curiosity. Ahmed nervously hovered in the background, occasionally bestirring himself to shoo away native children who, like curious small fry everywhere, had gathered to watch what was taking place.

No one gave Halla and David a second glance, or so I thought. Their disguises were perfect. In fact they were *too* perfect. I was in the midst of filming when a patriarchal old man entered the scene, stopped short, glared at us and then excitedly accosted Halla.

For a moment I stared with astonishment. The old boy—he must have been past seventy—waved his arms and poured forth a torrent of Arabic. He was obviously upset. David looked frightened and Halla's eyes were wide with bewilderment and growing apprehension.

255

I turned to Ahmed. "What's going on?" I demanded. "Are we starting a jihad—a religious war, or something?"

By this time a crowd of robed figures was gathering. It was growing dark and the atmosphere was ominous—or so it seemed to me.

Ahmed moved into the breach and tried to reason with the old man—but to no avail. He turned and hurried to my side. "We better leave, M'sieu Linker. He thinks your wife is Moslem and he is scolding her for posing!"

One look at his face and I knew he was not just putting on an act. I dismounted the camera, grabbed Halla and David, and hurried them away from the considerable crowd of spectators.

When we emerged from the Casbah, Halla had removed her veil. She was looking at me with a broad smile.

"Would you mind telling me what seems to be so funny, my dear?" I asked.

"Not funny, Hal-minn," she laughed. "I was just smiling because what I saw made me happy."

"What, for heaven's sake?"

"You're no longer limping!"

For a moment I stared at her and then I began to smile with her. In the excitement the stiffness of my injured hip seemed to have magically vanished. Although the bruise remained for a long time afterward the pain was almost completely gone. It was then a month after the injury.

Chapter Twenty-One

"The Greeks Had
A Word for It"

BEAUTIFULLY DECORATED in Turkish *décor*, the Istanbul Hilton Hotel, overlooking the Bosporus strait, which divides Europe from Asia Minor, is a glittering citadel of mid-twentieth-century luxury.

As we sat in our room which gave us a view of the Black Sea, I wondered what the old Romans, the medieval crusaders and, later, the conquering Ottomans would feel if they could return and gaze at this hotel.

Suleiman the Magnificent, who reigned here in the seventeenth century, at the height of the power of the Ottoman Empire, dwelled in what was then inconceivable luxury. An army of servants were at his beck and call. He had but to raise his hand and the treasures, fruits, and delicacies of a dozen lands were immediately available.

When I mused aloud about this to Halla she smiled. "We have more magic and power than even Suleiman had."

I blinked. "How so?"

"That telephone—and the hotel management," she said. "Pick it up and ask for room service—and within minutes we can have anything we want!"

It was, of course, true. The maître d'hôtel of the glass-enclosed night club had told us factually, rather than boastfully, that the Istanbul Hilton, catering to an amazing cross-section of cosmopolites has frequently been called upon to provide—hardly with reasonable advance warning—articles and services ranging from the unattainable to the impossible. And mostly via the room-service phone method.

"And are you able to comply?" I asked.

"To date our score has been 98 per cent," he replied.

Seated in our room I remembered that conversation and thought how fantastically magic our life would seem to Suleiman or even the fictional Aladdin who only had a magic lamp to rub. We are inclined to take our modern miracles for granted.

A magic carpet? I gazed at the stacks of more than 150 rolls of exposed color motion-picture film which I was in the process of identifying and packing, prior to shipping them back to the United States for developing.

It marked the modern magic of communication. After our return to Los Angeles I would edit the films, prepare narration, and then, by means of the electronic miracle of television, I would be able to share what Halla, David, and I had experienced with millions of people who, because of circumstances, rarely if ever got the opportunity to travel beyond the confines of their home towns.

A magic carpet? Ours was the "carpet" of airliners which had shrunk by more than 5000 per cent the girth of the world of Suleiman's era.

Should I desire to instantly dissolve the barriers of space? The quiet telephone cradled at my elbow could instantly connect us with Halla's parents in Iceland or friends in Japan, India, London, the United States. And as I reflected on all of this I once again offered humble, silent thanks for the wonderful life we had been permitted to lead. It was hard, exacting, sometimes nerve-wracking —this traipsing around the world—but the primary reward was the fact that the three of us could constantly be together, sharing the thrills, delights, and sometimes, chills of our family venture.

I gazed at the identification on one stack of exposed film: "Tangier—Gibraltar—Spain" and instantly highlights came crowding back to mind——

After our trip to the Casbah we had taken the ferry which plies between Gibraltar and Tangier—a four-hour crossing of the strait that separates Europe from Africa.

At the halfway point of the crossing the three of us had the thrill of being able to look in one direction and see the North African shoreline and then turn our heads to gaze at the looming European mass of the 1400-foot Rock of Gibraltar, known in the world of two thousand years ago as the Pillars of Hercules.

We rented a carriage and visited the city of Gibraltar which lies on the western slope of the promontory, facing the Bay of Gibraltar. After that we took a taxi and rode to the summit of the huge rock which, although famous to the world as a bastion of British might, is probably even more known to Americans as the trade mark used by a prominent insurance company.

Although in this age of nuclear weapons the Gibraltar fortifications, dug out of solid rock and reinforced by steel and concrete, are probably as useful as boulder-hurling catapults and bows and arrows, we could realize during our visit why the towering escarpment enabled the British to effectively seal off the Mediterranean during two world wars and make it indeed, for the Union Jack, "Mare Nostrum."

Visiting Gibraltar we found that the British military was maintaining the base with unswerving spit-and-polish regardless of whether jet bombers and hydrogen warhead-equipped missiles made the entire affair obsolete. Consequently it was frankly humorous, by virtue of amazing contrast, to be confronted by the bright-eyed, unpredictable, and mischievous Barbary apes, original garrison of "The Rock."

We ran into these inquisitive creatures near the top. A regimental sergeant-major who happened to be near by told us that, "the blighters are bloody awful nuisances sometimes but one generally gets used to them."

The legend has it that as long as there are Barbary apes on Gilbraltar, Britain will remain in control. During the worst of two world wars more than passing interest was expressed by both worried allies and hopeful enemies as to the ape population. Were they disappearing or were they remaining in full strength?

A somewhat apocryphal story claims that during World War II the apes started to die out due to starvation caused by lack of food donations by visiting tourists. At any rate (so the story goes) the British, cognizant of the legend, quietly recruited Barbary ape replacements from their original habitat in North Africa. If this is true, then the Axis counter-intelligence must certainly have been asleep at the switch.

Be that as it may, when I filmed the Gibraltar apes both they— and the British—were very much in strength, as the two have been for some 250 years, ever since the Union Jack first was hoisted over the Rock in 1704.

The Spanish border was "across the line." Since our trail would lead back through Spain to Italy and Greece before reaching Turkey for a pause prior to beginning our Russian adventure, we hired another taxi and were driven an absurdly short distance to the little border town of La Linea. On the British Gibraltar Crown Colony side we had to unload our gear and hand-carry it through Spanish customs (meanwhile declaring ourselves to Spanish *Inmigración*) to the chauffeur-driven automobile which awaited us. Although the atmosphere on the Gibraltar-Spanish border is fairly amiable, Spanish commercial vehicles are not allowed into the Crown Colony.

Although Franco's officials were painstakingly thorough in their search of our baggage and credentials they were polite, and quick about it. Within reasonable time we were speeding toward romantic Granada.

Along the route we noticed frequent patrols of soldiery. When we paused for fuel in a small town we had to pass another military "check." The officer in charge told us via our driver who spoke a passable English that "we weren't suspect." It was merely an "old Spanish custom" resulting from the days when bands of gypsies used to rove from one area to another, sometimes "liberating" possessions and livestock while en route.

It was on the tip of my tongue to point out that the modern-day gypsies were not only a decided minority but a long ways from their old, nomadic habits. Could there be a political undertone to this constant and cold-eyed scrutiny of travelers and their credentials?

And then the driver volunteered the information that this town was named San Roque.

During my youth, as a student at Georgetown University's School of Foreign Service, I studied Spanish for four years. Constantly drilled into me was the suggestion that to properly sound the Spanish letter R I should repeat to myself a little ditty which happened to contain a lot of words with that letter in them.

The ditty, as taught to me in college, was: *"El perro de San Roque no tiene rabo, porque Ramón Rámirez se lo ha robado."*

Hearing the name of San Roque instantly triggered my memory. To Halla and David's surprise I smiled and launched into the ditty.

When I finished I stood there, waiting for the officer to nod and return my smile. Instead his forehead gathered in a frown and his eyes grew icy, he seemed about to lose his temper. Our driver visibly paled. The smile on my lips wavered and then faded.

The officer closed our passports, seemed to hesitate for a moment, and shoved them into my hand. He curtly said: *"Pase,"* nodding to the road leading ahead and then turned and stalked into his office.

When we re-entered the car and the driver put it into motion I leaned forward: "Why did the officer get so angry when I spoke that little ditty?"

He shook his head. "Oh señor—I was very frightened—You realize these men, they live here in San Roque. You know what you say to them?"

"I said that 'The dog of San Roque doesn't have a tail because Ramón Rámirez stole it from him!' That's what they taught me in school in America. What's so terrible about that?"

Our driver turned his attention from the road and gave me a pitying look. "Oh señor—I fear they taught it just a little bit—" he made a gesture with thumb and forefinger—*"un poco diferente.* The original way says: 'The dog of San Roque hasn't got a tail because the people of San Roque stole it from him.' That means everyone used to say that from San Roque are only thieves!"

My jaw dropped. "B-but——"

"And these officers, being of San Roque, they think you know the old way, that everyone would be afraid to say to their face, and you just changed it a little bit."

I sat back and decided then and there that I would never again use any of those so-called language-training gambits I had received in college.

Granada, beautiful and romantic city where America's Washington Irving once lived and wrote his *Tales of the Alhambra,* offered to our eyes and my camera the magnificent Alhambra itself, one of the most splendid examples of Moorish architecture in all of Spain.

Completed after more than one hundred years of construction in 1354 A.D., the breath-taking buildings with its fabulous courtyards, exquisite mosaics, delicate tracery of columns and arches, and musical fountains fell into disrepair after the Spaniards, under Isabella and Ferdinand, won their freedom from the Moors.

To illustrate the former glory of the palace the story was told us that after the Moorish king, Boabdil, had to flee the Alhambra following the defeat of his army in battle, he turned back for a last look at his palace. Tears clouded his eyes and he began to sob.

His mother, who must have been a doughty person, is reputed to have said to him: "Don't cry like a woman—for what you could not defend like a man!"

We could sympathize with Boabdil after exploring the Alhambra. When Washington Irving first visited the Alhambra early in the nineteenth century he waged a one-man campaign, by means of his famous *Tales of the Alhambra* against the indifference of the Spanish Monarchy to the crumbling decay of this splendid monument. His literary efforts had the desired effect. Restoration was begun and today the Alhambra has been partially restored to its original splendor.

The rest of our trip through Spain had been a kaleidoscope of vivid color, sights, sounds. Sitting in the air-conditioned room at the Istanbul Hilton I recalled to Halla our visit to Seville—the amazing Hotel Alfonso XIII, the 400-foot Giralda Tower, built by the Spaniards after the Moors had been ousted from Spain, the groves of ripening oranges.

(Incidentally these oranges, grown in the streets by the city of Seville, are shipped almost exclusively to England for the manufacture of marmalade).

Since both Halla and I love grand opera we had to make a pilgrimage of sorts to the very cigar factory which Bizet used as a setting for his fiery heroine Carmen. From the factory we went to the Seville bull ring. Although it was shut down that day we could use our imagination and picture the stirring pageantry of the opera's conclusion which takes place between Carmen and Don José just outside while within Escamilio, the matador, triumphantly received the corrida audience's plaudits.

There was one other experience in Seville before we went on to Madrid where we boarded a plane for Italy. It was a rather personal one—for me. Before we left the "city of Carmen" I went to a barber. Halla manipulated the camera and took motion picture film of me satisfying a zany ambition—I was actually getting a haircut from "The Barber of Seville!"

On the next group of containers of exposed film I wrote: Naples, Pompeii, Sorrento, Athens——

When dictator Benito Mussolini had seized power in Italy, thereby miscasting that nation's volatile but essentially artistic people in the role of militarists, his hard-core followers always offered, as a sort of *raison d'être* for his fascistic regime: "Il Duce made the trains run on time in Italy."

The *rapido* express trains which whisked us from Rome to Naples was not only on time but an extremely comfortable and fast express.

That harbor city, situated on the bay and overshadowed by Mount Vesuvius, looked to the three of us like a vast picture setting for a tremendous light opera. From our window in the Hotel Royal we could look out over the harbor of Santa Lucia and watch the fishing smacks coming home to their moorings there.

Dominating Santa Lucia itself is the Castel dell 'Uovo—"Castle of the Egg." In the soft sunset we could hear snatches of song and instrumental music from boatmen and the various restaurants and sidewalk cafes.

When we went for a leisurely rowboat tour of Santa Lucia and the larger harbor our boatman, a thin, wiry Neapolitan who was in his late fifties reminisced about the fighting of World War II.

He himself had lost members of his family, many friends, under bombardment and during the vicious house-to-house fighting that took place later. He pointed to Vesuvius and, by means of his broken English and gestures, told us how, in the height of the campaign, it had erupted. Evidently it had taken some time for the Neapolitans to realize that the flame and rumbling of the old volcano signified that it was restless. Man's self-made eruption of shattering shellfire, aerial bombardment, and concussive explosions had overshadowed those of nature.

Pompeii, at the foot of 3900-foot Mount Vesuvius, was for us an eerie interlude. Despite the fact that the convulsion which destroyed the entire Roman city happened in the year 79 A.D., the imprint of that tragedy seemed to remain like a tangible thing. The effect was that of a recent holocaust rather than something which took place 1879 years in the remote past.

Perhaps it was the visible traces of old Pompeii which have been excavated on all sides. And, too, the museum with its mummified remains of victims, trapped by the volcano's gases, ashes, and lava flow, gave us the sensation of being surrounded by the aftermath of contemporary disaster rather than ancient catastrophe.

When we left to drive south to Sorrento, Halla, gazing with a brooding expression at the towering silhouette of the volcano, remarked: "Isn't it strange, Hal-minn. The war in Naples I know was a thousand times more destructive of life and property. Yet I feel more affected by what had happened to Pompeii." She looked at me. "Why is that, I wonder?"

It was a question I had been asking myself. I had personally experienced modern warfare. Yet the place had given me a similar feeling. "Perhaps," I slowly replied, "it is because war is, after all, man-made therefore, conceivably, man-preventable, if I can coin such a phrase. On the other hand an eruption, such as that which wiped out Pompeii, is a reminder of the unimaginable fury and force of nature itself. In spite of what we have invented and accomplished we are still as helpless as children when Mother Earth goes on a rampage. Pompeii is a reminder of how frail humanity really is."

The famous Amalfi Drive, cut into the hillsides fronting on the Tyrrhenian Sea, turned out to be a sun-drenched adventure in scenic beauty. Below us unfolded a continuous tapestry of coves, inlets, and small, picturesque fishing villages.

It was on this spectacular, winding road that we encountered the gay, sporting Romans who bow before the altar of the great God of Speed. Just as Spaniards and Latin Americans worship bullfighting, so Italians render homage to automobile racing. This is not too surprising. Italy's great houses of Ferrari, Maserati, Lancia, Alfa Romeo, and Fiat have, since the birth of the internal-combustion, reciprocating, piston-driven engine, produced most of the world's finest racing and touring-road thoroughbreds.

Road racing with sports cars and Grand Prix events featuring contests between single-seater outright racing cars constitute Italy's most popular form of spectator sport. Crowds of a size incomprehensible to American sports followers will line the course of the annual Mille Miglia, one of auto racing's most deadly contests from the aspect of participant and spectator fatalities and injuries. A turnout of 150,000 spectators to watch a weekend road race is commonplace.

The nice thing about the Spanish and Latin-American love of

Lisbon's Tower of Belem, Portugal.

Portuguese country
dancers.

Gypsies of Granada, Spain.

The Alcazar, famous castle of Segovia, Spain.

Segovia.

Boy dancer in Tangier casbah restaurant balances tray during dance.

Davey and some of his Greek Army Evzone friends. Athens, Greece.

At the Golden Horn, Istanbul, Turkey.

Russian guards marching to Lenin and Stalin's tomb in Red Square.

Famous big bell inside the Kremlin in Moscow.

In front of St. Basil's Cathedral in Red Square, Moscow, Russia.

The fan mail on our first anniversary on television thrilled us.

bullfighting is that the hazards of that sport, with the exception of Pamplona's "bull-run" is contained within arenas. Only the adversaries are exposed to disaster (with the possible exception of overly ambitious cinematographers, of course). Otherwise bullfight *aficionados* never practice that dangerous sport with animals on highways or side streets.

Not so in Italy. Everyone, from putt-putt motorcycle riders on up to the wealthy seated behind the controls of a $15,000 Ferrari sports coupe, considers himself—or herself—a born race driver, sharp of eye, unerring of judgment, and steeped in the lore of acceleration, gear shifting and "cornering" (navigating turns).

On the Amalfi Drive we discovered that Italian motorists cannot abide to be passed. Consequently we found ourselves in the midst of a dozen and one races. Our driver, evidently accustomed to frightened American passengers, wisely refrained from accepting challenge after challenge. But the others—that was something to watch.

At one point we heard a distant horn blaring behind us. We looked back to see a sleek, low, red-snouted coupe appear at least half a mile back. There was a crescendoing scream of engine and gears and then the car flashed past us like a crimson blur to take a sharp curve, almost literally sideways, with screaming tires, before disappearing.

I asked our chauffeur: "What was that?"

His face wore an enraptured, almost dreamy expression. "Ferrari, signore. The finest, the most magnificent, the greatest—!" He punctuated his statement with a shoulder-raising sigh.

As we followed "the finest, most magnificent, and greatest" around the same curve it was to come face to face with two tiny Fiat sedans, headed in the opposite direction, as they came racing one another.

On one side was a sheer drop, on the other a rising escarpment. Before I could so much as gasp, our driver, with sheer virtuosity, casually drove between the "contestants."

"Do people always drive this way here?" I finally asked.

"*Si*, signore." He glanced at me as though to say: "Don't people drive that way everywhere?"

Halla reminded me that drivers on Los Angeles's incredible network of freeways went almost as fast.

"Not with the same abandon, Elskan-mín," I answered. "If the traffic cops at home had to cope with these Romans our boys in blue would spend more time on psychiatrists' couches than patrolling on motorcycles."

Our trip from Naples to Piraeus, seaport of Athens, was actually a vacation interlude with a slight smattering of work.

Our vessel was the *Olympia*, a large, luxury cruise ship of the Greek Line. We set sail in a delightfully relaxed holiday mood during late afternoon and cruised over the rippling, "wine-colored" Tyrrhenian Sea—this time seeing Italy's coast with its fishing villages and the flashing, gleaming "race cars" of the Amalfi Drive rendered buglike by distance. Beautiful Capri, fabled island of enchantment, which lies almost opposite Sorrento, was a tantalizing blur just off our bow as the *Olympia* leisurely ploughed southeastward through gathering night toward the toe of boot-shaped Italy.

Early next morning found us navigating through the Strait of Messina which separates the island of Sicily from the Italian mainland. On a map Italy resembles a fullback's foot about to kick a ball which is Sicily.

In Homeric legend this strait was the abode of the monsters Scylla and Charybdis who plagued Ulysses. The "monsters" in reality were whirlpools and rocks which caused many ancient Greek, Roman and, later, Venetian and Genoan galleys to founder.

The *Olympia*, barely bothering to flex its mighty turbine-engine sinews, glided through the straits, passing beneath a high, arching power cable stretching from the mainland to the city of Messina.

Our ship tarried there just long enough for us to note that Messina, like Naples, has almost completely repaired the damage of World War II. From the promenade deck we could see, rising in the distance like a helmeted warrior, the snow-capped peak of Sicily's 10,741-foot Mount Etna. Looking across the straits, to the southeast, we could just barely discern the city of Reggio Calabria lying on the coast of the Italian mainland.

The balance of the voyage to Piraeus saw us completely surrender to the creature comforts of downy, sleep-inducing beds, swimming the *Olympia*'s pool, participating in deck games and eating much too often.

The delightful sailing interlude had lulled us into a blissful

266

contentment, a conviction that all was well with the world. This delightful feeling was enhanced when our ship negotiated the water traffic in Piraeus Harbor and after the usual "business" of mooring tied up at the dock.

Nor was it dispelled when a neatly attired young man of the Greek Tourist Office boarded the ship to extend an official welcome to his country and at the same time "facilitate" the clearance of our belongings through Greek Customs.

Before we had boarded the *Olympia* at Naples I had been instructed to label all of our baggage with the initial of our last name. The steamship-line official there had explained that after we docked at Piraeus our baggage would be taken ashore where, after clearing Greek immigration, we would identify it in the section reserved for last names beginning with the letter L, and have porters carry it for us to the customs office.

Standing on deck, awaiting our turn to debark, I spotted our baggage already in place at the prescribed location on the dock. Our young friend from the tourist office was working his official "magic" with the customs officers. The time came for us to walk down the gangplank onto Grecian soil. Without a care in the world we came to the place where I had seen our baggage.

Halla stopped short. "Hal," she looked worried. "Two of our suitcases are missing."

"Impossible," I exclaimed. "I saw them a moment ago from the deck—counted 'em in fact." I paused and checked. She was right. The two suitcases containing her clothing were gone.

We began to search the piles and heaps of other baggage laid out according to the alphabetical system. There were a thousand passengers on the *Olympia*. Most of them were Greek citizens returning from visits throughout the world. Many of them, too many of them in fact, had last names beginning with L. And since this unique system of "find your own bag and grab" meant that there was no way for anyone connected with either the steamship company or customs to determine whether or not a passenger had claimed his own or someone else's possessions, it meant that I got absolutely nowhere during the ensuing, two-hour search.

Our contentment had well-nigh disappeared by the time we realized that until, or unless, we found the missing luggage all that my wife had to wear was the dress on her back at the time.

And when, finally, we started to go through customs with the rest of our gear, the last vestige of our earlier good humor was replaced by mounting exasperation.

The young man from the Tourist Office stood by with a hopeless and apologetic expression while a cold-eyed customs officer arbitrarily ordered every bit of our luggage to be opened for inspection. We watched while he ploughed through our belongings as though he had had a tip-off that we were trying to smuggle contraband.

The weather was no longer velvety mild. It was downright hot and the office was confining. Furthermore we were irritated by the unexpected picayunishness of the inspector and upset by the mounting worry that Halla's entire wardrobe, which included a formal gown to be worn during our visit to Iceland later on, would be irretrievably lost.

The inspector let out an exclamation which, translated from Greek to English, undoubtedly meant: "Ah-hah!"

He had just seen my camera equipment and many rolls of film.

He began to jabber away, meanwhile grabbing up a large book of what obviously were regulations. Our Tourist Office man protested. The two argued. I cleared my throat.

"Can I enter this debate or is it a private matter?"

Our friend (angry as I was I could not help feeling sorry for him) turned an almost agonized face my way. "He is insisting that you will have to pay $3,000 duty in order to bring in your cameras and film!"

For a moment I could only stare. In my pocket I had letters from the Greek government officially giving us preferred "guest" status, explaining to all and sundry why we were visiting Greece, how our films would benefit the country. My face must have mirrored my mounting wrath because Halla, who had been watching, touched by arm.

I took a deep breath, produced the letters, and gave them to my Tourist Office ally. "Here," I tried to keep my voice calm. "Official letters of introduction, in Greek and English, explaining everything."

The inspector gingerly took the letters and skimmed over them. His expression was plainly skeptical. When he finished, he shrugged and returned them. His attitude was clear: it made no difference. Either I would pay a customs fee to clear my equipment or it would remain on the dock, undoubtedly without protection, in the section reserved for unfortunates whose last names begin with L— like Linker!

By now we had spent the better part of one and a half hours in this futile, seesaw debate. It seemed perfectly hopeless. I was on the point of throwing up my arms and paying the unwarranted fee. And then, abruptly, our friend and the inspector reached an agreement.

The former turned to me. "This is what must be done," he said, perspiration pouring down his face. "In your passport you will please allow me to write down the name, description and number of every bit of camera equipment you are bringing in!"

Without a word I produced my passport, took cameras, lenses, filters, rolls of unexposed film and watched him laboriously record everything on a complete page, in Greek. When he finished, the inspector rechecked everything he had written down. Then, and only then, did he grudgingly permit us to repack our remaining baggage and photographic equipment and depart from his domain.

Athens is too magnificent a country for even a petty, shrewish minor bureaucrat to spoil. Banishing the inspector to the limbo of memory we set about visiting and filming the "glory that was Greece." And glorious it not only was but still is.

Most spectacular was the Parthenon, finished in 437 B.C., which crowns the rocky hill of the Acropolis dominating Athens. Also in the vicinity of the Parthenon we were able to film the Erechtheum with the statuesque caryatids supporting its porchlike structure. The Temple of Nike (Victory), Temple of Theseus, one of Athen's best preserved classic structures, the Temple of Zeus, the Chapel of St. George on Lycabettus Hill and Hadrian's Arch left us with permanently enriched memories.

Our Tourist Office friend took us to the American College where we found both Greek and American instructors. Professor Demetrios Manos, a fascinating person, specialized in philology, the structure of language, as it pertained to classic Greek. Dr. John E. Hall, an American, was Chairman of the Department of English.

A senior student, Othon Athanassiou, undertook to accompany us on several of our explorations. He it was who called our attention to one of the Corinthian columns, some fifty-six feet high, in the Temple of Zeus. "In the Middle Ages a monk, doing penitence, lived on the top of that column for twelve years," he commented.

You may rest assured that I obtained footage of the site of what possibly was the first flagpole sitting venture ever known.

Othon explained the principle, known as "entasis," which the classic Greeks used when they erected the Parthenon. He pointed out how the columns not only taper toward the top but actually lean slightly toward one another, to create the illusion that they are perfectly straight. All of them had a slight convexity midway between top and bottom, and the corner columns were a bit thicker than the rest.

During all this time we thoroughly enjoyed our work and would have had a perfectly marvelous time had it not been for our worry about Halla's missing baggage.

The Tourist Office and the management of the Heraklion Hotel where we were headquartering persisted in a search which, conducted in a city of half a million people, seemed hopeless on the fact of it.

And then, after we had returned from witnessing and filming a presentation of *The Thesmophoriazusae*, a comedy by Aristophones, in the spectacular theater, the Odeon of Herodes Atticus, we found a happy message.

A lieutenant of the Greek Army had called during our absence. It seemed that he had been on the dock, waiting for his fiancée who had been returning from a visit to the United States. Since her last name began with L and her baggage somewhat resembled that of Halla's he had inadvertently taken off with it.

The very next day we arranged a meeting. The young officer, a handsome chap, was profusely apologetic about the mix-up. We were so happy to get her wardrobe back that we began to regard it as a humorous situation, to be related as a "remember-when" anecdote later on.

During our conversation he grew interested in what we were doing. At his suggestion we made official application for permission to film the Evzones, the fabled elite troops whose billowing, ballet-dancer type of dress uniform thoroughly belies their efficiency and bravery as fighters.

The officers and men gladly paraded for us, first in their truly ornate dress uniforms (a comparison can be made with the kilted Scottish troops, the "Ladies from Hell" who wear kilts). Later they put on a drill, this time in field kit, which made them look entirely different and grimly competent.

270

When the time came to leave Athens, this time by air for Istanbul, we really hated to say good-bye. We drove to the airport and I joked with the youth from the Tourist Office. "At least we're leaving by plane, not by sea. I won't be seeing our recalcitrant friend in customs at the Piraeus dock!"

He smiled and nodded. "That was difficult, wasn't it. But at the airport, all you do is tell customs you're taking out of Greece what you brought in and show them what's written in your passport. There'll be no more trouble, I assure you." He winked at Halla. "At the airport the customs men are more—shall we say—modern, in tune with the times? Besides, your plane doesn't leave for more than an hour."

At the airport the customs inspector "in tune with the times" stared at my equipment and then studied and restudied my passport in which had been laboriously listed each and every item. He looked at our friend and said something, meanwhile frowning and shaking his head.

My happy mood began to evaporate. Halla, with a "here we go again" expression, took David by the hand and went to a bench where she sat down, evidently resigned to a long, long wait. I tried to convince myself that we were at the airport. Customs people here were "modern." That's what the Tourist Office man had said with such assuredness.

Looking at him he did not seem so assured. He spoke rapidly, alternately pointing from my equipment to the page and then back again. The inspector who, at first, did not in the slightest resemble the original one, now began to look like his twin brother. I did not have to understand Greek to realize what he was saying.

Then my friend turned to me and said: "He's never seen anything like this. I mean, letting you bring this in here in the first place simply by listing everything in your passport."

"I know," I dourly cut in. "Now he feels it's against his 'regulations' to let me take it out of the country."

The other blinked. "Exactly, Mr. Linker. How did you know?"

"I'm clairvoyant!" I sighed and produced the letters. Since by this time I was becoming an old hand as a television program producer-director, I was interested in how the inspector would react. Would his "business" and "lines" parallel those of the first one? Or would he display originality? His reaction was almost identical.

271

Meanwhile the loud-speaker announced that our plane would be ready for boarding in twenty minutes. Great, I dourly told myself. We would probably watch the airliner take off and then spend the rest of the afternoon trying to convince the authorities that I had the right to leave Greece with my own property, carefully listed at our entry.

And then I had an idea. It worked before, why not now. Particularly since both inspectors seemed to have been poured into the same mold.

"Why can't the inspector check each bit of my gear against the listed descriptions and numbers on the page," I suggested to my friend. "It should be obvious that officialdom has already noted what I brought in, and since there is nothing here which has been added——"

"Excellent," he cut in and began jabbering away at the inspector.

The latter frowned, pulled his chin, stared at the ceiling. Finally he nodded, as though to say: "All right—let's get it over with."

But he did not merely check each item against the record. Oh no he selected *another* blank page of my passport and began to write in Greek, a description of each and every piece all over again. All I could do was stand there, shaking my head in disbelief.

Halla had to turn her head to keep from breaking out into almost hysterical laughter. David watched and then asked his mother: "Mommy, what is that strange-looking man doing with daddy's stuff?" Fortunately it was in Icelandic. Halla had spoken only Icelandic to Davey since his birth and he could speak Icelandic or English interchangeably. This often came in handy when he had a private comment he wanted to make. In self-defense I had also started to learn Icelandic.

Halla had to get up, take David's hand, and walk to a distant window where she stood gazing out at the field, her shoulders shaking while she went into a paroxysm of silent laughter.

It was finally done. The inspector handed the passport to me with a flourish and a bow. I accepted with a deeper bow and then, with my friend's help, hastily repacked.

We barely managed to board our plane. During the take-off for the short hop to Istanbul, Halla continued to chuckle over the incident. Noting my glum expression she put her hand on mine. "But really, it was so funny. Didn't you honestly think so, Halminn?"

272

"Funny—and a bit frightening at the same time!"

"Frightening?"

I nodded. "If we had so much trouble here, where we were actually invited, imagine what we're liable to run into when we get to Russia."

Chapter Twenty-Two

Odyssey to Odessa

I WROTE "TURKEY—ISTANBUL" on the last boxes of exposed films and leaned back.

It was late. In the morning I would ship the entire lot of film, the record of our journey thus far, to the U.S. When we boarded the Russian ship for our venture behind the Iron Curtain I would have only unexposed film with me. Should the Soviets say "*Nyet*" to my filming I would merely cut short our visit. At least there would be no danger of their arbitrarily confiscating everything I had previously shot in Spain, Tangier, Gibraltar, Italy, Greece, and here in this amazing and historic city on the Bosporus.

Halla sat by the wide picture windows, gazing at the moon-bathed Dardanelles with its border of stately minarets and contrasting modern office buildings.

David was sound asleep, doubtlessly dreaming about his seventh birthday which had just that day been celebrated in the Istanbul Hilton Hotel. As guests he'd had fifteen youngsters—Turkish, American, and European—and the maître d'hôtel had, on his own, asked the hotel orchestra to play "Happy Birthday." Highlight of his party was a surprise present from the Turkish Tourist Office—a valuable cap and ball pistol about 150 years old, and an ancient Roman coin.

As a country suitable for vacationing we found Turkey ideal. Insofar as photography was concerned we could have spent months filming the mosques, castles, palaces, and people and still would have fallen far short of covering all that this nation has to offer.

We necessarily confined ourselves to Istanbul (once known to the world as Constantinople) and tried to capture for our television and lecture audiences the richness, flavor and the magnificence of places such as the Mosque of Suleiman the Magnificent and the ancient Byzantine Hippodrome with the Column of Constantine.

One of the most picturesque subjects for my camera lens was the tremendous Aya Sofia, sometimes referred to as St. Sophia. Built a thousand years before St. Peter's Cathedral in Rome the building has a tremendous dome towering 179 feet from floor to ceiling. Architects throughout the world consider the structure one of the seven "wonder buildings" of the world.

The outstanding "incident" of our Istanbul stay took place at a small mosque. Seeking a vantage point from which to obtain a long, wide-angle shot of Istanbul's skyline with the famed St. Sophia and the equally renowned Blue Mosque built by Sultan Ahmed the First in 1617, I noted a small place of worship which boasted a tall, solitary minaret.

When I asked our guide if it would be permissible for us to climb to the top of the minaret and film from there he shrugged as though to indicate "why not."

The place of worship was not only ancient but run down, as though it had been abandoned by the faithful for many years. The winding stairway leading to the top of the minaret was narrow and many of the stone steps had been almost completely worn away.

Our climb was a slow, laborious process. However when we reached the top the effort turned out to be a good investment. From this towering camera platform we could see not only the fascinating city spread out below us, but also the harbor and straits dotted by shipping of every conceivable type.

While Halla, David, and the guide stood to one side I set up the camera and began to film. And then, in the midst of my concentration, I noticed that a newcomer had just crowded in with us. He was a youth—hardly more than eighteen. He gazed searchingly at us and then whispered to our guide. The latter seemed hesitant. I paused, wondering if we had been trespassing after all.

And then, to our astonishment, the youth turned his back upon us, and began to call the faithful to prayer.

In the faith of Islam devout Moslems are summoned to prayer several times daily by the call of muezzins from the minarets of the mosques. We had observed this ritual many times before from afar—in Pakistan, the Arab settlements of Israel, and in Egypt.

But never before had I imagined I would be right there on top of a minaret during the ceremony. Our teen-aged muezzin cupped one hand around his lips. The other was funneled around one ear. I could only assume that this was done in order to let him decide, by means of resonance, how well his voice carried.

When he opened his mouth his voice was a clear, melodic chant in Arabic. Below us people paused and dropped to their knees.

Haldun Sel, our guide, was plainly troubled by this unexpected turn of events. Halla and I hesitated. The platform was over-crowded. If I dismantled my camera and we started to crowd past the muezzin we would interrupt him and that would be immeasurably worse. I decided to stay put, making myself as unobtrusive as possible, but filming the whole event.

As the muezzin uttered his summons to prayer Haldun whispered a translation.

"Allah (God) is great." This was repeated four times. After pausing he twice said: "I bear witness that there is no God but Allah." Following another short interval he twice called out: "Come to prayers: come to Salvation. There is no other God but Allah!"

During the ritual he moved from one section of the minaret to another, as though summoning the faithful to prayer from the four cardinal points of the compass. As he moved to each new station the four of us would hastily but quietly edge around sideways out of his way.

Haldun said nothing while I shot the footage. The young muezzin himself merely eyed me as he moved from station to station. When the interlude finished the grave-faced young man left without so much as a word or backward glance. Haldun looked relieved. Frankly so were we.

"Had I known that this mosque was still in use I would not have brought you up here." Haldun said.

Halla and I felt concern. He seemed upset. I began to profusely apologize and then offered to destroy the footage I had taken rather than run any risk of offending his religion.

He smiled. "That is kind of you, Mr. Linker, but it won't be necessary."

As we made our way back down the rather tricky winding stairs Halla remarked on the youth of the muezzin. "I thought muezzins, being like our priests, were older men."

Haldun shook his head. "He isn't a 'priest' as you put it. Anyone qualified can be appointed a muezzin. That young man is obviously a student of the Koran, our bible. His position shows that he is highly esteemed by our religious leaders."

I mused upon that. "In a Christian Church he would be like a vestryman."

Haldun nodded. "If I understand you correctly I think so—yes!"

When we emerged from the minaret he grew more cheerful. "We are called to prayer several times each day, from dawn until dusk," he volunteered.

"Are the words the muezzins use always the same?" Halla asked.

He shook his head and grinned. "In the morning he adds a line at the end which says: 'Prayers are better than sleep.'"

When we first arrived in Istanbul I had taken the precaution of calling on the agents of the Russian steamship line to make sure that our accommodations were in order.

The people in the office checked. Yes, they had word of the Linkers, Americans, family of three. Yes, the Linkers were traveling deluxe on the Intourist plan. The ship, the *Pobeda,* was en route from Cairo via Beirut and Piraeus.

"How big is the *Pobeda?*" I asked.

The clerk shrugged. He actually did not know.

"Do you have any deck charts, showing the location of our accommodations?"

He did not have that either.

"Do you at least have a drawing or a photograph of the *Pobeda?*"

Again the answer "*Nyet.*"

When I had relayed this amazing admission of utter lack of information to Halla she had shaken her head. "Maybe there is no ship coming. Maybe it's just a figment of Intourist's imagination."

"There's a ship all right. And it's named the *Pobeda.* But as far as I can tell it could be anything from a four-masted sailing bark to, perhaps, the old cruiser *Potemkin* converted to a passenger ship!"

On the appointed day of our embarkation we rode with Haldun in a limousine to the ship's moorings in the Golden Horn. Halla and I both had a certain amount of worry. The mystery surrounding the *Pobeda* had served to sharpen the uncertainty of venturing through the Iron Curtain.

When we arrived at the dock we noticed an impressive ocean liner, every bit as large as the S.S. *Olympia.* Moored behind it was a low, somewhat dingy-looking freighter. I stared at the freighter and my heart sank. "Dollars to doughnuts that's the *Pobeda*," I muttered.

Halla shook her head and pointed to the big ship. "No—this one is the *Pobeda*—see—there's the Soviet hammer and sickle emblem and the name on the bow!"

The day became much brighter. We went through Turkish customs (a mere formality as compared with our Greek experience) and were about to bid Haldun and Istanbul adieu before boarding the liner when I had a sudden idea. "Is it possible to hire a rowboat here?" I asked.

Both Halla and Haldun looked blank. "Rowboat?" he answered. "I think so——"

My wife smiled. Her eyes sparkled mischievously. "Did you change your mind and decide to *row* us to Odessa, Hal-minn?"

David clapped his hands. "That'd be fun, Daddy!"

"Nothing like that," I said. "I'm planning to take motion pictures in Russia. Although 'Comrade' Spiridinov in New York told me it would be perfectly okay I want to make sure now and not after we sail, when it's too late, that we can do so!"

My audience still looked mystified. "But what has a rowboat got to do with it?" Halla asked.

"I want to be rowed around the *Pobeda* while I take pictures of it, in fully view of the captain and crew. They'll see me at work, with the camera. If they have any objections they can voice them now, before we go aboard. If they do object—" I took out my camera— "we'll just cancel our trip and travel elsewhere!"

Haldun shrugged. "Wait here," he said and trotted away.

The craft Haldun secured was a picturesque affair called a caïque. As we rowed around the Russian ship I stood up, balancing myself in full view of the people on the *Pobeda*'s decks and bridge, and began to film. If nothing else I would at least have pictures of this hitherto mysterious vessel.

When our boatman returned us to the dock it was time to climb the gangplank leading up to the *Pobeda*'s deck. We shook Haldun's hand feeling that we were saying good-bye to the western world and then began the ascent to the head of the gangplank where we saw uniformed men regarding us without expression.

Halla looked pale. "Worried?" I whispered.

"Petrified," she answered.

At the moment we were the only souls boarding. I felt as though we were climbing into the lair of some ogre. "Look unconcerned," I told Halla. "Be nonchalant, as though going on a cruise to Russia is the most natural thing in the world for an American family."

Thus we stepped onto "Russian territory," our faces void of apprehension and my camera jauntily carried in one hand. The uniformed men at the head of the gangplank were joined by a heavy-set, stolid-faced woman who wore a similar uniform.

The foremost man looked inquiringly at me. "Linker," I said. "Hal Linker" pointing at myself. "Mrs. Linker, my wife, and David Linker, my son." I indicated each of them in turn.

He consulted a list in his hand and nodded. "Yess—Leenker. Ve aspacktink you. Vallcom—" He turned to the woman and said something in Russian.

She nodded and silently reached to relieve Halla and me of our hand baggage. The man remarked: "She ees cabeen hattandant. Follow her, pliz!"

There was no move made toward my camera. As far as they were concerned the cases of obvious photographic equipment being brought aboard did not mean a thing. I thanked the man, who was the chief purser, and we began to follow our Amazon-like "cabeen hattandant." On the way we passed some pleasant-looking suntanned young men and several attractive young women. I assumed that they were passengers. Later I found I was correct. Many of them were Russian government employees who were returning from posts in the Middle East for home leave.

Our guide halted before a door, produced a key, and unlocked it. She stood to one side and watched us. Her brown eyes, set far apart beneath bushy brows, now had an expectant glint. We momentarily hesitated. She smiled and nodded toward the door. Her smile swept away her previous stolidity and we saw that she was actually a pleasant-looking woman.

Halla entered our cabin first. She stopped short.

"Hal-minn," she gasped. "This is unbelievable!"

I entered and my mouth opened. When Intourist said "deluxe" they were not spoofing. Our quarters were a tremendous suite consisting of a combination foyer-reception room and baggage-storage area, a huge living room which, in addition to padded furniture and gleaming coffee tables, also featured a mammoth mahogany desk.

Our guide's eyes were now dancing with delight. Evidently the *Pobeda's* crew was proud of the deluxe suite. And our obviously impressed reaction suited her to a T.

She hurried by us and threw open the doors leading to the bedroom. This chamber, as large as the living room, was paneled with colored wood inlays. Tremendous drapes, more suitable for a palace than a cruise ship, covered large windows. Our guide smiled, said something in Russian which we assumed to mean that she would "see us later" and then she hurried out.

"She's probably going to tell the crew how surprised the Amerikanskis were to see so much luxury on a proletarian ship," I remarked.

"Well—it's luxurious all right," Halla said, gazing about the suite. "The three of us will be lost in all this space!"

When the *Pobeda* got under way we went on deck to enjoy the excitement of another sea-voyage departure. Although we are firm believers in air transportation and indebted to the broad wings of globe-circling airliners, I must say that when it comes to the heady aroma of travel excitement and glamor, airline terminals must take a back seat to ship departures.

The sudden hoarse blasts of the *Pobeda's* whistle sent delicious thrills up and down our spines. The huffing-chuffing tugs swinging the long, towering hull (our ship weighed over 25,000 tons), the smell of salt water and the constantly shuttling boat traffic back and forth on the Golden Horn all served to make us "old hands" as excited as beginners at traveling.

The dock dwindled behind us and with it the solitary, waving figure of Haldun, our guide who had remained there until the moment of sailing to take us back in case we were refused permission to board.

The ship pointed its prow up the Bosporus which is some twenty miles long and narrows to a mere 1800-foot passage at one place. As we slowly navigated toward the Black Sea I began to boldly and openly take panoramic shots of the castle of Rumeli-hisar erected by Mohammed the Conqueror and the anti-submarine nets which reminded us of the chilling possibility that the "cold war" could quickly ignite into flame.

As we ploughed along the western reach of the Black Sea the *Pobeda* "shook down," as the saying goes, into the languid, pleasant routine of a typical cruise ship. As on our sojourn on the

Olympia we lazed, partook of innumerable but uninspired meals, swam in the pool, and made shipboard friends.

The atmosphere was anything but proletarian. We were all "capitalists living in luxury."

The Russians aboard were intrigued by our presence. They said the same thing Spiridinov had said to me in New York: we were the first Americans ever to visit Russia via the Black Sea-Odessa gateway. To them we were "their Amerikanskis." They seemed friendly. Their curiosity about the United States was boundless. However, not once did anyone comment on politics or the international situation. Instead they were openly concerned with the cost of living, price of shoes, food, cars, apartment rents. And since they refrained from bringing up any controversial subjects we followed the same tack.

We put into Varna, the "verboten" Bulgarian seaport thirty-six hours after having left Instanbul. An impressive city it was named Stalin in 1949. However when the old Bolshevik dictator died and fell out of favor the Bulgarians changed its name to Varna once again.

The second purser, a handsome blond, blue-eyed man who looked more Scandinavian than Russian, spoke fairly good English minus the Akim Tamiroff accent of some of the others. As the *Pobeda* inched toward Varna's dock he told us a bit of the city's history and pointed out that in the year 1444 the conquering Ottoman Turks wiped out a European army in the nearby hills.

Our ship was scheduled to remain in port for some two or three hours. We stood on the promenade deck, leaning on the railing and rather wistfully watched our fellow-passengers stream ashore to stretch their sea legs.

Our passports bore the stern State Department admonition that we were permitted to *transit* Bulgarian waters only.

The second purser hurried by, saw us standing there, and came over. "Why don't you go ashore for a while?"

I explained about the restrictions. He snorted. "Oh that," with a deprecatory wave of his hand. "Go ahead. There won't be any trouble. You can take some pictures. As long as you come back in plenty of time it will be all right!"

I stared down at the dock. Debarking passengers, I noticed, had to pass through a gateway manned by armed, uniformed guards.

"Suppose we do leave the ship and get by those soldiers. What if they won't let us return, what then?"

He shook his head. "Don't worry about it. I assure you it'll be, how do you say, 'okay!'" And then, still seeing the uncertainty on our faces, he laughed. "Come—I'll prove it. Come with me!"

With misgivings and, at the same time, mounting excitement I led Halla and David down the gangplank after him to where a nattily uniformed Bulgarian officer, in his late twenties, stood supervising the activity. Our friend spoke to the Bulgarian and then introduced us. To our pleasant surprise the officer spoke more than passable English.

"Americans? You want to see a bit of Varna? Why not!" He beamed at David and smiled with open admiration at Halla.

"But will you promise that we'll be able to get back on board?" I asked.

"Don't worry, Mr. Linker. You have my word!"

I took a deep breath, gave Halla a "keep your fingers crossed" look.

He said: "Let me have your passports, please, for a moment."

We watched while he made a little notation to the effect that we were going ashore. I held up my camera which dangled by a strap from my hand. "Okay?" I asked.

The Bulgarian nodded. "Okay," he answered.

We marched to the gate where the armed soldiers were on duty. I said to Halla and David: "Just stroll right by them. If you act as though you have every official assurance in the world they won't ask any questions."

With Halla on one side and David on the other, my camera dangling in full view and the cut and styling of our clothing plainly indicating that we were anything but Russian or Bulgarian we strode through the gate, smilingly nodded at the soldiers and found ourselves in Bulgaria.

Varna, with a population of more than 80,000 people, was bustling and clean but had a curiously quaint aspect. This was due, to a great part, to the noticeable absence of Western-type office buildings. Traffic, such as it was, moved at a leisurely pace. The people were well-dressed. Later we were to find that they wore better clothing than did Russians in Odessa.

We wandered along several streets, filming a church, traffic policemen in their Russian-styled uniforms, typical shops and passers-by. Halla began to grow increasingly nervous. She just could not bring herself to believe there was not some sort of trick involved.

"But they said they won't be leaving for two, maybe three hours dear," I pointed out. "We haven't been gone an hour."

"I'll feel better if we went back," she said. "What if they change their minds and sail before we return. Then we'd be in a fine mess —stranded in this country!"

"All right. Rather than have you worry, we'll return to the *Pobeda.*"

We hurried back to the dock and stepped up to the gate. My stomach muscles tensed in spite of myself. The soldiers glanced at us, nodded and looked away. We hurried to the gangplank, trotted up to the deck, and finally relaxed. It had been a greater nervous strain than I had imagined.

The following day saw us approaching Odessa. To the east, evidently putting out to sea, was the grey hulk of a formidable-looking Soviet Navy heavy cruiser, a reminder that the Russian Black Sea Fleet was potent reality rather than propagandistic rumor.

As we entered the harbor we saw numerous naval vessels ranging from what appeared to be mine sweepers on up to destroyers, cruisers, and a large sprinkling of submarines. Odessa, scene of bitter fighting between the Nazis and Russians during the Second World War, obviously was a major base for the Red Fleet. I carefully refrained from filming these since I knew of Russia's strict regulations about military scenes.

The procedure for clearing Russian customs, we were told, would consist of the inspectors coming aboard rather than the passengers filing down to the docks, à la Piraeus.

As the inspectors marched up the gangplank I began to feel increasingly nervous. "I'll settle for nothing worse than our Greek experience and feel thankful," I told Halla.

When it came our turn an inspector merely checked to see that we had a Russian visa. He yawned at my camera equipment and gave a negligent wave of his hand, indicating that he was finished with us! I simply could not believe it. We all felt almost trancelike as we followed baggage-laden porters to the dock. There another surprise was in store. An English-speaking man stepped in front of us. "Mr. and Mrs. Leenker?"

We nodded.

"I am from Intourist. I am here, with car, to take you to hotel!" He pointed to a long, black sedan which resembled a Packard, vintage of 1941. The make was Zis and the manufacturers had deliberately copied the old Packard styling.

Thus far the efficiency of Intourist was impressive. We were driven to the Hotel Odessa, the only hotel in the city for that matter, and ushered into the lobby.

Built in 1910 during the czarist regime the establishment had obviously not been updated since then. The lobby itself was a huge, cavernous affair. And instead of the familiar reception desk we found an official-looking individual seated on an elevated dais, like a judge. And like a jurist he ruled the roost. He examined our passports, consulted his register, and assigned us to rooms.

Feeling as though we had been brought before a bench, judged and sentenced, we followed our porters into an openwork, birdcage sort of elevator that moved upward at a snail's pace.

Our suite consisted of two lofty-ceilinged rooms. At first the layout was confusing. One room, obviously intended as a living room, had a small bed set up for David. The other chamber contained two single beds arranged head-to-head so that when we retired Halla and I faced away from each other. Leading from this bedroom we found another room, almost as large. In it an old fashioned tub, mounted on four ball-claw legs circa 1910, bulked along one wall.

It was obvious that during the days of the czarist regime only nobility patronized the hotel. And since they evidently had less need for bathrooms than servants' quarters it was apparent that the big bathroom had once been the maid's room in the old days. And giving this suite a private bathroom was just a "modern" idea!

Intourist, we quickly discovered, ran tours according to hard and fast rules. In the armed forces we used to describe it as "by the book."

Our daily $87.50 rate spelled out precisely what we were entitled to, when, and where. The fine print specifically stated that we each were to have four deluxe meals per day (one a "snack"). For this we were issued, on our arrival, coupon books which contained separate stamps marked breakfast, luncheon, tea, dinner.

Each coupon was good for the value of the indicated meal so you could combine them and splurge if you wanted to.

The afternoon we arrived I told the Intourist director, a frosty-eyed man of about forty-five, that we wanted to make an early start the next day—about 7:30 or 8 in the morning.

He merely looked at me and said: "Your car will call for you at ten tomorrow morning."

"But I want to make an early start—"

"Ten o'clock," he repeated. "Rules!"

I swallowed my pride. Although, to my way of thinking, a running tab of $87.50 per day should entitle a person to some sort of choice of starting time, I realized that arguing with this Odessa version of a Washington bureaucrat would be useless.

The next morning, after having dutifully appeared in the dining room for the coupon-breakfast, we went outside. There, on time to the minute, stood a Moskevitch sedan, a bulky, four-door automobile which looked almost identical to the 1954 model American Ford. A meek young girl in her mid-twenties, named Lili, was assigned to accompany us.

Before we left for our first tour of Odessa two other tourists, both Americans, got into the car with us. One was a woman, a "writer" who came from our own home town, Los Angeles. The other was a man, a Kansas schoolteacher. Both seemed to be bubbling over with enthusiasm simply because they were in Russia.

Although Halla and I were bored by their "fellow traveler" attitude we did not particularly care. If the Russian idea seemed to be their idea of the "pot of gold at the end of the Rainbow," that was their business or hard luck, whichever.

Odessa looked like an overgrown small town. Most of the buildings, of pre-Revolutionary architecture, were two to three stories high.

Although we did not see signs of war's destructiveness, such as we had encountered in Naples, our guide assured us that Odessa's main streets had been devastated. "It is just that we rebuilt as quickly as we could," she added with pardonable pride.

What puzzled Halla and me was the fact that in their rebuilding effort they had determinedly recreated not only the old style of architecture but had managed to reproduce, with authenticity, a stained, plaster-peeling weather-beaten aspect! A large city, with a population in excess of a million, Odessa at the time of our visit was almost depressing.

People had a sort of threadbare look about them. We observed how they conducted themselves, the stores with rather meagerly stocked shelves, and the small fly-specked restaurants. We saw how drab their lives seemed to be.

Without asking us where we wanted to go, our guide whisked us to the outskirts of town to a small sanitarium consisting of a collection of quite dilapidated-looking buildings situated on large, nicely landscaped grounds. We were led from the car into the main building where we were greeted by a woman doctor.

She was heavy-set, hair severely combed, and clad in a long white smock. Her attitude was coldly professional or professionally cold, I could not decide which. At any rate her look told us that she did not particularly care for "Amerikanskis." Her disdainful attitude irked us but I silently vowed to try to be polite. After all, we were their guests, although very well-paying ones!

Like it or not we were started out on a tramping tour of this incredible place where people come for therapy. Our home-town woman "writer" was enraptured. The flaking paint on the walls, the obvious dilapidation did not exist for her.

We were shown patients taking steam baths, immersing themselves in mud packs in rusty bathtubs, and a dental patient being treated for infected gums by a frightening-looking concoction which looked and smelled like tar! During this curious "tour" which would have been depressing even if the place had been the most advanced rather than the wretched patchwork it was, we found ourselves growing constantly more irritated with the attitude of the Los Angeles "writer."

When we were shown a room where, according to the interpreter, "heart patients were treated," the Amazonian physician-in-charge who had accompanied us all this while addressed a question, via our guide, to the writer, while showing us an electro-cardiograph machine.

"Do you have such modern treatment of heart disease in the United States?" was the way the question was translasted.

It was on the tip of my tongue to say: "We have—and even our county medical charity setup beats anything I've seen here," but I refrained.

To my astonishment the writer shook her head. "Oh, no," she breathed, "we're very backward in heart disease in the United States. We've nothing like this back home!"

As they say in the comic strips: "That did it."

I confronted our compatriot and coldly told her that since she was obviously not professionally equipped to discuss medicine she had no right to imply to these people that American medical science was backward!

My expression and tone of voice clearly told the cold-eyed physician what I was saying and how I felt. As for the writer, she merely looked aghast, as though I had uttered blasphemy. For a long moment there was a strained silence and then our guide cleared her voice and said: "Are there any questions?"

By this time I was seething. "Yes," I snapped. "I have a question. Why were we brought here in the first place? I did not take your 'deluxe tour' to visit depressing establishments like this which, for your information, are not even up to the facilities we have in third-rate American cities!"

There was another silence. Halla later told me that her heart sank. She felt sure the doctor, attendants, and guide would summon the OGPU and we would be thrown into Odessa's bastille. The guide shrugged. "If there are no other questions we will continue with our tour."

The ride back to the hotel was accomplished in painful silence. I was seething. I strongly felt that Russians had every right to be proud of their scientific accomplishments and their rebuilding efforts after the war. But I resented being treated like a country child being given its first trip to the big city, and being expected to show awe at fourth-rate accomplishments. After luncheon we were taken to a typical summer camp for Communist youngsters, who are called "Young Pioneers."

The sign over the entrance read "Dobro Pojalivat" which, translated, means "Welcome." Inside we found an establishment much like a typical U.S. summer encampment with playgrounds, a rather attractive fountain, and droves of cheerful, healthy-looking, handsome children. Although loud-speakers blared music at an ear-deafening volume we found the visit enjoyable and photogenic. Of course, after the "sanitarium" anything would have been wonderful by contrast!

We were informed that the camp was "typical of the Socialist methods of the U.S.S.R." in that the costs were 90 per cent paid for by the management of the factory where parents of the children worked. The remaining 10 per cent was contributed by the fathers and mothers. The children slept six to a room, where we would have accommodated two in the same space in any summer camp.

During the occasions when we were able to strike off on our own, we managed to wander through the streets of Odessa. We watched adults and children buy drinks of what is called *kvass*, something like our Prohibition "near beer" which, non-alcoholic, is made from fermented black bread.

On some corners we saw kiosk-like affairs where they sold periodicals and confectionary. Chocolate bars, we learned to our amazement, cost the equivalent of $2.50 each in American currency. Little wonder that Russian children there merely stared with wistful longing at the gaily wrapped candies.

In the big squares of the city we saw large bulletin boards. These truly king-sized affairs, show photos of the citizen workers who have accomplished something heroic during a specific period —like raising more pigs than anyone else, for example, or gathering more eggs. This honor takes the place of a raise or a bonus for a job well done.

The day before we were due to leave Odessa by plane for Kiev, we went down to the beach to film Halla and David with sunbathing vacationers. For some odd reason a policeman walked up to me, waving his arms and volleying in Russian, implying that it was forbidden to take pictures.

I looked to our guide for help. She stared at a woman bather some distance away. I smiled at the policeman, shrugged, and continued to take pictures. His face flushed and he stepped in front of the lens. Now I began to wave my arms and argue, in English which was incomprehensible to him, that I was an "Intourist deluxe" guest, as were the members of my family, that his own government had given me permission to bring my camera to take pictures and that I was merely taking films of my own wife and son!

He kept shaking his head and saying "*Nyet*" and I continued to shoot and nod and say "*Da*," and before long quite a crowd of bathers gathered around us.

Although the Russian bathers did not understand my words they knew what *he* was squawking about. To our happy surprise it turned out that they were sympathetic to us because men and women, perfect strangers to us, began to argue with him on our behalf. While this took place I continued to take my pictures while Halla grew noticeably more worried.

The harassed policeman suddenly waved his arms and bellowed the obvious Russian equivalent for "For crying out loud shut up, *all* of you!"

The bathers momentarily obeyed but merely stood there, arms folded, their expressions plainly indicating that they considered him something less than idiotic!

By this time our guide reluctantly came to our rescue. She listened to my story and then spoke to the policeman. When she said that I was merely trying to get pictures of my wife and son the audience started to bob their heads and loudly berate the policeman for being such a spoilsport. Again, this time with a livid complexion, he shouted them down. Then he snapped something to our guide.

The latter shrugged, turned to me and said: "He wants you to follow him to the police station!"

Halla gasped. By this time David had noticed that something was amiss. He trotted up and stood clinging to his mother's hand. The Russians noticed this and a sigh of sympathy went up from them. I looked at the policeman and then I began to take the camera from the top of the tripod. "I am sick and tired of being abused," I snapped at the guide. "I am a guest of your government and I insist on being treated as one. You can tell this dismounted 'Cossack' that I definitely will not go with him to his police station or any police station!"

Without another glance in their direction I turned to my family and said: "Come Halla, it's time we were returning to the hotel."

I led the way to where our car was parked, Halla and David silently followed me. Behind I could hear the heated debate between the guide and the policeman. At any moment I expected to hear pounding boots and then feel a rough hand grab me.

Instead, just as we reached the car, we heard applause from the beach. We turned and looked. Evidently the guide had won her point because the policeman, shaking his head with obvious defeat, was beating a retreat while the Russian bathers were expressing their pleasure with our "victory" by heartily applauding!

Chapter Twenty-Three

Inside The Kremlin

OUR FLIGHT TO KIEV was scheduled to leave at seven in the morning. This was the "deluxe non-stop" flight. Intourist had warned us not to take the uncomfortable local flight, a DC3 type.

Our plane, which resembled an American twin-engined Convair, sat on its tricycle landing gear awaiting us. We checked into the terminal. Our tickets were in order. When we asked for help with our baggage we discovered that there was no such thing as a porter. When it came to help with our personal gear, we had to do it via the *Tovarich* (comrade) method: to wit, carry it ourselves.

More asleep than awake we sat in the small terminal restaurant and drank tea. Finally a loud-speaker mumbled something in Russian. I caught the name: "Kiev."

"That's us, Elska-mín," I said rising to my feet.

Halla sighed, reawakened David. We began to load ourselves with baggage and started from the terminal building to the waiting plane. And here we found that there were no substantial steps such as are used elsewhere to board the plane. No indeed. Russians are hardy people. There was a stepladder, of all things, like the ones used on air force planes in wartime. It hung down from the doorway.

A figure appeared at the door. I squinted. It was a female—a frowsy, sleepy-eyed woman of perhaps forty who must have weighed at least 180 pounds. She wore a long, double-breasted jacket that hung like potato-sacking below her broad hips almost to her knees. Her hair tumbled every which way, as though she had just stepped out of an electric-shock treatment. There was something like the look of a uniform about her jacket. And then it dawned on me: that was our "stewardess."

She lounged in the doorway and watched us struggle up the

ladder. I had to make several round trips to get everything on board. When I looked inquiringly around the interior of the cabin, trying to make it obvious that I wanted to know where to leave our possessions, she yawned and pointed to a cleared space on the floor toward the tail.

The baggage was unceremoniously dumped in the tail of the plane rather than in special compartments; such as is the case beyond the Iron Curtain. Nor was the heaped baggage tied down.

As I helped Halla and David aboard and took them to the seats indicated by the "stewardess" I thought of the unsecured baggage. Should anything happen on take-off or during a landing or were we to encounter rough air—I shuddered at the mental picture of the possible consequences of the baggage flying helter-skelter on top of the passengers.

Evidently the official Soviet attitude toward air travel is that only two classes of people fly: those under government orders (and they wouldn't *dare* complain) and capitalists such as ourselves. And who cares what happens to a capitalist?

The interior appointments were, shall we say Spartan? Other travelers panted and puffed their way up the ladder into the cabin, dumped their baggage on top of ours, and glumly chose their own seats. The crew in the cockpit started the engines. The noise was unusually loud. The cabin began to rattle and vibrate. I leaned forward and reminded Halla and David to be sure and fasten their seat belts. She twisted around. "What seat belts, Hal?"

There were none.

As I contemplated the unpleasant possibilities implied by the lack of that basic measure of passenger safety our pilots released the wheel brakes, blasted the engines, whipped the plane around on the axis of its main landing gear and briskly taxied to the take-off position.

Elsewhere airline pilots pause and check their engines, one by one, prior to leaving the ground. Not these boys. Maybe they'd landed from a long hop before we got to the field. Perhaps the engines were already sufficiently warmed up. At any rate no sooner had we reached the end of the runway when the pilot revved the engines again, spun the ship around, and without the slightest pause began to take-off!

We did not immediately begin to climb. Instead the plane seemed to hover mere yards above the blurred earth. I uneasily recalled travelers' tales of how Russians liked to hedgehop, just over the treetops. I took a deep breath and resigned myself to a bumpy, earth-hugging flight that would just skim trees, houses, and hills, when abruptly our pilot hauled back on the controls and we zoomed up into the sky!

He leveled off the ship at a comfortable altitude, however. Our cabin altimeter (an excellent idea, incidentally) told us that we were cruising at 5000 feet. The rest of the flight, although noisy (the engines sounded like lawn-mower motors!), was fortunately uneventful. Even so Halla and I vowed then and there that we would never again use Russian airlines. For the balance of our stay we'd travel by train, automobile, trolley, bus or, if necessary, on yak-back. But no more Soviet airliners, deluxe or plain. *Nyet*, *nyet*, *nyet!*

After Odessa, Kiev was almost like another world. The city, a mixture of medieval churches, narrow streets, modern structures, and broad, tree-lined boulevards sprawls along the bank of the busy, sparkling Dnieper River.

When we landed there and after I finished the chore of climbing up and down the ladder three times to off-load our baggage we were greeted by our new guide, once more a woman.

A slender, dark-haired, vivacious person in her late twenties, she stepped up to us, hand outstretched and a pretty smile on her face.

"Welcome to Kiev, Mr. and Mrs. Linker. I am Djana from Intourist and I want you to know that we have much nice things to show you in Kiev to make your visit most interesting and memorable!"

Looking at her Halla and I felt better. She was definitely a vast improvement over the dour, crusty monitors of Odessa. And then Djana looked at David and her eyes twinkled. "And this is your son David—" She shook his hand. "*Pojalivat*, David. That means welcome in Russian. You just wait. We have a playground for children here with all kinds of things, such as you've never seen!"

Her warmth was almost overwhelming. Driving to our hotel she asked what would become the inevitable opening conversational gambit on the part of Russians for the remainder of our trip. "Is this your first visit? What do you think of Russia? Of Russians?"

We nodded to the first part of the question. As to the second

I could say with all honesty, that we had only seen Odessa thus far. Halla replied to the third part. "If your countrymen are as nice as you I'm sure we'll like Russians!"

Djana laughed and actually blushed. "Ah, Russians are people—good, indifferent, a few—" She shrugged. "Like Americans, *da?*"

"All countries have their 'black sheep'—their bad specimens," I answered.

She gazed at me. "Ah, that I know. You travel a lot?"

"Quite a bit."

Djana sighed. "I, too, have traveled. To East Germany." She thoughtfully gazed at David. "My husband is an army officer [she pronounced it "offitzier"] stationed there. I lived there three years with him."

"Is he back home now?" Halla asked.

She shook her head. "No. He is still there."

"Then you have traveled quite a bit yourself," I said. "Perhaps to England where you studied the language?"

She laughed. "No—I study English in gymnasia—school. I saw English, French, Americans, Swedish—in East Germany."

Halla leaned forward. "How did you like West Berlin? We hope to visit there, maybe next year!"

Djana shook her head. "I never even visited *East* Berlin!"

"Well—what other countries did you visit while you were with your husband?" I asked.

"None. I stayed in East Germany."

Halla's eyes widened. "All the time?"

Djana nodded. "We were not allowed to leave our German village. But"—she rubbed her hands—"now I am back again, home."

Although not as ornate as those in Odessa, our Kiev hotel accommodations were more cheerful (or was it because of the unexpected friendliness on the part of Djana?).

While we were checking in I told her that we wanted to change from airline to railroad for the trips from Kiev to Moscow and Leningrad and, finally, to Helsinki. When she looked questioningly at us I thought it best to say, "It's because when you fly you really see nothing of the country, the people. A train, on the other hand, brings you close." We didn't want to tell her the truth.

The Kreshchatik is the main thoroughfare of Kiev—a mixture

of Main Street, Broadway, Wilshire Boulevard, and the Champs Elysées—stretching almost from one end of the city of a million people to the other.

As we drove through a mellow summery afternoon I remarked on the newness of many buildings. Djana nodded. "Yes. During the Great Patriotic War almost all of Kiev was destroyed by the Germans."

"You mean World War II," I corrected her.

"The Great Patriotic War," she firmly insisted.

I pondered on that. Later when she took us to various statues and monuments erected in memory of the bitter fighting between the Russians and Germans I discovered that most of the people living in the Soviet Union regarded the tragedy as their own burden. The Stalinist government had successfully kept hidden from its people the truth about the extent of the involvement of the United States and Great Britain in the struggle against the Nazis. When we tried to mention something of what the U.S. had done in the war the expression of polite skepticism on her face discouraged us.

I tried a new tack. "In Odessa they also claimed that they had to rebuild the city after the fighting. Yet we honestly could see no solid evidence of that."

Djana reached down into a briefcase and pulled out a sheaf of photographs. "Look," she said. "This is the Kreshchatik as it looked right after we drove out the Germans."

Halla, David, and I silently examined the pictures. The devastation had been incredible. But even more surprising was the fact that in the process of rebuilding, the people of Kiev had faithfully, painstakingly reproduced the original, prewar aspect of the Kreshchatik, including the buildings put up in the 1920s.

Looking about us as we drove down the street it was as though there had never been warfare here. It dawned on us that the people of Odessa had probably done the same thing: restored the prewar city exactly as it was, but with shabbiness included.

Our sedan, (interestingly enough also called a Pobeda, the same name which identified our Black Sea liner) turned off the boulevard and brought us to a square on Lenin Street. Here we found a towering polished red granite statue of Vladimir Ilyich Lenin, the shrewd-faced, bearded Bolshevik who, in 1917, overthrew the Provisional Government which had ousted the czarist regime, and then established Communist rule.

Djana looked on with approval while I filmed Halla and David at the foot of the statue. It was obvious that to the people of Kiev the memory of the "Father of the Russian Revolution" was holy.

During this interlude a number of passers-by paused to watch from a distance with friendly curiosity. Unlike the cop of Odessa's beach a Kiev policeman happened by, recognized Djana, nodded to her and, after a casually interested glance in our direction, continued on his rounds.

The language spoken by the people around us resembled Russian as "the mist resembles the rain."

Djana reminded us that they spoke Ukrainian, a tongue which had started to differ from Russian as far back as the eleventh century A.D. She spoke glowingly of the history of Kiev, the Ukrainian capital, of its medieval splendor under the suzerainty of the Czars.

"Our languages became even more different after the Tatars [Mongols] invaded Kiev in the thirteenth century," she added. "You know, of course, we Ukrainians are not 'Russian.' People from Moscow [she pronounced it Mosk-va] and Leningrad are called 'Big Russians.'" Her brown eyes danced. "We Ukrainians are 'Little' Russians!"

Little by little, during our stay in Kiev, we were to find traces of a stubborn nationalism which is nurtured by the Ukrainians despite the fact that their "independent" republic is part of the union of fifteen socialist republics of the U.S.S.R.

When Djana took us to the summit of the Vladimirskaya Hill overlooking the Dnieper with its many bridges and its heavy traffic of river steamers, barges, innumerable pleasure and excursion boats, she urged me to be sure and obtain pictures of the statue of Prince Vladimir nearby.

"He is one of our heroes," she explained. "In the year 988 he brought Christianity to Russia!"

While I filmed this monument of a medieval warrior prince who was remembered for having brought the teachings of the Prince of Peace to a nation whose leaders now deny God, I was amused to overhear a somewhat one-sided conversation between Halla and Djana.

"You've told us very interesting things about Kiev," my wife said, "but did you know that Kiev was conquered in the year 882 by Vikings led by Oleg, the son of a Viking named Rurik?"

Djana shook her head. "I didn't know they were *Vikings!*"

Halla went on. "Oleg and Rurik were Viking Varangians who had first conquered parts of Northern Russia, 'Big Russia' as you put it. When Oleg came here the Vikings called themselves Ros or Rus. That's where the name 'Russia' actually came from."

Our guide's eyes widened. "How exciting," she said. "This I never heard before. How is it that you, an American, should know about it?"

Halla's chin proudly lifted. "Because I was Icelandic before I met my husband and came to the United States. You see, the Vikings who settled in Iceland in 874 A.D., were my ancestors, and came from the same race which marched through Russia and captured Kiev eight years later. It is taught in schools to all Icelandic children."

Djana clasped her hands. "How marvelous!" she exclaimed. "I cannot wait to tell my friends of this." Then she paused and stared at my wife with fascination. "That means that your little country is as old as Russia! Amazing!"

A short sail on the Dnieper River in an excursion boat which could accommodate fifty to seventy-five passengers took us past clean beaches jammed with swimmers and sun bathers. At frequent intervals we saw men seated in rowboats just offshore. From the way they kept a critical eye on swimmers we assumed they were officials of some sort. When I questioned Djana she nodded: "They're 'Spasatyelnayas'—" Her brows furrowed as she tried to mentally translate. "You know—if people can't swim——"

"Oh—lifeguards."

"*Da, da*—yes!" She thoughtfully repeated to herself: "Lifeguards, lifeguards, 'Spasatyelnayas'—lifeguards."

But we also saw many men in rowboats, just fishing. Maybe they would never get their photo on an "honor board" but they seemed to be enjoying themselves just the same—as fishermen should.

Kiev's cultural life regards the ornate Shevchenko State Opera House as its heart. Djana arranged for us to attend a performance, by an Estonian company, of a rather turbulent Russian opera entitled, appropriately enough, *The Demon*.

Although the opera had good costuming, passages of good music, and several rather excellent folk dances, the production as a whole was not top notch.

Several nights later we returned to the theater, this time to be enthralled by a presentation of the "Swan Lake" ballet. In both instances I was able to obtain color footage of the actual performances. The sequences, later televised in the United States, had tremendous, favorable audience response.

Over breakfast Djana said: "Now today we will visit a most unusual place." She eyed each of us. "It's a little, how should you say—'fearful.'"

"Scary," volunteered David.

"Da—'scary." She nodded.

Halla and I looked questioning.

"We're going to the Kievo-Perchersky Monastery. It's very, very old and built over caves and there are catacombs."

On the way to the monastery which, I learned, was also called the Lavra, we paused by a huge obelisk, 150 feet high, which was dedicated "to the Patriots who died in the Great Patriotic War." Again it was on the tip of my tongue to set Djana straight about what the rest of the Allies had accomplished, including some plain, blunt truths concerning our own campaign against Japan.

What's the use, I argued with myself. Maybe she would believe, maybe not. In any event it would turn into an argument and by this time we were too fond of her to cause any unpleasantness.

Before reaching the monastery we paid a short visit to the Shevchenko University, a modern and fairly large university where a faculty of 705 teachers instruct a student body of 6200 students, "mostly in science," Djana pointed out.

The monastery itself had been badly battered by artillery fire during the war. When we arrived the restoration of the churches was still incomplete. However the catacombs below were intact.

We got in line with droves of Russian visitors and were given tiny pencil-like candles. Before we started to descend into the catacombs, which were actually natural caves, we all lit the candles. It was a weird, funereal sight—the fitful gleam of the small flames casting strange leaping shadows on the walls hewn out of solid rock while we carefully negotiated the worn steps that led into an almost Stygian gloom.

The whispering of Russian on all sides echoed and re-echoed. Combined with a musty odor and a dry, rather penetrating chill which made us involuntarily shiver, the over-all effect was almost as "scary" as Djana had predicted.

Djana had told us that the government wanted to preserve the monastery with its "barbaric relics" consisting of the actual mummified remains of long dead monks, priests, and bishops of the Russian Orthodox Church.

Halla had asked: "But if the Soviet government no longer believes in religion why does it go to the expense and trouble of maintaining the monastery?"

"To remind our people how decadent the 'old Russia' used to be when the Church had even more power than the czars," Djana had instantly replied.

Now, gazing at the shrunken figures lying in their robes which had been preserved by the dry air, I watched shadowy Russian figures furtively place prayer candles by certain bodies. I looked at Djana to see how she reacted to this visible evidence that many of her country's people still believed in religion. Her eyes watched them but her expression was inscrutable.

It was a relief to climb back to the "land of the living," even if it was a police state. Djana seemed preoccupied as she led us back to our Pobeda. When we started to drive she remarked: "Now we will visit the Cathedral of St. Sophia. You'll find it interesting." And then she surprisingly withdrew into herself.

She was correct. It turned out to be an impressive example of Russian architecture of the style which was so heavily influenced by Asian culture. Built in the year 1037 the cathedral provided Russia with its first library.

The main bell tower reared 250 feet into the air. Surrounding it were the onion-shaped towers of the main church, eight of them. All were covered by hammered gold leaf. For centuries the "golden church towers of Kiev" had been a world-famous symbol of Russia.

As I filmed the exterior and, later, the priceless collection of ikons and wall paintings within the huge structure where lies entombed Prince Yaroslav the Wise, I felt amazed at the incongruous attitude of the Kremlin.

On one hand they viciously propound that "religion is the opiate of the masses" and, as such, should be destroyed. Yet, in almost the same breath, the rulers turned right around spent fortunes restoring ancient symbols of the very thing they professed to hate.

When we were alone I mentioned this to Halla. She shook her

298

head. "I think the churches and relics are beautiful. And so do the Russian people. If the government authorities think that their people feel otherwise about it, they're just plain foolish!"

When we emerged from the cathedral, Djana suddenly became her former, friendly, smiling self. She grasped David by the shoulders and exclaimed: "Poor Davidschka—all these dismal, dusty dead things. NOW I will take you to the surprise I promised, the place where children have fun!"

David beamed. Djana enthusiastically herded us back into the Pobeda. Her eyes sparkled and there was color in her cheeks. Halla and I could only exchange wondering glances.

Our destination was Siretsky Park. Djana had not been exaggerating when she said it was a place where children could have fun. The major attraction was an actual, although scaled-down, railroad system consisting of electric locomotives, freight and passenger cars, switches, trestles, and several stations. One was called "Pioneerskaya," the other "Teknicheskaya." While grown-up technicians supervised the operation, the actual running of the railroad was accomplished by boys and girls up to fourteen years of age.

Djana's explanation that this was part of a carefully conceived "training" program still did not alter the fact that the setup was truly a children's paradise. David was immediately "adopted" by the other kids after Djana told them who he was. I began to film our son as he rode with his newly found Russian playmates in one of the trains.

Authenticity was the keynote of the entire procedure. The Russian boys and girls actually wore the uniforms of real trainmen—hip-length white jackets, red neckerchiefs, and white caps with visors.

The "engineer" would solemnly look back for a signal from the "conductor" while his "fireman" tolled the bell. If the conductor at the rear of the train unfurled a red flag the train remained still. When the conductor (either boy or girl) rolled up the flag it was the equivalent of the American railroad "highball," and off the train would go!

Halla and I were finally invited, along with Djana, to go for a ride. And before we left, David had ingratiated himself enough, without knowing a word of what the others were saying, to ride in the locomotive cab, undoubtedly as a spare fireman.

I chuckled and said to Djana, "Now there is 'feather-bedding' with a vengeance." She looked rather blank so I dropped the subject rather than find myself struggling in the quicksand of American railroad labor-management relations problems.

When the time came to leave Kiev we genuinely regretted having to say farewell to Djana. Our feelings were reciprocated. Before we boarded our train I tried to get her last name. She declined to give it, mumbling a vague excuse which did not make sense.

"But we'd like to write to you," I explained.

There was a pained look on her face. "I know," she nodded, "but we're not allowed to have correspondence with foreigners."

It was a sad reminder that this was still communist Russia. What had made Kiev so pleasant had been a warm, gracious human being named Djana who, alas, was not permitted to live like one.

Our train was an overnight express to Moscow. The cars were typical of European *wagon-lit* design: long corridors or "vestibules" down one side with separate compartments placed crosswise to the axis of the car, opening upon the corridor.

However there was a certain amount of substantial comfort in our first-class car. I stood in the vestibule and began to take pictures of Djana and the other people on the platform.

Abruptly a white uniformed porter appeared and motioned that picture-taking was "verboten." The train started to glide from the station and while he shook his head and remonstrated in Russian I managed to take a few feet of film.

Rather than argue I shrugged, lowered the camera and entered our compartment which contained four berths, two uppers and two lowers.

A loud-speaker was blaring with ear-deafening martial music. I had been warned that Russian trainmen considered passengers hard of hearing and that if they decided to play music it would be music of their own choice and loud enough to almost shatter eardrums.

For a while I tried to find some way of shutting off the malevolent loud speaker, but to no avail. And then a key was inserted in our door and the porter ushered in an utter stranger.

Well! The newcomer was a man who spoke no English whatsoever. He smiled uncertainly at each of us, settled his suitcase by his side and sat down. It dawned on me that we were going to have him with us all the way to Moscow. Our tickets called for the occupancy of three berths. And since the compartment had a fourth one——

I went out into the corridor and searched for someone with authority to whom I could make myself understood. I drew a blank. There was a woman clad in a gray uniform seated at the end of the car. Her official duties were to brew tea on a small samovar for the passengers and assist in the various duties of portering.

I tried to communicate by means of sign language, showing our tickets, holding up three fingers, nodding and smiling, holding up the fourth one and frowning and saying *"Nyet, nyet"* and then producing a sheaf of rubles to indicate that I was willing to pay for the fourth berth to secure privacy.

She stolidly watched me. I let my arms fall to my side and sharply exhaled my breath in frustration. Suddenly she smiled, nodded her head, exclaimed: *"Da, panymayoo, panymayoo,* (I understand)" and began to pour a cup of tea! It turned out that when I had exhaled it had sounded to her, as though I was cooling off some tea.

*"Nyet choroshaw—*no good," I exclaimed. "Privacy, peace and quiet!" And then I made motions indicating that the music was giving me an earache.

She nodded, reached down under the little table which supported the samovar, and flicked a switch. The sudden silence was wonderful.

When the time came to retire we looked at our Russian friend and he looked at us. He smiled and made gestures indicating that he would be gone for a while. Obviously he knew what was troubling us. During a tactfully prolonged absence it gave Halla a chance to disrobe and tuck herself into her uncurtained berth. We were all lying in our berths in darkness when our companion finally timidly returned. There were no curtains for any of the four berths in our compartment.

Later on, Halla and I both agreed that the incident had its humorous aspect. But at the time, lying there, listening to a perfect stranger going through the routine of disrobing and then climbing into bed, almost alongside, was strange, to put it mildly.

Our Moscow arrival was not only exciting but relieving as well, although our unknown traveling companion had kept himself as unobtrusive as possible. I've often wondered what kind of thoughts ran through his mind. The trip for him may have been as embarrassing as it was for us.

We nooded good-bye to the man, with distinct mutual relief, and parted. When we started to walk into the large, smoky terminal, we were accosted by our Moscow Intourist guide.

I began to chat with him, only to be brought up short when he shook his head and said: "No *panymayoo* English—*Hablo solamente español!*"

Fortunately my Spanish is fluent. At one time during my formative years I instructed in the language. I exclaimed: "*Muy bién, pero porqué es necesario hablar en español, señor?*"

He gratefully smiled and explained that the Moscow office "had run out" of English-speaking guides. Evidently there were many other tourists there, either American or from the British Commonwealth. The management had picked a guide who spoke Spanish, the nearest thing to English they had available!

Our hotel, the National, was located a block away from the walled-in Kremlin. From our window we looked toward the famous Red Square, an enormously wide area that received its name during the days of the old czars. It was then called Krasny Square which meant "Beautiful Square." Through the years the word "Krasny" gradually came to mean "Red," and so Beautiful Square gradually became Red Square, with no political connotations at all.

It was in the hotel dining room that we first encountered a smothering sensation of being watched—a feeling that would gather and increase and not leave until we finally left the country.

We noticed a heavy-set, middle-aged-looking man dressed in a dark suit, who had "detective" written all over him. He sat at a table close to ours and minded his business, elaborately so. We noticed that he wore a hearing aid. But what made us suspicious was that whenever we sat down at mealtime he invariably appeared. If we dawdled, so did he. If we ate hastily, by some odd happenstance he, too, had things to do necessitating hurry. And when we left he would wait for less than a minute and then also rise and leave.

Now it could be that our imagination was working overtime. But when I happened to spot him in the background of several places we visited I grew more convinced than ever that "Big Brother" was watching.

Our Spanish-speaking friend was replaced, in "mid-Moscow

stream" by a girl, tall, attractive, and smartly dressed (for a Russian woman). Unlike Djana she did not have an outgoing personality. Her name was Gala. She was polite and tried as much as possible to be helpful but at all times she made us conscious of the fact that she was merely doing her duty for the sake of Intourist. We sensed that we were not "gay companions" insofar as she was concerned.

We strolled around the tremendous walls of the Kremlin and then visited the huge government-owned GUM department store where only a small part of floor space is actually used by sales counters because of its strange layout.

We marched to one end of Red Square and inspected the truly remarkable St. Basil's, formerly a church which was built in 1555 by Czar Ivan the Terrible to commemorate his defeat of the Tatars at Kazan, an event which incidentally lifted the yoke of Mongol oppression from the Russian people after three hundred years of almost abject slavery.

We noticed that Russian tourists who were obviously visiting their capital for the first time, always spoke in lowered tones as though fearful that they would be overheard.

This automatic "near-whisper" way of living was to remain with us for the duration of our trip through "Holy Russia."

Later during our exploration of Moscow our "girl guide" grew curious about Halla and the life of a housewife in the United States. Her questions were guarded and yet probing. Halla began to talk about conveniences which, in our country, are taken for granted, such as electrical appliances.

"Oh but we have such things—even better," our guide said.

"Where?" was Halla's skeptical reply.

"Come. I show you!"

She led us back to a department store and ushered us into their appliance section. There we stared at electric washing machines which had been outmoded since 1930 in the United States. The machines did not even have switches. To turn them off a person had to yank the power line plug out of the socket. To turn them on, the archaic procedure was reversed.

The girl's curious insistence that this was "progress on a par with, if not greater, than that in the U.S." made itself again evident when she took us to a "fashion show." There models wearing "specimen" gowns made in Czechoslovakia by Czechs who

303

had pilfered the original lines from Paris in the first place, paraded before a group of expressionless women, most of them quite heavy-set.

When we asked where the gowns could be purchased and for how much our guide said: "Oh they're not for sale! Whichever design appeals the most to the majority here will be reproduced in patterns. People will be able to buy the patterns in stores and make their own gowns. They're just *voting* on the styles now."

No visit to Moscow is complete, for either "faithful" or "heretic," without a visit to the tomb of Lenin and Stalin. There is always a queue of people patiently waiting their turn to enter the granite mausoleum which is located in Red Square right under the walls of the Kremlin.

We had eyed the line-up. And its length was discouraging. To our amazement, our guide arranged to slip us in at the head of the line. In our country you can just imagine the howls that would go up when people who have been "sweating out" a line waiting to enter a theater suddenly find some privileged foreigners being admitted ahead of them. The Muscovites, however, did not even blink when we were ushered in ahead of them. It was the custom.

The interior was permeated with a deathlike hush. No one may talk there. Guards are posted at intervals of ten feet. We followed our guide to the subterranean chambers where the bodies, amazingly lifelike, of Lenin and Stalin lie in their coffins.

We stared with fascination at the mortal remains of the two men who, during their lifetimes, had so startlingly altered world history.

Our guide closely observed our reaction. When we got outside, she exclaimed: "You were impressed. Don't deny it!"

"Of course we were impressed," we answered. However we did not go into details of what we had been *really* thinking of their heroes.

During Stalin's regime the gates to the Kremlin were closed. Now the public is permitted to enter and visit certain sections, particularly the really impressive museum and art galleries.

The museum contained an awe-inspiring collection of some of the world's most magnificent and priceless collections: crowns, jewels, weapons, carriages—an accumulation of wealth that is not only staggering to the imagination but a fascinating outline of

Russia's history extending from the remote, pre-medieval era through the pageantry of the czars up to the present.

Outside the museum, adjacent to the bell tower of Ivan the Terrible we stared at the huge, 200-ton Czar bell which had been first cast in 1735.

This monstrous affair, which has yet to be hung in any tower, has a huge chunk broken off. In 1737 while it was on a scaffolding prior to being installed, a fire broke out and the gigantic affair crashed to the ground, breaking off an eleven-ton fragment and solidly burying itself in the earth below.

I could not learn whether it had even been sound-tested. Later during our stay in Moscow we happened to encounter the noted American jurist, Judge Samuel Liebowitz and his charming wife. He was staying at our hotel on a combination vacation and study of the Soviet judicial system (at their invitation). When we mentioned having seen the bell and also the fact that, for most Russian tourists, it was a favorite "prop" for snapshot taking he wondered, as did we, what the monster would have sounded like if its clapper could be put into operation.

Halla afterward said the thought made her shudder. "It would probably be loud enough to wake up the dead— Maybe Lenin and Stalin!"

"Or Ivan the Terrible," I added.

Delightful high spots of our Moscow sojourn were our visits to the puppet shows and Bolshoi Ballet. The artistry and beautiful presentation are outstanding.

Moscow's "modern city" with its peculiar "skyscrapers" was impressive enough, in a 1920 style, but terribly old fashioned by modern standards. An interesting sequence for my camera consisted of the Lomonosov University, a thirty-two-story structure, located in the Lenin Hills.

On our next to the last day in the Soviet capital we "shot" the changing of the guards around the Lenin-Stalin mausoleum.

The soldiers are clad in olive-drab uniforms with long, shirtlike blouses gathered in at the waist by heavy belts, jodhpur-like breeches and heavy, high, hob-nailed boots. On their heads they wore stiffly crowned caps adorned with the red-star insignia. Their weapons were bayoneted rifles. And they marched in a sort of goose step that made their hob-nailed strides echo and re-echo along the walls in front of the sprawling Kremlin.

Just before we left the inside of the Kremlin for the last time, Halla stared at the active government buildings that are out of bounds to the public and asked which one used to house Stalin's office. Our guide pointed it out. And then both Halla and I noticed a curious thing: the yawning muzzle of the tremendous old "czar's cannon," a famous landmark, was "zeroed in" squarely upon the building.

Our journey from Moscow to Leningrad, once called St. Petersburg and later Petrograd, was on another night train. This time we had the entire compartment to ourselves—a considerable improvement over our first experience.

In Leningrad we were to meet an entirely different breed of Intourist agent, a young, red-haired individual who never stopped chattering from the moment he greeted us at the station until he brought us to our hotel, the rather plush (for Russia) Astoria.

During our drive through the busy and interesting streets he babbled away about how pro-American he was, how during the war, as a boy, he had gotten to know American sailors and how they had been kind to him, showering him (and other Russian kids) with candy and food. Of course, the generosity of American servicemen is legendary.

But to suddenly have an Intourist man talk this way, especially after their closed-mouthed, cold attitude in Odessa and Moscow, was a puzzler. And when he began to tell how he hoped someday to leave Russia, that he was trying to save money and obtain a visa— "Maybe become an immigrant to your wonderful country"— my puzzlement turned to suspicion.

The first accommodations they gave us were slightly larger than broom closets. I acted like the indignant, money-paying capitalist I was and demanded rooms "fit for a deluxe tour!"

It worked. We were transferred to a monstrous-sized suite consisting of three tremendous rooms with immense baths and furnished in a rococo gilt decor that would have delighted Grand Duke Nicholas himself—as perhaps it had at one time or another, since the hotel had been built in the year 1913!

The city guide assigned us by the headquarters office turned out to be another girl, named Ella, short, pretty, and perky. Since our hotel stood on St. Isaac's Square opposite the cathedral of that name built by a French architect in the nineteenth century our coverage of Leningrad started from our very doorstep.

We noticed a different, more European atmosphere about Leningrad. People there seemed better dressed, more prosperous-looking, and walked with a certain amount of briskness.

This city, second largest in the Soviet Union, with a population of about four million, is "new" compared with the other cities and hamlets of Russia. Founded by Czar Peter the Great who had decided, at the turn of the eighteenth century, to learn Western ways in order to raise the standards of his own backward nation, Leningrad (then St. Petersburg) was scientifically laid out as not only a model city but a military and naval bastion as well.

The metropolis maintained that name until 1914 when Russia and Germany went to war. Because St. Petersburg sounded too German it was changed to Petrograd—still using the monarch's name. However after the Revolution it was renamed Leningrad (guess why).

At various times exposed to the destructive forces of war (from 1941 to 1944 it was constantly shelled by long-range and short-range German ordnance) Leningrad has also served not only as a center of government but of learning and culture as well.

The profusion of palaces and art galleries is staggering. To list the masterpieces we devoured with our eyes, the treasures we examined, would cover dozens of finely printed pages.

Their subway, although not as ornate as that of Moscow, still gave us pause, especially the beautifully decorated stations. It obviously must have cost the government many, many rubles and much thought to make the subway stations gleam and sparkle with their tasteful designs and conveniences. Russian workers seemed to barely earn enough to get by. They could afford only the skimpiest of clothing and crowded shelter and, of course, *chleb*—bread. But their government poured money and time into making the subways show places, as a substitute for the drabness of their daily lives. The subway stations were their personal palaces, the promise of the future for them.

The sprawling Admiralty buildings provided grist for my camera, as did the hut which Peter the Great used when he first came to the original marshy site and remained to supervise the construction of the city-to-be.

307

At the water's edge on the Neva River, guarded by sailors, the cruiser *Aurora* was moored. Like the *Potemkin* of the early 1900s, it is a landmark in the Russian Revolution. The *Aurora* was the battleship which, under Bolshevik orders, steamed from Constantinople (Istanbul) to Leningrad and attacked the Winter Palace, then headquarters, of Alexander Kerensky's more moderate "republican" army. With the downfall of Kerensky the extremist Bolsheviks under Lenin and Trotsky took over and the first links of the grim Iron Curtain began to be forged.

Towards the end of our Leningrad visit we had one of those surprising and pleasant "small world department" experiences.

It took place during our visit to the rather grim Fortress of Peter and Paul, so named because it was there that Peter the Great's own son, the Czarevitch Paul, was condemned to death and executed for having "plotted" against his father.

While I took different camera angles of the bastions, towers, and old cannon a group of visitors appeared at some slight distance from where I posed Halla and David. One of the newcomers kept staring in our direction. His expression indicated that I was someone familiar to him. I was puzzled because I was positive I had never seen him before.

And then the stranger confronted us. When he spoke, he said, "Say—aren't you people Hal and Halla Linker." His eyes glanced at David. "And isn't that little David?"

We could only stare in utter amazement.

"I'm sure you are," he grinned, thrusting forward his hand. "Recognized you right off the bat. We always watch your program on our television channel back home in Des Moines, Iowa!"

The morning of our farewell to Russia was nerve-wracking with suspense. I had exposed over 7000 feet of color film behind the Iron Curtain. To my mind came memories of warnings that experienced travelers in Russia had voiced prior to our departure from the States.

"Getting your film into Russia isn't too much of a problem. It's getting it out again—that's the rough part of it. Sometimes the Russians will confiscate it and tell you they'll develop it themselves and censor it before they'll send it to you. When that happens you might as well kiss all your expense and effort good-bye. You'll never see it again!"

I had, of course, relied on Mr. Spiridinov's implied assurance that it would be all right to film in his country. But sitting in our hotel room in Leningrad the day of departure I realized that that gentleman was a long way from where we were now.

Halla noticed my worry. When I explained my fears she patted my arm.

"All we can do is hope for the best," she said.

We boarded the train. Since the crossing from Russia to Finland was to be done in daylight hours it meant an early start. I piled the cases of exposed film where they could be seen immediately so as not to be accused of trying to smuggle them out and then sat back to wait.

For an interminable length of time the train clattered and swayed on the track which skirted Lake Ladoga. And then it began to slow down. It finally came to a halt. I peered outside. We were standing by a large signal tower. Several uniformed officers tramped by our car.

There was a long pause. And then I heard the sound of approaching boots. The door to our compartment opened and a stern-faced Russian Officer stepped in. "Passport," he snapped, extending his hand.

I silently watched as he checked our visas. He grunted and returned the precious documents. His eyes flickered over Halla and David and then rested on the almost mountainous-looking cartons of exposed film, seventy of them. For a moment none of us breathed.

He pointed to the film. "Yours?"

I could only nod mutely.

He hesitated, gave us one more searching glance and then, wearing a frown left our compartment. I crossed my fingers and looked at Halla. "Hold everything," I whispered.

The train suddenly lurched, glided a few yards and then stopped again. Once more we heard the approach of heavy boots. Again the door opened. Another officer wearing an entirely different uniform, entered. "Passports!" he asked.

Once more I offered him the three documents and watched him riffle through the pages. "Do you speak English?" I ventured.

He nodded.

"When will we get to Finland?"

He stamped a page in the passports and handed them back,

"You're *in* Finland now," he smiled. "That was the border you just passed!"

For a moment we just sat there staring at him, and then Halla, David, and I embraced each other with relief. The Finnish officer laughed, said "Welcome to our country," and went on his way, shaking his head with evident amusement.

The train started again and began to pick up speed. The clickety-clack of the wheels on the rails seemed somehow smoother and happier. The passing countryside looked neater. The houses we passed were freshly painted. People along the roads waved to us. We could feel the freedom in the air.

As we watched the blessed free world pass by our windows Halla leaned back, humming to herself and stroking David's head which rested against her shoulder.

I watched my two precious "partners" and then gave silent thanks for the miracle which had dictated that we three should be born in the free world, so that we could continue to enjoy the "Wonders of the World" with our three passports to adventure.

Epilogue

THE THREE OF US were seated in a comfortable American-made airliner which had just taken off from Iceland and was now winging us closer to our beloved homeland. Halla and I chatted, in order to get our minds off the clouds and overcast through which we were ascending. Our program would have been on the air for about three consecutive years when we got back. "Wonders of the World" had been sold all over the United States.

In Los Angeles, where our program originated, each week's episode was done "live," when we were not traveling abroad. All three of us appeared in person to narrate the films of our travels. In all the other thirty cities the twenty-six episodes of the series were shown on film.

The income from all the cities in which we were being seen had already started to flow in. It looked as if the lean years were finally over. I could see by the relaxed smile on Halla's face that these same thoughts were passing through her mind.

"Do you remember, Hal-minn," she said softly, "when we were returning from lectures and we used to coast down long hills with the motor turned off in our car so we could save gasoline? In a way," she continued, "I'm glad we went through those days."

A fleeting shadow crossed her face then disappeared.

"I hope we never have to go through them again," she went on, "but if we must we'll come through all right, I *know* we will."

A few moments later I picked up a notebook from my brief case

311

and started scribbling furiously. Halla got up to make sure that David was comfortable in the seat beside us where he was taking a nap, completely relaxed. When she returned she glanced at me.

"What's that, Hal? Some notes about Russia?"

"Russia?" I murmured absentmindedly. "Russia? Oh, the Russia trip. Oh no. I was just making some notes about where we should go next summer." I started to warm up to my subject. "After all, we haven't been to Alaska yet and then I've always wondered what Borneo is really like. But maybe a trip through South America is what we should do first." I pulled out a map. "Let's see, we could stop off in Mexico and then go down to Peru to see the Lost City of the Incas at Machu Picchu. From there we could fly over the Andes to visit the Upper Amazon at Iquitos and meet the interesting Indians they have there. Then at that point we wouldn't be very far from Bolivia so we might as well not miss that. After that we——"

I stopped because Halla was smiling at me—that special warm smile that tells me that I was talking about places that she, too, would like to see.

She took my hand again. "Hal-minn, I'm sure I've told you this before, but I'll say it again. Wherever you want us to go we'll go with you. Davey and I know you'll take good care of us and watch out for us."

"That's absolutely right, Poppy," said a tiny voice, "we trust you!"

Davey had not been asleep after all. All three of us burst into laughter. A few of our fellow passengers looked at us. We were secure in our own little world of faith in each other and in our hope that we would continue to travel together to see, film and share with our viewers all the marvelous wonders in our world.

The gleaming broad wings of our airliner suddenly emerged from the overcast blanketing Iceland. Ahead of us stretched a crystal-clear, deep blue, cloudless sky.

C